The Naval Brigades
of the
Indian Mutiny

The Naval Brigades of the Indian Mutiny

Two Accounts of the Brigades of H.M.S. Pearl
& H.M.S. Shannon

The Cruise of the Pearl
E. A. Williams

The Shannon's Brigade in India
Edmund Hope Verney

LEONAUR

The Naval Brigades of the Indian Mutiny
Two Accounts of the Brigades of H.M.S. Pearl & H.M.S. Shannon
The Cruise of the Pearl
by E. A. Williams
and
The Shannon's Brigade in India
by Edmund Hope Verney

First published under the titles
The Cruise of the Pearl with an Account of the Operations Naval Brigade in India.
and
The Shannon's Brigade in India

FIRST EDITION

Leonaur is an imprint
of Oakpast Ltd

ISBN: 978-1-78282-144-1 (hardcover)
ISBN: 978-1-78282-145-8 (softcover)

http://www.leonaur.com

Contents

The Cruise of the Pearl

THE ATTACK OF FOUR SEAMEN UPON A PARTY OF SEPOYS AT AMORHA

Contents

Advertisement

H.M.S. Pearl

Introduction

The only excuse I can offer for publishing the following brief and imperfect narrative is, that it gives an account of the services of seamen on shore of an unprecedented character. This is, I believe, the only example in English history of officers and seamen of the Royal Navy leaving their ships, and taking their guns seven or eight hundred miles into the interior of a great continent, to serve as soldiers, marching and counter-marching for fifteen months through extensive districts, and taking an active part in upwards of twenty actions. I have refrained from making any remarks on the services of the Naval Brigade of H.M. ship *Shannon*, with which I had not an opportunity of being sufficiently acquainted. But the events I have endeavoured to depict with reference to the Naval Brigade of H.M. ship *Pearl*, to which I was attached as chaplain during the two harassing and trying campaigns of 1857 and 1858, I have had ample opportunity of knowing, either from personal observation, or the statements of those on whose veracity I can rely.

Although the Narrative does not tell of thousands slain in battle, or describe the shaking of nations under the crash of contending armies, it nevertheless embodies an account of services rendered to the State, great, when compared with the means employed. The country acknowledged these services in the thanks of both Houses of Parliament having been passed to the Royal Navy and Royal Marines as well as to the army; and Sir Michael Seymour, the Naval Commander-in-Chief, expressed his high approbation of the gallantry and good conduct of the Naval Brigades. "Their services," he remarked, "won the distinguished approval of Her Most Gracious Majesty and the Lords Commissioners of the Admiralty," and their "brilliant campaign he had viewed with pride," feeling "that the honours so gallantly won by the Naval Brigades in India are reflected upon the navy at large." The opinion of one so deserving of respect, gives me reason to suppose that a narrative of what was done by them in the Upper Provinces of India may prove acceptable to the public.

It is not that more credit can be claimed for this small force than for any other equal number of Britons under similar circumstances; but it is considerations arising from the difficulties that were overcome, the isolated position that was occupied, totally unsupported by Europeans, for many months; the holding of an advanced post exposed to constant attacks, and removed from the rest of the army so far that its services and dangers have been little known, that afford an additional excuse for describing the part taken by the Royal Navy, and which may fill up a hitherto vacant niche in Indian history; and adding as it did to the strength of the army in artillery when troops were few, and that arm of the service in particular was loudly called for in the country, I hope the following Narrative may show how it contributed a *quota* towards the many triumphs in India which shed lustre on the British arms.

London July 22nd, 1859.

CHAPTER 1

Armament of H.M.S. Pearl

On the 24th of December, 1855, H.M's screw steam-ship *Pearl* was commissioned by Captain Sotheby, R.N., at Woolwich, When ready for sea, she proceeded to Portsmouth, where it was intended she should join the fleet which was assembling for the third expedition to the Baltic.

The *Pearl* was the first of the new class of 21-gun corvettes, which had been commissioned. Her armament consisted of 8-inch guns, having one 95-cwt. pivot-gun; and, considering her tonnage, draught of water, weight of metal, and steam power, she was regarded as a most effective ship, and well suited to the Baltic, and, consequently, likely to see much active service. For these reasons the command of her would naturally present more attractions to an enterprising officer than a line-of-battle ship, which would in all probability spend most of her time at anchor.

In the spring of 1856 she went to sea for a fortnight on a trial trip, and, after encountering a severe gale, returned to Spithead without suffering any damage, and proving herself to be an admirable sea-boat.

The Russian war being now over, peace was proclaimed; and as there was no prospect of a Baltic expedition, the *Pearl* was got ready for a foreign station. With the utmost speed she was fitted out for a long voyage, and, when ready for foreign service, was ordered to sail for the South American and Pacific station.

We left Spithead on the 30th day of May, 1856, steamed through the Needles, and bid farewell to the shores of old England, not knowing what changes would take place, what scenes we were destined to witness, or what service was destined to await us between that day and the date of our return. On the following day we called in at Plymouth, and in the afternoon were again at sea.

On the 9th of June we arrived at Madeira, where a few days were pleasantly spent. There were two American men-of-war at anchor at Funchal, the *James Town* and *St. Lewis*; the former, a corvette, was the commodore's flag-ship; the latter was a smaller vessel which accompanied the commodore. Their station was the West Coast of Africa, and they had come from thence to spend the summer months at Madeira, and thus, by avoiding the intolerable heat of an African sun, they wisely discovered a very agreeable method of passing away a commission on "the Coast." At this time the feeling between England and the United States was not very amicable, and at first some doubts existed as to who should take the initiative in the formulae of civilities. However, the ice was soon broken, and the best of goodwill soon prevailed.

The United States' Consul invited the officers of the *Pearl* to a ball, and their Transatlantic friends lost no time in inviting them to "liquor." One would begin, "I say, stranger, will you liquor?" In the first place, the health of the queen, for whom they entertain the greatest respect, would be loyally proposed. This would be quickly followed by the health of the President and Congress; then he would propose the health of themselves; next, the health of the Crimean heroes; then, if he could not think of anyone else, he would propose the health of the queen again. This process being perpetually repeated, health after health following each other in quick succession, so that, when taken by storm with this kind of Transatlantic friendship, it required some firmness of purpose to avoid the natural consequences. At any rate, whatever disputes disturb cabinets, it is quite clear that there is in the navy a happy knack of settling them by a glass of Madeira, as well as by stronger measures.

On the 13th of June we weighed anchor and left Madeira, proceeding on our voyage towards Rio de Janeiro. The morning was fine, and the wind was fair when we left behind us the narrow dirty streets of Funchal. At this time, however, it was unusually clean. The Royal yacht having lately arrived there on a cruise, gave rise to a vague rumour that the queen would visit the island during the summer; and in consequence of this report, by a general order of the governor, the houses were whitewashed and appeared in a new dress. The scenery, the work of nature, presents a pleasing contrast with the town, the work of man. The lofty mountains and sunny valleys, where the rose, the pink, and geranium grow wild, and where the fuchsia and the fern flourish in harmony together, are a great relief to the eye of the traveller when he emerges from the narrow, toasting, grilling pavements of Funchal.

July 12th. We anchored in the magnificent harbour of Rio de Janeiro. It is supposed to be unequalled by any harbour in the world except that at Sydney. The scenery is exceedingly picturesque. The entrance is not much more than a quarter of a mile wide, and protected by a strong fort; and, after entering, it opens out into a splendid haven surrounded by mountains. In the distance, at the further side, the Organ mountains rise majestically, and add all the beauty that hill and forest can give to a beautiful sheet of water studded with picturesque islands. St. Sebastian is situated on the south side of the harbour, and is the chief city in the empire of Brazil. It is much improved of late years, and gives evidence of being the seat of government of a rising kingdom. Since their declaration of independence in 1822, great strides have been made, trade has increased, and education has been promoted.

In a beautiful valley near the summit of the Organ mountains,[1] is a sanatorium for the people of St. Sebastian. It is named Petropolis, after Peter the Second, Emperor of Brazil. The colony is chiefly inhabited by Germans, with a mixture of French, English, and Brazilians. Here the emperor has a country palace, where he can retire when the heat of the plains becomes excessive.

The system of locomotion from the capital to Petropolis is made as easy and convenient as possible: a steamer conveys passengers to the upper end of the harbour; from thence to the foot of the mountains they are conveyed by a railway; and from the railway terminus to Petropolis, the means of conveyance is by a small carriage, drawn by four mules at a canter, up a well-made macadamized road—the ascent being regular and gentle from the bottom to the top, a height of about two thousand five hundred feet. The road is about ten miles long, and is a splendid piece of engineering; it winds through the deep indents, and round the spurs of the mountains, presenting at every turn a new and varied prospect.

Education also seems to be the object of the chief care of the government. Here two excellent colleges for boys are established, and a seminary for young ladies, in addition to numerous schools for the lower classes. The population seems industrious and prosperous; their

---

1. Or Terra San Salvador.

cottages are neat and clean; and crime is rare among them. The climate is as tolerable as can be expected on the borders of the tropics; and on the whole, there is the appearance of a thriving colony, and the advantage of a cool retreat to the merchants of the capital during the heat of the summer months.

July 22nd. Left Rio harbour, and, sailing southward, on the 8th of August entered the Straits of Magellan. At eight o'clock the same evening we anchored off Cape Possession, on the coast of Patagonia. Each morning early the steam was got up and we were under weigh by daylight; and every evening at dusk we came to an anchor. The water was as smooth as a mill-pond. We were fortunate in meeting neither fogs nor gales of wind; and on the 13th, after four days, we emerged from the straits into the Pacific Ocean, and thus succeeded in cheating Cape Horn of the accustomed homage which ships usually pay in pitching and rolling in an unmerciful manner. We stopped for half a day at Sandy Point, where the Chilians have a military settlement; and we stopped a day at Fortescue Bay, when, the weather being threatening, it might have been dangerous to pass through the narrow channels.

The climate was by no means so cold as we expected to find it at this season of the year. The mountains were covered with snow, but it did not reach down to the water; and a great coat was as much additional clothing as was required. The Chilian settlement at Sandy Point was formed after the mutiny which broke out at Port Famine about four years previously, when the governor was killed, and the convicts were let loose; some of whom were afterwards executed at Valparaiso.

From the entrance of the straits up to this place, the land on both sides is rather flat and uninteresting, being only occasionally varied by a precipitous cliff or bluff headland, or a hill some distance in the interior; but from this place until the waters of the straits mingle with the vast expanse of the Pacific Ocean, the mountains rise from the water's edge, sometimes abruptly, sometimes gradually, covered with trees and verdure, until the trees and verdure in their turn are covered with snow. Sailing along, we observed in the clefts of the mountains several beautiful glaciers of a light azure tint which seemed like some mighty torrent arrested in its course, and frozen into rocks of ice before it had time to fall.

The straits vary from a mile and a half in the narrows to five-and-twenty or thirty miles wide, and are upwards of three hundred miles in length. The population is scanty, and those who are seen along the shores seem to be about the lowest in the scale of uncivilisation, living little better than the wild beasts of the forest, their food rancid fish or seals; and inhabiting hovels or wigwams made of the branches of trees, which do not exhibit so much ingenuity in their (construction as that of the ant or the birds of the air; while the country through which they roam, untutored and ungoverned, is most picturesque in its features, splendid in the barren magnificence of its cliff's and mountains, and strikingly majestic in the bold headlands dipping down almost perpendicularly into the sea.

Having left the Straits of Magellan on the 13th August, we arrived at Valparaiso at the end of the same month. The *Pearl* then continued on the Pacific station, for which she was originally intended, until the 5th of April, 1857. She touched at various ports on the coasts of South and Central America; but during this time nothing of importance occurred beyond what usually occurs to most men-of-war, except the capture of two Peruvian gun-boats, which took place on the 28th of March, a few days before leaving the station—a punishment which they brought down upon themselves by committing an outrage on the English flag.

The government of Peru was at this time, as usual, what might be called remarkably "shaky." Revolutions in small republics on the coast of America are of ordinary occurrence, and in Peru the number of general officers is so great compared with the rest of the army, that they very often find themselves out of employment, and, for the want of anything better to do, set up a claim to be President of the republic; but, in order to obtain this enviable appointment, it is necessary to oust the reigning President. To effect this object he is not attacked in the Congress on the ground of misgovernment, and got rid of by the opinion of the country; but they appeal to arms!—a revolution is stirred up, and as many adherents are collected together as have not had any share in the government offices or appointments for some time previously, and who are of opinion that they have as good or a better right to administer justice as well as expend the public treasury as those already in power.

It is never very difficult for a clever adventurer, or rather patriot, to collect around his standard a cloud of these wronged and neglected heroes, who are ready to fight for a due share in the administration, or die in the attempt. It was during one of these patriotic struggles that our lot was cast in Callao Roads, when General Castillia being President of Peru, Señor Vivanco considered that he was not the right man in such a place. General Castillia was a brave old soldier who never shrunk from danger, who won the President's seat by the sword, and was resolved to retain it by the same. He had the sympathy of the army and the mass of the people on his side, while Señor Vivanco had the sympathy of the higher classes, but more particularly of the ladies, who exercise a great influence in the politics of Peru. The naval force was not quite equally divided, the greater portion of their navy upholding the cause of Vivanco, while only a few took the side of Castillia.

Such was the condition of the country when one fine evening (Tuesday, the 24th March, 1857) a *soiree* was given by the officers on board H.M.S. *Pearl*, to which many of the inhabitants of Lima and Callao were invited. During the entertainment, intelligence arrived that two small war-steamers, whose officers and crews had espoused the cause of Vivanco, stopped our mail-steamer, the *New Grenada*, on her way to Panama, and having boarded her, placed sentries in different parts of the ship, searched her, and abstracted thirty-two thousand dollars, besides bales of goods and articles of less value which had been shipped under the names of merchants at Valparaiso, but in reality had been sent up by Castillia to pay his troops in the northern part of the country.

According to orders given by Admiral Bruce, we weighed anchor next day about noon, and sailed northward in search of the *Loa* and *Tumbes*, which were the two vessels that had committed the outrage on the English flag.

On the 28th March we arrived at Lambeyaque, where the *New Grenada* had been plundered, and where it was expected the vessels would be lying at anchor. It was so arranged by Captain Sotheby that we should arrive by daybreak, and take them by surprise. About six o'clock in the morning ships were seen ahead, and as it was impossible to tell but that resistance might be made, the bugle sounded to general quarters, and the *Pearl* was ready for action. On nearing the ships, the *Loa* and *Tumbes* were recognised; and all hands on board seemed to be at general quarters also. Coming upon them in the grey dawn, they at first mistook the *Pearl* for the *Apurimac* (44 guns), which was the flag-ship of Vivanco's fleet, and the officers in command were in full dress ready to pay their respects to their admiral, until the English ensign being hoisted at the peak, as the *Pearl* steamed up alongside, dispelled the illusion, and the unpleasant truth became apparent that a foe instead of a friend was approaching.

20

Our boats having been manned and armed, Mr. Turmour, the first lieutenant of the *Pearl*, went on board the *Loa*, which was the senior officer's ship, and demanded the 32,000 dollars and bales of goods which had been abstracted, and also the officers and men who had committed the outrage; and in default of the fulfilment of these terms, in five minutes, an immediate surrender. It was impossible to comply with the first of these terms, as the cash had been distributed among Vivanco's needy dependents as soon as it was captured. The captain, in consequence, came on board the *Pearl* and surrendered, offering to give up his sword, which was refused, as it was not the object of the expedition to capture them as enemies' ships, but simply to inflict punishment for a predatory excursion, and keep them as hostages until they could inspire hopes of their better behaviour for the future. The captain of the *Tumbes* followed the example of his senior officer.

The officers and men who had taken no part in the affair of the *New Grenada* had their option to go ashore at Lambeyaque or proceed to Callao. The latter they preferred, being desirous to remain with their companions and await the issue of the matter. Lieutenant Radcliffe was ordered to take charge of the *Loa*, with a few of the *Pearl* crew as a guard; some of her own officers and men being left on board to assist in working the ship, while Lieutenant Grant took charge of the *Tumbes* with another party of men, to conduct them back to Callao, there to await the investigation of the affair, and the decision of the commander-in-chief of the station. The *Loa* and *Tumbes* were two fine gun boats, built in England for the Peruvian Government, the former carrying four guns (long 32-pounders) and the latter two guns of the same calibre, each having one brass gun in addition.

Some of the crews of the gunboats having been drafted on board the *Pearl*, and some of the *Pearl's* men having been sent to them in exchange as a guard, while a sufficient number of their own crews were left on board to do the rough work, including their engineers, who were Englishmen, we left on the same afternoon, and steamed back towards Callao with one gun-boat on each quarter. Nothing of any importance took place on our return except the inconvenience of having so many additional hands on board. It was, however, quite clear from all that could be made out of the conflicting statements of the officers that they had used unpardonable violence, some of them acknowledged much that others, wishing to shield themselves from blame, were very vehement in denying; and he who had been the principal actor in the affair, and had placed the sentries in the ships when the dollars were abstracted, we were afterwards informed had been originally an owner of a cart which conveyed goods from Callao to Lima, and subsequently had been promoted to be a master of a trading vessel on the coast, and finally attained the rank of an officer in the Peruvian Navy.

Under these circumstances it could scarcely be expected that he should have known much of the law of nations. One incident, however, produced a little excitement. Late in the evening a light was seen ahead. It was conjectured that the admiral on board the *Apurimac* might have had tidings of the pursuit, and was coming to their assistance; there was a rumour that she had sailed northward, and this strengthened the conjecture. The bugle sounded to general quarters, and precautions were taken against a surprise. The Peruvian officers were puzzled, not knowing what to think of it. In the countenance of some, consternation was depicted, some affected indifference to the rumour. But among all for several minutes there was a breathless silence. Certainly, it must be acknowledged that if an attempt had been made to cut out the ships it would have been very unsatisfactory to those Peruvians on board the *Pearl* to be made a target for the shot and shell of one of their own ships which came to their rescue. The suspense, however, did not last long; the light ahead soon disappeared, a retreat was sounded and the excitement subsided.

On the 31st of March, having returned to Callao with the two vessels, great excitement was produced among the inhabitants. The beach was lined with spectators to witness the return of the *Loa* and the *Tumbes*; they were exceedingly wroth, and expressed their indignation in no measured terms, at their ships having been brought in, as they said, like pirates, without their flags flying; and the *Pearl*, which had been previously tolerably popular, suddenly sunk in general estimation. One of the vessels was given up to the party from whom she had been taken, and the other was kept for some time as a security that such a depredation should not be committed again.

Castillia had offered a large reward of several thousand pounds for the capture of these two steamers, which, no doubt, would have been promptly paid if they had been delivered up to him; but as it was not the intention of England to take an active part in the support of either party, they were therefore not given up to him; in the meantime, however, he took advantage of the blunder made by his opponent, and the consequent embarrassment that his blunder entailed, by sending troops to the north to attack Vivanco's forces. The Peruvian soldiers, most of whom are Cholos, that is, the original natives of the country, chiefly from the hills, are a strong hardy race of men; they are for the most part of low stature and swarthy complexion, their limbs are thick and their shoulders broad; they are capable of enduring much fatigue, and making very long marches. There is a plant called the "*Coca*," the leaves of which they chew, much in the same way as tobacco is used by some Europeans, but its effects are very different. It is said that the soldier of Peru will go a great number of hours without food if he has the coca leaf to chew, which seems to soothe, and dispel the feeling of hunger, and although it is so great a stimulant, it leaves no bad effects behind. Under its influence they undergo much fatigue, and march surprising distances with the greatest cheerfulness and endurance.

It is by these intestine feuds that Peru is becoming gradually de-populated, and its once fertile provinces are rapidly falling into desolate wastes. In these revolutions brother rises against brother, and father against son; the ties of kindred seem to be no barrier to the shedding of blood. In fact, there is a certain policy in the members of the same family adopting opposite politics, this plan sometimes works with advantage to the parties concerned. When one side gains the day, the victor generally has interest enough to secure the pardon of the offending brother; his point has been gained, he has got into power, and is in a fair way of making a competent fortune. When party feeling has subsided he no longer thirsts for his brother's blood; natural feelings take their proper place and assume their rightful prerogative, and he is reprieved.

Such a state of things is ruinous to the country; the thinking portion of the community regret it, while they are too few to have weight enough to reform it. Morally, physically, and socially, the contrast this country presents with the account we have of it under its former sovereigns, the Incas, is most striking. Prosperity has never attended the footsteps of the conquerors. The first stone of their power was laid in a thirst for gold which was gained by injustice, treachery, and blood—that thirst has never been slaked. No settled, well organized government remains as an evidence of the power, wisdom, and sagacity of the victors, the inhabitants are rapidly diminishing in numbers, and the lands show no signs of fertility. The depopulation which has been going on for years may be attributed to various causes. From many millions at the time of the conquest they have dwindled down to about three millions, or a little more.

This may be attributed to the bad government which has existed, to the tyranny which has been practised, and to the civil wars and riots which have perpetually prevailed, as well as to diseases which have been introduced without medical men in sufficient numbers throughout the country to apply remedies, and to many other causes. Added to which, a constant series of revolutions which have followed each other in rapid succession, as one wave follows another, has disturbed the country for years.

A president is elected for five years, but before three years have run their course, some unhorsed, hungry general raises a party to put him out. This struggle, which is tantamount to a change of ministry among other nations, lasts, perhaps, for a year or two, when one or other conquers, and is put out in his turn by some other aspiring competitor. Wise heads make a mercantile speculation out of these revolutions; they lend money at a high interest to the contending parties. Whoever attains office pays handsomely, while the defeated are sometimes not only beggared, but beggar their friends and supporters also. They all sink or swim in the same boat, their contentions do not seem to be even tinged with patriotism. Their disregard for life is great, they hold it cheap.

Their insatiable thirst for gold has descended through the line of their Spanish ancestors, but their energy, enterprise, and chivalry have formed no part of the inheritance. Travelling in the country is neither very safe nor convenient, and so weak is the government that the most dangerous roads in the empire are those within ten miles of Lima, the principal city, where the traveller would expect to find the police the most efficient. In that neighbourhood, if alone, he is more in danger of being robbed and plundered by assassins and gangs of liberated negroes than in any other part of the country.

Of the ladies I have little to say, except that they are usually seen by candlelight, when they appear pleasing and good looking. Their figure is graceful, and their manners easy and affable. It is not the custom to visit during the day, except on Sundays or holidays; but in the evening their reception rooms, which, in Lima, are the first apartments on entering the house, (no hall leading from the door to the drawing room as in England,) is illuminated by many lights; and if not lit up, with the ladies dressed as if for an evening party, it is evident to the visitor that the inmates do not intend to receive visits that evening, or are gone to spend the evening with some other friends. Their greatest expenditure seems to be on the furniture of their reception rooms, and their dress; on these they spare no expense. They have no carriages, because they have no roads to drive them on. The men use riding horses when going a long distance, but the ladies are too fond of the *dolce far niente* to appreciate such violent exercise.

The Peruvian Navy did not seem to be so often called into action as the army in their late revolutionary movements. This may have arisen partly from the fact that the greater number of the ships were in the hands of Vivanco. The only one that Castillia possessed which was a match for the *Apurimac* being the '*Amazon*, which had been abroad for several months. Report said that Castillia avoided the risk of a naval engagement, not having confidence that the officers and crews would be true to his standard. Once only while the *Pearl* was lying in Callao Roads, there was an attack made by the frigate *Apurimac* on the forts at Callao, and a small steamer called the *Ucayali* with the intention, if possible, of cutting her out. The *Ucayali* was close inshore, alongside the mole, or pier, on which several guns were mounted.

The Peruvian admiral conceived a plan of surprising this vessel, expecting to sink her if he could not succeed in her capture. Just before the dawn of day one misty morning she steamed stealthily close up to the mole where she was anchored, and delivered a broadside; so well was the surprise conducted, that the first intimation given of her approach was a shot through the surgeon's cabin, which aroused him from his peaceful slumbers; consequently there was ample time to discharge several rounds of shot and grape before the fire was returned. The fight then lasted about half an hour—it was hot work on both sides. Spectators in the different merchant ships were aroused by the booming of the cannon. The gunnery of both parties was not calculated to inspire anyone with fear except those who had nothing to do with the affair.

From the fort and the mole many shots were fired, but few took effect, considering the close proximity of the belligerents. Several men, however, were wounded, and three or four were killed. A request was sent to the surgeon of the *Pearl* to lend his aid, which was at once complied with. Most of the shots fired at the *Ucayali* were too high, they did not calculate on such close quarters. If the gunnery practice had been as good as the manner in which the vessel was brought into position, and if the manoeuvre had been carried out as well as it was planned, it would have met with better success. But so high was the elevation of the guns that many of the shot went over the houses in the town, carrying terror into the homes of peaceful citizens, and causing them to fly in alarm and dismay along the road which led to

Lima. Among other casualties, it was reported that a child was killed in the arms of its mother, which she afterwards carried to the President, no doubt to excite his commiseration, and to show what misery these civil feuds entail.

CHAPTER 2

Orders to Sail for India

In the afternoon of the 5th of April we weighed anchor and left Callao Roads, on a long voyage across the Pacific to China. Having fair winds and fine weather, we arrived at the Sandwich Islands on the 9th of May, and on the morning of the 10th steamed into the harbour of Honolulu. This city, containing five or six thousand inhabitants, is situated on the Island Oahu. Some of the houses are built of wood and some are of stone, so that, it presents the appearance in its architecture of an American rather than a European city: Americans and American interests also predominate. The king of this group of islands, of which Honolulu is the chief city, is Kamehameha the Fourth. He is an intelligent man and very much in advance of his predecessor. Both himself and his Queen Emma, who is partly of European extraction, seem to be popular among their people.

The population of the Sandwich Islands, which is about 75,000 or 80,000, is now in a very different condition from what it was thirty years ago, the inhabitants, from having been wild and uncivilized, are now all nominally Christians. It has been stated that when they use an oath, it is in the English language, having no words to that effect in their own. What a slur on a people, civilized, and professing a pure Christianity! Much credit is due to the American missionaries, who have worked with energy and zeal for many years, and much success has attended their labours. The Kanakas[1] are simple-minded and docile, but being naturally idle and immoral, are often more easily led astray by the allurements of vice offered to them by Americans and Europeans who do not feel the restraints of religion, than persuaded to follow the path of virtue by those who labour among them for that

1. This word means, in the Hawaiian language, "man," and is used to express "native of the islands."

27

object.

One of the missionaries gave it as his opinion that the boys go on-ward and upward under the influence of education, while the girls go backward and downward in sin and vice, and if other means and fresh appliances are not used to arrest this great evil, the prospect for the fu-ture generations is sad indeed. This statement, however, applied chiefly to the Island of Oahu, where foreigners are numerous. The population of the rural districts in the other islands is on the increase, while in the seaport towns, where vice prevails, it is diminishing.

They have several large churches in Honolulu, and the congrega-tions are as numerous and attentive as in any English church. Each missionary station has now settled down, and assumes the character of a parochial charge rather than a missionary settlement. Some years ago the parent missionary society in the United States resolved to reduce the expenses, which had been considerably on the increase, and ac-cordingly proposed to contribute a certain reduced amount, and that the rest should be raised by the native congregations or other means; and if the missionaries found it impossible to carry on the work with the reduced allowances, the board was ready to defray their expenses home again.

Most of them, however, remained. A large sum is subscribed an-nually by the native congregations who can afford it towards the sti-pend of the pastor and the support of the church. The work went on as usual, and the expenses of the home society were considerably diminished. One congregation in Honolulu contributes upwards of 600 dollars or 120*l.* annually towards the stipend of the pastor; and although the Hawaiians are naturally selfish, yet when Christian prin-ciple takes root, they have afforded many examples of generosity.

If we were to judge from the number of schools in the island, and from the law of the land which obliges children between the age of four and fourteen to attend, we should be led to suppose that educa-tion was flourishing. The teachers certainly seemed to attend to their work; but the materials, as may be expected with all races which have recently emerged from barbarism, are not the most promising to work upon. The race has not yet received the culture and training of cen-turies, and therefore the minds of the young do not possess that grasp and capacity which is found among European nations. The children are quick in picking up some things until they arrive at a certain point; but to urge them one step in advance requires a considerable effort, both on the part of the teacher and the taught.

The rudiments, such as reading, writing, geography, and arithmetic, are easily acquired, but it is difficult to get them much further. Their memory is good—it seems to be their best faculty—but few give evidence of a high order of intellect; time, patience, and perseverance, have, however, done much, and, no doubt, will produce greater fruit in future. The present race of teachers have been their instructors for many years, and as the system of instruction varies and improves in the process of time, like most other things in this age of progress, it might not be amiss if fresh blood was introduced in that department.

In one or two of the schools there is a great mixture of races. You might see English, Irish, American, and some half-caste boys as well as natives. I have also seen the children of a Tahitian and a North American Indian. Under these circumstances it would be productive of much good to introduce the English language more than it has yet been done, and which, if energetically attempted, many of the apparent obstacles would vanish. Some years ago it might easily have been done; their own language containing so few words, it was found necessary to coin a multitude of others to express and describe various new things which were introduced. If these things had simply been called by the English name, the language might almost insensibly have been introduced.

The children in the schools are much gratified at being noticed by visitors, and are vociferous in their "*aloha*," meaning "peace," which is their method of salutation, and is suitable either to a meeting or parting. Their complexion ascends, through various degrees, from a light copper colour to a shade nearly black. Their dark bright eyes, when their fuzzy black hair is combed off their brows, present a tolerably intellectual spark. I observed that when one of the boys, in reading English, came to a word which he did not know how to pronounce, he miscalled it, and tacked on an "s" to the end, supposing that he could thereby manufacture an English word. This seems to be a common habit. The mottoes suspended in some of the schools are truly characteristic of the States, of which the following is an example:—

Be sure you are right,

(then)

Go ahead.

The male population are a good height, athletic, and well proportioned; but neither men nor women are prepossessing in appearance, although they have the reputation of being good-tempered and not easily aroused into anger.

The ruins of an old temple are still to be seen about six miles from Honolulu, near Diamond Hill. It is said to have been built by Kamehameha the First, after the conquest of the island. It is called Heiau. Here, in the days of heathenism, were offered human sacrifices. The victim was chosen either by the priest or king. The messenger of death entered his abode while he slept, and he met his end by strangling. He was then dragged off as an offering to the sanguinary god. Some affirm that the priests ate the flesh of the victim, but for this there is but little foundation; and it is now thought that the people in general never were cannibals.

Although the light of truth has dispelled much of the mist of ignorance and error, there are, however, still some of their former superstitions deeply rooted among them. In the healing art they are sometimes absurdly apparent. Their native doctors have recourse to charms and incantations in preference to medicine, of which they are totally ignorant. These learned sons of Æsculapius will put a row of charmed stones about the diseased part of the body which is to be cured, and walk round, uttering screams and yells, and making strange grotesque grimaces in order to restore the sick to health.

One of these distinguished practitioners found himself incarcerated one day in consequence of one of his unsuccessful experiments terminating in the death of the patient, a catastrophe which could not by any possibility be brought in *secundum artem*. He had been called in to try his skill on a man who was deranged. The sufferer had, although unintentionally, been partly the innocent cause of the death of another man by drowning. Subsequently (probably by the accident preying on his mind), he became deranged. The doctor having duly considered the case, and thoroughly investigated the cause of the disease, prescribed that he should be cured by water. The water-cure was forthwith resorted to. With the assistance of four strong men (his wife and friends consenting, and being fully convinced of the efficacy of the cure), he was bound hand and foot, and then tied down with the water up to his chin.

The men who were stationed to watch him, and who ought to have observed the progress of the cure, lay down and fell asleep. When they awoke the man was drowned. The doctor and his accomplices were of course taken up and tried. The wife of the deceased was so fully convinced that the treatment was correct, although it unfortunately failed in this case, that she made every effort to procure the acquittal of the culprit. She again had recourse to another doctor, who supplied her with pills, which she was to take when the case came on in court, and by means of which the jury were to be so spell-bound as to give a verdict in his favour. The case came on; law was more potent than charms. The four accomplices escaped on the ground that they were hired servants of the doctor, but the doctor himself was safely lodged in jail.

There is another superstition prevalent among the lower class. They fancy that some men are gifted with the power to pray their enemy to death. It sometimes occurs that if a man has a quarrel with his neighbour who happens to obtain one of his garments, the man who lost his garment would be in a great state of alarm lest the other got possession of it in order to have a spell or charm over him. And very often the fear of their enemy praying them to death so works on their imagination as to produce the effect. They do not believe themselves endowed with the power of praying a white man to death. They have had a practical example of their impotency in this matter. It was once tried on John Young, who had been a boatswain in the American ship *Eleanor*. He was detained on the island in consequence of the taboo having been laid on the canoes, which were not allowed to leave the shore. The ship put to sea without him, and on finding himself a resident on the island, he married a native lady of a noble family, and was himself created a chief.

Having had a quarrel with one of the natives, he resolved to pray him to death. So he built a hut on the top of a hill, and periodically went up to his lofty retreat to pray John Young to death. His friends told him that his end would soon come, for his enemy was praying him to death. The brawny tar had been travelling too long over the world, and had weathered too many storms, to be alarmed by such a tale; so he collected several of his friends, and sallied up the hill. They soon built a hut alongside that of the man who was praying for his death, and both he and his friends united in one voice a counter-supplication, which so terrified the unfortunate native, that he went home discomfited. He felt that it was all over with him, and that he had been out-prayed; becoming melancholy, he subsequently died. After this failure the natives became thoroughly convinced that it was quite impossible to pray a white man to death.

In the rainy season, when all is verdure, the scenery is exceedingly picturesque and beautiful. There is a road leading from the town through the valley of Nuanu, where there are many neat and commodious villas belonging to the merchants. At the extremity of the valley is a deep precipice called Pali,[2] down which it is said Kamehameha the First, on his invasion of the island, drove the natives headlong in a terrible battle. The direct road to the opposite side of the island is by a winding pass, cut out of the face of this precipice. The island is divided by a range of mountains, stretching east and west; and on each side of the Pali they rise to a great height, looking like the huge lofty portals of this narrow gorge, through which the north-east trade-wind rushes violently, and sometimes with great fury, encountering the traveller as he commences to descend the opposite side.

Here a noble prospect of the plain or district of Palikoolau amply repays the visitor for his ride. To the right and left the range of mountains which forms the backbone of the island, rise majestically and nobly. Towards the south they slope gently towards Honolulu and the sea; but on the north side they rise from the plains below like a perpendicular wall, varying from two to three thousand feet and upwards in height. Against this huge gigantic barrier the north-east trade-wind hurls dark and solemn clouds big with rain, which break against the rocky towers, cutting deep fissures in its haggard face like wrinkles wrought by the rude hand of Time.

At a few miles distant to the east and west, spurs of smaller hills extend outwards from the main range towards the north, forming a mighty and extensive amphitheatre, encircling a valley, beautiful in its rich tropical luxuriance. This group of islands are of volcanic origin; in some there are volcanoes now in operation, but in Oahu they are entirely extinct. If, upon further investigation, it could be proved that this valley had ever been the crater of a volcano, with one side now burst out by some great convulsion of nature, we may be able to form some idea of the magnitude of this monarch of fires in the days of its activity.

To all this natural beauty one historical incident invests the Pali with a kind of respect and awe in the estimation of the native. To the Kanaka his sea-girt home is his kingdom; it is his little world; he has his ancestors, and his stories to tell about them as well as ourselves; he can tell of the conquest of Oahu, when the forces of Kalani Kupule and Kaiana were routed by the victorious troops of Kamehameha the First, and how many of them, after being driven up the valley of Nu-

2. In the Hawaiian language "*pali*" means "precipice."

anu, were precipitated headlong down the Pali and destroyed.

But from the Pali another scene of peculiar interest is presented to the view. It is when the eye is turned from contemplating the works of God in all their sublimity and grandeur, to the little missionary station of Kaneohe, about four miles from the foot of the pass, where you may see a self-denying-missionary and his family making humble efforts to bring back the wandering and reclaim the lost. There you may see the house of prayer, the school-house, and missionary's residence, where exertions are made not merely to reclaim the waste lands of the smiling valley, but, what is of infinitely greater importance, to reclaim the lost and ruined sons and daughters of Adam, whose souls present a waste, a moral wilderness, more appalling and more deserving of our utmost solicitude than the wastes and wilds of nature.

For ages Satan reigned supreme with undisputed sway over the ruins of this section of the human race; but now men's hearts are moved towards the heathen, and feel themselves bound to obey the orders of our Divine Master in proclaiming peace to them who are afar off as well as to them who are nigh. There is also a Roman Catholic missionary settlement here, as well as a school for the better class, which is also under their control. These missionaries were forced upon the islanders by the French, who sent ships of war there for the purpose of reducing them into compliance. They do not seem to be well received either by the government or the mass of the people; but when restless spirits get tired of the religion in which they have been educated, or take offence at the minister who may be placed over them, they change sides and attend the Roman Catholic chapel, which is intended as a punishment to their former pastor, and thus a considerable congregation is collected.

14th May.—Set sail from Honolulu, and passing by the Philippine Islands, cast anchor on the 19th of June at Hong Kong. When war was proclaimed with China, some of the vessels on the Pacific station were ordered across to take part in this expedition. The *Pearl* was one of the ships selected for this service, and it was for this reason that she was directed to make a voyage so unusual and so distant from the station to which she was originally sent. Troops were on their voyage out from England, and extensive preparations were making to strike an effective blow in reducing the Emperor of the Celestial Kingdom to terms, and convince him of the necessity of opening his ports to the commerce of the world. But no opportunity was afforded to the *Pearl* to take a very large or active share in these operations. More important military achievements were to be accomplished, and more valuable service was to be done.

During the month the *Pearl* was in China, her men were only once in action against the enemy, when they were sent on a boat expedition to destroy some Chinese pirates. The method adopted to distinguish between a pirate and an honest trader is not very consonant to our ideas of discerning character. When a Chinese guide was once asked by the commanding officer whether the vessels seen ahead were the pirates, he recommended, as a test, that a few shots should be fired among them, remarking that honest men would not run away, but remain quietly in their ships; but that if they were pirates, they would "*makey woilo*," that is, they would desert their ships and make their escape. This would be rather an unsatisfactory test to the innocent ones, if any such there be; doubts are afloat on this point, however, arising from the fact that numbers of the Chinese vessels are armed, and it is strongly suspected that if they do not succeed in carrying on a little trade legitimately, they do not scruple to try the other way. They do not object to make money honestly if they can, but at any rate they like to make money.

It was when we were lying at anchor at Hong Kong that the intelligence of the atrocities committed in India reached ns. At first it was scarcely understood: it was not known whether it was a partial outbreak or a national revolt; but matters appeared to wear a more gloomy aspect when the report spread abroad that the Governor-General of India had despatched a most urgent requisition to Lord Elgin to send the troops to India which were daily expected out for the Chinese war. The truth then seemed to show out in all its alarming extent.

On the 15th July orders were issued to H.M.S. ships *Shannon* and *Pearl* to prepare for sea, and next day both ships weighed anchor and sailed for Calcutta. Lord Elgin was on board the *Shannon*; and three hundred of the R.M.L. Infantry having lately arrived in H.M.S. *Sanspareil,* were immediately sent in the same vessel to Calcutta.

On arriving at Singapore, we found that H.M. 90th Regiment, which had a short time previously been wrecked in the *Transit,* was awaiting a passage to India. Two companies were sent on board, and the ship being got ready for sea, we steamed through the straits, and made the best of our way to the mouth of the Hoogly. On arriving at the sand heads on the 7th of August, no pilot was to be procured;

they were taking their ease in Calcutta, while for three days we were beating about in search of one, tossed by a tempestuous south-west monsoon, at a time that the country was in a state of revolt and troops urgently required; and while their detention might have been most disastrous, the crisis in the capital of India being at its height.

After capturing one of these valuable functionaries, we proceeded up the Hoogly to Calcutta, and made fast to moorings off the Esplanade. The two companies of the 90th Regiment disembarked on the 12th of August, and were immediately sent up country.

H.M.S. SHANNON

CHAPTER 3

Naval Brigade Embarked in the Chunar

At the time of our arrival one panic at Calcutta had just died away, and another was coming to a head. The *Mohurrum*, which is the great Mahomedan festival, was about to commence, and fears were excited that Mussulman fanaticism, which is generally brimful, would now boil over. Reports were spread of arms concealed, of rebels ready to rise, and *sepoy* ripe for massacre. Calcutta was put into an attitude of defence, some of the large public buildings were garrisoned by the volunteers who enrolled themselves in the ranks for mutual protection. The Royal Marines which came from China were quartered in Fort William, and orders were issued that the crew of the *Pearl* should be in readiness, the men being frequently landed for drill and the exercise of light field-guns.

At last the *Mohurrum* passed away, and the alarm along with it—the preparations were too much for any Bengalee rebellion. The authorities were becoming wide-awake to the magnitude of the exigency; and, if the truth was known, it is highly probable that the natives were as much alarmed at the military arrangements that were made, as the Europeans were at their deficiency compared with the extent of the apprehended danger. At any rate, the *Mohurrum* went off more quietly than usual; whether it was that the Mussulmans were disappointed at their hopes being defeated, and their designs being frustrated, or fear lest the smallest disturbance would give occasion for an attack by European troops, from whom they had no reason to expect mercy, deponent saith not. The fears, however, of the European population who had taken refuge on board the ships on the river a few weeks before, became allayed; and the knowledge that the destructive broadsides of two ships of war could have been brought to bear on the city, burning the native population out of house and home, no doubt contributed to hush the murmurs of rebellion into silence, and render general the sense of security.

But the aspect of affairs was still gloomy:—a cloud hung over India; Delhi had not fallen; Lucknow was in the hands of the rebels; and shortly after a *chuckledar* waved his standard over the rich and fertile province of Goruckpore.

Captain Peel, R.N. had volunteered, on his arrival, to bring the crew of H.M.S. *Shannon* and his heavy guns to the walls of Delhi. His offer was gladly accepted, and he left Calcutta about a week after his arrival. This design, however, was not carried out, but subsequently his guns were brought into position before the city of Lucknow. Captain Sotheby, R.N., also volunteered his services to the government, which were accepted; and on the 12th of September, 1857, he embarked a part of the crew of H.M.S. *Pearl*, on board a small paddle-wheel steamer, called the *Chunar*. The first detachment of the Naval Brigade to be followed by another company a month subsequently, consisted of 158 men of the *Pearl*, including seamen and marines; one 12-pounder howitzer, one 24-pounder howitzer, and 24-pounder rockets.

The *Chunar*, I believe, was one of the best steamers that could be obtained at the time; but bad was the best. If the stream was running strong, she was warranted "not to go;" in fact, a more deplorable conveyance for sending troops expeditiously up country could scarcely be found. The absence of railways was now experienced to be a want that no other means could so adequately supply, when a quick transport of troops would have been of such advantage to the State.

There is little of interest in the river scenery. Rank tropical luxuriance everywhere prevails; the banks of the river are low, and for some miles from Calcutta you may see large houses belonging to European merchants or native *baboos*. The burning *ghats* near Calcutta are a novel sight. Here the bodies of the deceased Hindoos are committed to the flames: the smouldering corpse is deserted by those held dear in life, and the last offices of the dead are left to be performed by strangers who are regarded as the lowest caste, and despised for their profession and their pains. No friends remain to see the last offices performed with decency or order; but dogs, vultures, and adjutants frequent the spot to pick up the fragments that remain.

Sometimes the ghastly corpse of a Hindoo whose friends are too poor to buy fuel for the burning pile, floats down the river, on which a vulture or carrion crow sails along to obtain his wonted repast. Such customs, like many others, are repulsive to Christian ideas of decency and propriety, and, like a multitude of other Eastern usages are the reverse of our own.

Occasionally a herd of cattle may be seen swimming across the river to the opposite bank, guided by the herdsmen, who cling to their backs with all the tenacity of monkeys. Their numerous heads just appearing above water, present an odd sight; more particularly so when a passing steamer suddenly blows off steam with a loud noise. Then there is a precipitate hurry-scurry and helter-skelter. They make as much haste as possible to escape. We need not, however, be surprised at the alarm of the dumb animal, when even their sable masters exhibit a similar fear. It is not uncommon to see them, while gazing from the banks on the "fire ship," take fright, and scatter in all directions, at the sudden blast from the blow-pipe. Bengalees are an exceedingly timid race. I have seen villagers run from the banks when a spy-glass was presented to the eye, supposing it to be a gun, and some who stood courageous for a few minutes, when a spy-glass was presented a second time, thought discretion the better part of valour.

16th September.—Passed the site of the battlefield of Plassey, which decided the fate of India one hundred years ago, (as at time of first publication). For many years a well-known tree was flourishing here called Clive's tree; but the river has no respect for trees or fields, so it has washed away the one, and flows over the other. On the 17th, anchored off Burhampore. Near this place is Moorshedabad, where the government has built a noble palace for the *nabob*; in which, however, he is not supposed to reside. It contains a fine suite of apartments for show, but his private residence is adjacent, where he spends the greater part of his time. When coals were shipped, we proceeded steaming next day up the Bhaugaretti, and on the 21st entered the Ganges, that mighty artery of India.

We had not gone far up the river when the pilot lodged complaints against a Brahmin called Chummun Sing regarding his threats to maltreat or murder the river pilots if they continued to bring steamers up the river for Europeans, telling the people that the Company's *raj* was at end. To permit this Brahmin to spread these reports, and use these threats with impunity, would have been productive of much inconvenience to the public service in terrifying the pilots from their duty or rendering them disaffected; it was therefore deemed advisable to bring the offender at once to punishment. On arriving at the village where he resided, a messenger was sent by Captain Sotheby, who was in command of the Naval Brigade, to summon the head policeman of the village, who requested to be excused on the grounds of being sick.

Another policeman was procured, who rather reluctantly accompanied a party of marines to apprehend Chummun Sing. On being found, the policeman played false by denying him; but being unmistakeably identified, he was brought on board the *Chunar*, and the case was investigated. The policeman was reported to the magistrate of the district, for attempting to shield the prisoner from punishment, and the prisoner was sent to the same magistrate to be dealt with according to his offence. During the rainy season the land in many parts of Bengal is covered with water, and presents the appearance of a dismal swamp, while the huts of the inhabitants looked wretched and comfortless in the middle of a land inundated with waters. It is the former, however, which renders the country a fertile garden; and the latter, though so miserable, seem to satisfy the wants of a simple people, who are averse to change, even for the better, the construction of their hovels.

There is very little in the scenery to relieve the monotony of a dull cruise up the Ganges: it was not sufficient to know that the barren and desolate-looking banks from which the waters were fast receding, would, in a short time, be covered with crops and vegetation, the eye wanted something attractive to rest on as well as the imagination. From Moorshedabad to Dinapore, which was reached on the 7th of October, there was no station of any importance except Rajmahal, Bhaugulpore, and Monghyr. The first was once a royal residence, as its name imports; and there are still to be seen the fine old ruins of a palace, with some curious arches and tracery-work remaining; but the greater part of the building has fallen to decay, or has been precipitated into the river by the stream, which has not ceased for years to undermine its foundations. The second is a civil station, with the usual staff of civilians for the management of the district.

Here missionary operations are carried on with considerable vigour and success. The Santals and Hill men, among whom the missionary labours, have fewer prejudices to break down, and present fewer obstacles to the embracing of Christianity than the Hindoo, and therefore afford a favourable field for labour. Monghyr is also a civil station, and one of the most picturesque on the river. It is an old square fortress, surrounded by high walls with a ditch outside, enclosing within a considerable space, sufficient for many fine houses and gardens. It is also defended by small towers and bastions; but not having been repaired for years past, they are falling to decay. Within these spacious grounds there is a church, as well as one at Bhaugulpore; but neither having a government chaplain, they are dependent on the voluntary services of missionaries for ministerial duty. Monghyr also lays claim to the name of a manufacturing town, and has been denominated the Birmingham of India; though by what right its friends assume for it that title I am at a loss to discover. The natives here possess the faculty of manufacturing chairs, tables, and other furniture; they can carve ornaments in wood and horn, such as bracelets, chains, and ornamental walking-sticks; they also manufacture fire-arms and other iron work; but their ingenuity does not seem to be of a very high cast, or to take a very wide range.

On the 7th of August, on arriving at Dinapore, the 24-pound howitzer was left behind to be sent back to the ship; since no gun-carriage fit for land-service could be procured for it, either from the arsenal or at Dinapore. One 12-pr howitzer and two 12-pr mountain train-guns were supplied in its place.

Captain Sotheby received orders that the Naval Brigade under his command should proceed to Buxar and garrison the fort there. Having reached it on the 10th, the guns, ammunition and baggage being landed, they took up their quarters in the fort which had been prepared for their reception. Buxar was once a civil station, and is soon to be so again, but its importance at that time chiefly consisted in one of the principal government studs for breeding cavalry horses being in the neighbourhood. And in consequence of the mutiny of so many cavalry regiments, it was of considerable importance to keep a good look-out for those that remained in order to supply the place of those that had been taken off by the mutineers. During the time that the Naval Brigade was quartered in the fort at Buxar no time was lost; the men were drilled daily, and were exercised at gunnery with unremitting care. In a short time, they were proficients in the exercise of the field-guns and the management of the artillery horses; in fact, they were rapidly becoming soldiers.

On the 23rd of October orders were received directing the Naval Brigade to proceed immediately to Chupra, an alarm having arisen from a report that a body of rebels were hovering on the borders of the district of Sarun. This district was rich and fertile, the treasury was full and tempting, and therefore precautionary measures were urgently required to prevent it meeting with the same fate as some others. That evening a detachment, under the command of Lieutenant Grant, R.N., was sent over in a small river-steamer, the distance being about five-and-thirty or forty miles.

And on the 26th the remainder, with the guns, ammunition, and baggage, followed, landing at Chupra Ghat in the afternoon of the same day. The schoolhouse was fitted up to receive them, but these quarters were not long enjoyed. As soon as *hackeries* and baggage-carts could be procured, they marched to Sewan, a small town forty miles to the north of Chupra. This town had, some time previously, been abandoned by the European residents on the occasion of the incursion of the rebels in that quarter; but was at this time reoccupied by a regiment of Gurkhas, having lately arrived, and giving some degree of security and confidence to the peaceable portion of the inhabitants.

The rebel forces began collecting in formidable numbers on the borders of the district; and threatening a friendly *rajah* at Mujowlee, not more than six-and-twenty miles distant, it was deemed advisable to take up a more advanced position; and consequently, by the orders of Captain Sotheby, R.N., the force, consisting of the Naval Brigade and a regiment of Gurkhas, made one march to Myrwa in advance. This movement had the effect of diverting the rebels from attacking Mujowlee for that time. Prospects of a most serious character seemed to threaten the valuable districts of Sarun, Chumparun, and Tirhoot. The *sepoys* at this time managing to inspire the public with a very exalted idea of their courage and dangerous ferocity, serious apprehensions of consequences of the most calamitous nature were entertained by men in authority, if the rebels should succeed in making a sweeping invasion of the districts north of the Ganges with artillery, while there were no available troops to augment the Sarun field force, and enable it to make a determined resistance.

It was felt that even Patna, to the south of the Ganges, was not safe: peril of no ordinary character would have hung over it if the districts on the other side of the river had fallen into the hands of the insurgents. The paucity of the European troops at this period of the war was felt in every direction. The only Europeans that could be spared to defend these extensive provinces was the Naval Brigade, which had lately been augmented by another company under Lieutenant Radcliffe, R.N., numbering altogether about two hundred and fifty officers and men. Some of them had been raised by volunteers among the merchant seamen at a time when every European was of such great value; but the great majority were men-of-war seamen belonging to H.M. steam ship *Pearl* and her detachment of Royal Marines.

It may seem a misapplication of a name to apply the term "Brigade" to so small a number as two hundred and fifty men; but the Naval Brigade in the Crimea having consisted of a very strong force, to it the term may with propriety have been applied; and no definite name being generally given to a body of seamen when landed for service on shore, they seem to have inherited that title from the distinguished band who served on shore during the Russian war; and hence it seems to have been adopted, without reference to numbers, by seamen engaged in land service. It was not unusual to read in some of the Indian newspapers, during the time of the mutinies, about the movements of some Naval Brigade consisting of a hundred merchant-seamen serving in different parts of India; consequently, if this is admissible, it need not be considered out of place to denominate a body of seamen and Royal Marines of H.M. Navy by the same name.

The difference between service on shore and afloat now presented commissariat and other difficulties, which in an incredible short space of time were overcome. Lieutenant Grant, R.N., who had previously been given charge of the treasure-chest, was also appointed staff officer, and in addition acted as paymaster and commissariat officer—offices which he continued to fulfil for several months, until it became necessary (the brigade being augmented by other European troops) to have a commissariat officer. Lieutenant Bolton, attached to the force. On the 27th of November Colonel Rowcroft, who had commanded the 8th Regiments of Native Infantry which mutinied at Dinapore, arrived at Myrwa to take command of the Sarun Field Force. Operations were to be carried on entirely on the defensive, and at this time, on no account was Goruckpore to be entered, as the force was not sufficiently strong to attack the enemy with effect, and other troops could not be spared.

For several weeks the force was encamped at Myrwa, and no enemy showed himself; occasionally a Brahmin, a spy or *budmash*, would be captured and executed; but there was no advancing army reported. The men began to despair of seeing the mutineers; they began to think that they were brought up country for nothing, and thought it very hard to be left in the background where there was no opponent, while others were pressing to the front. Disappointment became general that they could not have a "crack" at the *sepoys*. This state of repose was not destined to last long.

On the 13th of December a report was brought in that the rebels had attacked Goothnee, a village about eight miles distant, had plundered the magazine, and had driven out the small garrison of Sikhs which were left to defend the town. Colonel Rowcroft ordered a detachment of the Naval Brigade, with four guns, a detachment of the Ramdhul regiment of Gurkhas, and a detachment of the Royal Marines, to march without delay to Goothnee, and drive them out. On arriving at the place about noon, a true account of the affair became known.

The alarm was occasioned by a small force of the rebels having crossed the river during the night, the Sikhs were taken by surprise, being utterly unprepared for an attack: and their *jemadar* in command, being an old Brahmin, maintained no discipline, and allowed them to live in a disorderly manner; and who, when the Sikhs were assembled, would not lead them out against the insurgents. The *jemadar* was made prisoner and sent to Dinapore for trial.[1] The Sikhs were ashamed of having left their post, volunteered any service to retrieve their character, and threw the blame on the *jemadar*. On the other side of the river which flows past Goothnee, the rebels were numerous, but it was not considered prudent to attack them with so small a force, and in the evening the men returned to Myrwa.

On the 18th our camping ground was changed to a more desirable position on the left bank of the River Jurrai, and strong piquets were posted in front and on both flanks. This movement was necessary, arising from the fact that the information was not always reliable, and the number of the insurgents might turn out to be (as subsequently was discovered) much greater than at first reported; it was, therefore, deemed desirable to have the river as a defence in front, instead of being a barrier immediately in rear of our camp, in the event of the enemy coming down with very superior numbers. The rebels being usually short-sighted, and not probably understanding the cause of this apparent retreat, were emboldened by it to advance; and encouraging their followers with the notion that we were weak and retreating, crossed the little Gunduck at Mujowlee on the 22nd, and a day or two afterwards took up a position about seven miles in our front, in topes (of trees) near the village of Sohunpore, where they threw up earthworks in front of their camp. This apparent retreat, which was only intended as a precautionary movement, had the effect of drawing them on to an engagement in the open field; an opportunity which, in

1. He was afterwards transported.

44

all probability, would not otherwise have been so freely given.

The Sarun Field Force only consisted, at this time, of 250 of the Naval Brigade, with four guns, including a detachment of forty-five of the Royal Marine Light Infantry, and about 450 of the Ramdhul regiment of Gurkhas, fifty of them having been left at Sewan with a small detachment of seamen. On the 24th, the day before Christmas, the alarm was given of the approach of the enemy, which numbered several thousands. The troops were soon under arms, and the artillery horses were got ready for the guns. After waiting an hour without any prospect of an enemy, the spies who were sent out for intelligence, brought back word that quietness in every direction prevailed, and no rebels were to be seen beyond their piquets, a few *sowars* who were observed on the road on a reconnoitring excursion causing the alarm.

All prospect of seeing the rebels that day was banished, and the men went to their tents disappointed. Next day being Christmas, and having no prospect of a plum-pudding. Jack jocularly expressed his disappointment at not having a "sea-pie" (*sepoy*).

CHAPTER 4

Action at Sohunpore

December 25th.—This morning the Field Force received a reinforcement of the Gorucknath regiment of Gurkhas, 500 strong. It
was now our turn to produce a little alarm among the enemy; but
having come by forced marches from Segowlee, they were too much
fatigued, footsore, and hungry to march again that day; and consequently the Christmas-day was passed in peace and quietness. Notwithstanding this augmentation to our force, the prospect was not
particularly promising. The insurgents numbered several thousands,
the Gurkhas were still untried, and they were armed with the old
flint-lock muskets, which were by no means equal to the Brown Bess
of the Sepoys; nevertheless, it was resolved to attack and beat them the
following day. The Nepalese did not rejoice in a strikingly Hyde-Park
appearance; but they turned out occasionally to have plenty of "pluck"
when led by Europeans.

Each regiment numbers about 500. The Ramdhul had red coats,
and the Gorucknath blue: the cut is not very describable; it was evidently intended to be after the fashion of the *coatee*. There was a scarf
over their shoulders, rather brownish, but intended for white; and
trousers of a similar colour, the cut of which was something between
French and Turkish. The religion of the men in the former regiment
was Hindoo, regarding the ox as a sacred animal; and consequently
orders were issued by government that no bullocks should be killed in
the vicinity of their camp, that their prejudices should not be violated.
The other was raised in that part of Nepal bordering on Tibet, and
would eat the flesh of the buffalo without any conscientious scruples.

Christmas-day passed in peace. Towards evening rumours were
afloat that the rebels were to be attacked next morning. Orders were
issued a little later in the evening by Colonel Rowcroft that put it

beyond all doubt, and all went to rest awaiting the results of the morrow.

December 26th.—Having breakfasted earlier than usual, the force under the command of Colonel Rowcroft left the camp about eight o'clock, a.m., to meet the enemy. One hundred Gurkhas, fifty matchlock men of the Hutwah *rajah*, and a few seamen were left to protect the camp and guard the bridge across the Jurrai, which was on the high road leading from Myrwa to Sohunpore.

The force which got ready to march was the Naval Brigade, 180 men and four guns, 12-pr howitzers under the command of Captain Sotheby, R.N., including thirty of the Royal Marine Light Infantry under Lieutenant Pym, fifty Sikhs under the command of Lieutenant Burlton, 500 of the Ramdhul regiment of Gurkhas, and 350 of the Gorucknath regiment, under the command of Captains Weston and Brooks. The Hon. Victor Montagu, midshipman, was appointed acting *aide-de-camp* to Colonel Rowcroft, and Mr. F. H. Stephenson, midshipman, was acting *aide-de-camp* to Captain Sotheby, R.N. This duty they continued to fulfil throughout both campaigns. Mr. Foot, midshipman, was attached to Lieutenant Turnour's light field battery; and Lieutenant Radcliffe was in command of the naval column.

The line of march having been previously arranged, the force kept along the road leading from Myrwa (where the camp was left standing) to Sohunpore, about seven miles distant. Along the line of march the column was in sections, preceded by the Sikhs in skirmishing order; and the Marines, under Lieutenant Pym, followed as a reserve to the Sikhs, in case of an attack.

It had been ascertained that the rebels were posted in two or three large *topes* (groves of mango-trees) near the village of Sohunpore, on both sides of the road leading to Mujhowlee, and that three of their four guns, with a numerous body as a support, were posted behind a high bank, with the additional cover afforded by a large tank. Having arrived within a mile of this position, the force deployed into line, taking ground to the right. Lieutenant Pym, with a detachment of the Royal Marines, and Lieutenant Grant, R.N., with a detachment of seamen, advanced skirmishing on the right Lieutenant Burlton, with the Sikh skirmishers, were on the left. The four 12-pr howitzers were in the centre; at some distance to the right of the guns, the naval column deployed into line; a detachment of the Gorucknath regiment were between the marines and the naval column; and the Ramdhul regiment formed line on the left of the guns; a reserve of two companies of Gurkhas were in rear of the line, and the spare artillery bullocks, spare ammunition carts and elephants, were drawn up in rear of the reserve with a rear-guard.

As it was the intention to follow them up as closely as it was possible with infantry, and hold all the ground that might be gained, two days' provisions and two or three tents were brought with the force, no other baggage being allowed to leave the camp. The first gun was fired about ten o'clock, a.m., and disclosed the enemy's position. *Sowars*, or Native Cavalry, were seen hovering on the left, while on the right and in front were large bodies of infantry. Our force deployed into line in a large open *maidan* or plain; but intervening between our men and the enemy were fields of high crops, such as sugar-cane, *dhal*, and other grain, and which grew so high that a large army might lie concealed in it, while the country would present the appearance of the most placid repose. The enemy pushed forward numerous skirmishers into the topes (woods) and high crops, opening a heavy fire of guns and musketry.

Our skirmishers, though few, also advanced, steadily and boldly, driving them back, and doing much execution with their rifles. Notwithstanding the thick cover by which they might have been concealed, the noise and tumult which prevails in a native camp soon discovered the position of their main body. Their left was resting on the village of Sohunpore, and their right on a small village in which they had planted two guns. As soon as our line had advanced within range, it was received by a heavy fire from the guns which were in position in the village on the left. These guns enfiladed our line, which then fell back and changed front.

The Naval Artillery in reply fired several rounds of shot and shell in rapid succession. The line advanced, and approached close to the village, from which a fire of musketry was still kept up. Other guns opened fire on our line from our front, and a brisk cannonade was kept up on all sides. The firing of the Naval Artillery, under Lieutenant Turnour, R.N., was kept up with great precision and telling effect, silencing two of the enemy's guns, which were posted on our left, in half an hour. Once the *sowars* made a movement as if with the intention to charge; but the incessant fire of the artillery produced a change in their movements, and checked their advance. A few well-directed shell, pitching in the midst, scattered them in all directions.

A large body of infantry then moved towards a village on our left,

48

apparently with a view to outflank us; but the Sikhs, supported by two companies of Gurkhas, advanced, and took the village, which they held throughout the day; while the Royal Marines under Lieutenant Pym, and a party of seamen under Lieutenant Grant, R.N., entered Sohunpore on the right. Their movements then becoming completely paralysed, they retired in great confusion. After a three-hours' hard fight, the enemy was completely dispersed and driven off the field. They were expelled from the *topes* and village, which was then entered. Their camp was taken and burned, some tents were carried off by the Sikhs, while their dinner and other articles, including earthenware culinary utensils, were left on the ground.

Their number was estimated at 6000; of which 1200 were regular *sepoys*, and 150 were cavalry. Their loss was supposed to be about 150, and their principal leaders were Hurkishen Sing and the Naib Nazim Mushuruff Khan. A few of them held the village for some time after the main body had fled, to cover their retreat, as on entering, it was discovered that they had gone for some time with their guns, flying precipitately by Mujhowlee towards Goruckpore.

Throughout the action they never ventured nearer to our line than four or five hundred yards, the shell and rifles keeping them at this respectful distance; and as our line steadily and firmly advanced, they judiciously, but precipitately, retired. The Gurkhas, under the direction of Captains Weston and Brooks, behaved steadily and stood firmly throughout the day; but their arms, being the old flint-musket, did little execution, and therefore to the shell and rifle success was universally acknowledged to be due.

Disorganized and routed, they were followed up in hot pursuit. If cavalry had formed a part of our force, their defeat would have been rendered still more disastrous. On approaching Mujhowlee, the rear of the rebel forces came in sight. The Marines, a part of the Naval Brigade, and four companies of the Gorucknath regiment were ordered to push rapidly on after the Sikhs, who composed the advanced guard, in hopes of capturing the guns, as they were fording the river. They were soon pounced upon by the Sikhs; one large iron gun was taken with limber completely full of ammunition, and several of the enemy were killed. Two tumbrils, one full of ammunition, and the other of powder, were also taken.

But one circumstance above all others which is a matter of wonder as well as thankfulness, is, that, while inflicting so severe a blow on the enemy, so little loss should be sustained by ourselves. There was only one killed, and he was a camp-follower; several, however, were wounded, although only one or two, who were Gurkhas, severely. Fortunately the gun and musket-firing of the rebels is generally too high, the balls passing over the heads of the troops in the line, tearing up the ground, and ricocheting harmlessly in the rear.

The day by this time was drawing to a close, and the men had had a hard day's work of ten hours, and a fourteen-miles march under an Indian sun, when they returned to the village of Mujhowlee, and bivouacked for the night. They were fagged, and tired with running, and required rest. The excitement for a time took away the thoughts of heat and hunger; but a bit of bread and a glass of grog was not to be refused. The *rajah* came out to meet the troops and give a hearty welcome, as also did the villagers along the road, who supplied water to quench the parching thirst of the men while marching in thick clouds of dust and under a burning sun.

Their *salaams* were most humble, and apparently as sincere as most Hindoo compliments. They were, at any rate, glad to make friends with the winning side, and no doubt felt the difference between the conduct of our troops and that of their own countrymen, who for several days had been looting all the villages in the vicinity of their camp. On the other hand, a locomotive bazaar or market having been established, marched when our force marched, and the natives, finding the trade so lucrative, were glad to bring their goods, knowing that they would obtain a ready sale and a good price.

The Rajah of Mujhowlee had suffered severely by the looting and plundering of his villages; and they coolly told him that, upon becoming masters of the country, they would divest him of a portion of his landed property, but that a portion of it he should be permitted to retain. The rajah also stated that the insurgents advanced with the full persuasion of being able to surround and destroy so small a force, and then to overrun Sarun, Chunparun, and Tirhoot, raising the districts in rebellion.

There are few actions on record, if any, in which so small a number of European troops encountered and completely defeated an enemy so numerous; and seldom has one day's work been known so completely to clear a district of a horde of marauding rebels, rescuing many villages from plunder and oppression.

Asiatics can by no means be compared to European troops, and never can be so depended on; and although the Nepalese may be active in climbing the crags of their native hills, and be formidable when defending the fastnesses and homes in their native jungles, yet that an enemy numbering 6000, or perhaps more, should be dispersed and scattered when 200 European troops were engaged, aided by these Nepalese, is an evidence of what the boldness and daring of British troops will do. And when it is remembered that they were British seamen and marines, the former of whom were entirely out of their element—who, from being sailors by profession, were marshalled as soldiers—who, from riding over the boisterous billows of the foaming deep, were drilled to ride the horses of the Naval Artillery, and while they pursued the enemy with a rapidity and perseverance not to be outstripped, the 12-pounder howitzers discharged shot and shell on their retreating and broken ranks with a precision and effect not to be surpassed, eliciting the praise from the commanding officer that the "troops behaved as British seamen and marines ever do, most excellently and gallantly. Captain Sotheby, being everywhere present with the guns in action, having paid great attention to the drill and training of the men for land service," for which "they are now ready, horses having been trained for the guns, and seamen to ride them and act as gunners."

And thus, under the influence of good discipline, artillery practice and drill, the men invariably gained the approbation of those by whom they were commanded, for valour in the field as well as good conduct in the camp.

During the halts at Sewan and Myrwa the brigade was exercised daily at battalion and light-infantry drill, rifle-practice, and light field-piece drill. The horses at first were fresh and unbroken, and when yoked to the guns, carried away the traces; but in a short time they were so well managed, that when they came into action, they had advanced to a high degree of efficiency, not only in those duties in which the requirements of their profession as men-of-war's men caused them to be acquainted, such as rifle-practice and gunnery, but to their wonted activity in the management of guns was added a speedily acquired expertness in the management of the artillery horses. But the difficulty of raising this corps to such a high state of efficiency was more than ordinary, arising from the impossibility of procuring the necessary stores from the arsenals.

Guns were supplied; but spare ammunition-wagons, limbers, and horses were deficient, and when with great difficulty and perseverance horses were procured, it was found necessary to get the greater part of the harness made in camp not being able to get sufficient saddlery supplied; and, instead of having spare ammunition-wagons and limbers drawn by horses, which is necessary to the efficiency of a battery, the only substitute that could be procured was *hackeries*, or native carts drawn by bullocks, and warranted to go two or two and a half miles an hour by a vigorous application of the stick. A limber or spare ammunition-wagon was nowhere to be procured until after the first action, when those taken from the enemy, on that and other occasions, were, by the vigorous ingenuity and diligence of the ship's carpenter, Mr. Burton, converted to our own use, affording an example of that readiness with which a sailor can turn his hand to anything, and get out of a difficulty while many a man would be thinking about it.

Inconsiderable as this force may seem to have been, the results and moral effect of this victory were of great importance, when it is remembered that a few days prior to the engagement, some of the most valuable and productive districts in India, from which a large revenue is collected, were threatened by several thousand rebels, many of the *zamindars* being disaffected and likely to render assistance to the enemy, and, as has since been discovered, their plans and expectations had been to surround by their superior numbers and cut up the little force at Myrwa, and then march direct and unopposed into the district of Sarun, where there was not a European soldier from the banks of the Ganges to the frontier of Nepaul, except the Naval Brigade.[2]

But the tide turned; the wave which seemed destined to sweep over the fertile plains dashed against a rock, from which it receded broken and abased. Confidence was restored in the district, disaffected *zamindars* paid their rents in silence, and thus, though the force employed was small, the advantages derived from the success were considerable. And when it is remembered that it was obtained without the loss of a single man, a few only being wounded, ought we not to be led to believe that the High and Mighty One who is the only Giver of all victory, showed a favour unto us, crowning our arms with success.

For several days successively, prisoners continued to be taken, one of whom was a *sepoy* of the 10th Regiments of Native Infantry. Following the routine at that period of the war, he was blown away from a gun in the presence of the assembled troops, explanations having been given to the Gurkhas that this was not the English method of treating prisoners taken in war, but was only inflicted in this special case when the crime committed was stained with peculiar heinous-

---

2. About this time the Bengal Yeomanry Cavalry crossed the Ganges at Patna into the district of Tirhoot, in number 200.

ness. As was usual with these men under similar circumstances, he walked up to the gun apparently with perfect indifference, was lashed to it with his back to the muzzle, and met his end with remarkable apathy. He acknowledged having been engaged on the 26th, and he must have been zealous in the cause he had espoused, for he had gone out to the battle unarmed, waiting to take the place of some fallen comrade, whose arms he could appropriate.

The Rajah of Mujhowlee was well pleased with the departure of the rebels, and often came into camp like a feudal baron, attended by the chief men of his household and armed retainers. His palace, however, did not present a very baronial appearance; nor did it appear to afford what we should regard as plain English comfort.

On the 27th the tents and baggage came from Myrwa to Mujhowlee, where we remained encamped until the 30th, when the camp was struck and the force crossed the Chota Gunduck, and pitched the camp on the right bank of the river, near the village of Sulempore. During the halt here the time was occupied not only in discovering and punishing those who had been active in their opposition to government, but in getting the best intelligence that could be procured regarding the retreat and probable movements of the rebels at Goruckpore.

Many of the peaceably-disposed inhabitants who came to pay their respects and make their *salaams* to the magistrate, complained bitterly of the plundering of the rebels in all directions; in fact, when poultry or mess stock was sought for along the line of march, the invariable reply was that the *budmashes* had looted it all. But as many of them were rebelliously disposed when European troops turned their backs, they were not so much to be pitied; and it is to be hoped that, having tasted the "*Raj*" of their own people, they may for the future be better contented with that of the British.

After a succession of marches, the force arrived at Roodurpore on the 11th of January, from which the *rajah* had fled, taking with him his treasure and moveable property; a great part of which was afterwards discovered and captured. The town was nearly deserted, and the houses locked up. It was a case of "*like master like man*." The *ryots* follow the steps of the ruler. If he is a rebel, the chances are they will be rebels too, although they have no very clear conception of the reason for being so. Here the force remained encamped until the 22nd. During the halt a sale of the *rajah's* property and effects took place, and the magistrate was enabled to organise a police, and get that part of the country a little settled. On the 22nd the camp was struck, and the force left Roodurpore and marched to Gowra, a small village which carries on a trade in the boiling and preparing of sugar. The camp was pitched in a *tope* of trees, and without any prospect of a move for a few days. Some of the principal residents of this village were said to have been killed at Sohunpore, and many others in the vicinity were known to have been disaffected.

Next day a detachment was sent to Pyena, about five miles distant, to punish some of the principal offenders; and the day following the force made a short march to Rajpore Ghat, on the River Raptee. Having been deluged here by a heavy fall of rain, the river was not crossed until the 27th, when the baggage, guns, &;c., crossed in boats, and the men followed in the afternoon. There was some trouble in crossing the baggage and guns in boats, but none in crossing the elephants. They take to the water as naturally as a spaniel, and swim. Their bodies disappear completely under water; the mahouts stand on their backs, while the huge proboscis appears over the surface, through which he breathes and occasionally utters most uncouth sounds. Along the river, as well as on the adjacent *jheels*, there are abundance of wild duck, widgeon, a kind of snipe, and geese, affording plenty of occupation for sportsmen.

The Ramdhul regiment of Gurkhas proceeded to Azimghur the same day as an escort for percussion-muskets (I believe 4000 stand of arms), which were to be brought back for the Nepalese troops with Jung Bahadoor, their own arms not being considered effective. The day following we marched to Burhul, on the left bank of the Gogra, which was on the high road from Goruckpore to Benares; and some importance being attached to the keeping of the *ghat*, there was a halt here for several days, until, by the advance of the Nepalese troops, by whom Goruckpore had lately been taken, after a feeble resistance, and with whom the Sarun field force was to act in concert, the insurgents were known to be entirely driven far to the westward. There was reason to suppose that four regiments of cavalry and 4000 infantry were at Fyzabad, not more than five or six marches distant, and therefore there was an additional reason for keeping a good lookout on this part of the river, boats being required for the construction of a bridge across the Gogra for Jung Bahadoor's army which was marching to Lucknow.

The time occupied by these numerous halts was not altogether thrown away, as an opportunity was given to the magistrate to make

54

arrangements for the reorganisation of the police, and the settlement of the district, while at the same time punishment was inflicted on the refractory *zamindars* by the destruction of their houses, and in such other ways as was most suitable. This, it must be acknowledged, does not seem to be a very chivalrous method of bringing the delinquent to terms, savouring something of the Goth; but to the native of India it is a most severe punishment, and peculiarly humiliating, being regarded as a great disgrace, and serves to keep up a wholesome dread in the minds of others, lest a similar fate should befall themselves. It is reported that at this part of the river, about Pyena and Burhuj, some of the most influential men impose a sort of duty or tax on boats passing up and down even in peaceable times, and therefore their punishment may be looked upon as an example of retributive justice for a double offence.

CHAPTER 5

Battle of Phoolpore

By the 8th of February, 150 boats were procured, and a small steamer called the *Jumna* was in readiness to accompany them up the Gogra as far as Gai Ghat, Along her sides, bulwarks, and around her upper decks fascines were attached, to protect her as much as possible from shot, and the fire of musketry; presenting, in some degree, the appearance of a moving battery. The following day Mr. Fowler, an officer of the Naval Brigade, was sent on board the *Jumna* to take charge, and on the 10th the fleet of boats proceeded up the river as far as Ghopalpore, where the field force were encamped, having marched from Burhul the same day. The intelligence as to the state of the Oudh side of the river was not very favourable to such an undertaking.

Various reports arrived as to the strength of the rebels in the different forts that overlooked the river, and from which a few rounds of shot and shell would not only destroy the boats, but even long before this would be effected, every native boatman would have fled in dismay and alarm, leaving the boats to their fate. It would, therefore, have been hazardous to allow the fleet to advance further up without a strong escort. It was ascertained with tolerable certainty that four or five thousand rebels were at Tandah; a town at no great distance from the place where the boats were required, from which a flying column might be detached by an enterprising and daring enemy (which fortunately experience showed was not their character), and being brought to bear on any one point, might sink the boats.

Intelligence being defective, the whole of that part of the country on the Oudh side being entirely in the hands of the insurgents, the escort, if taken by surprise, might not only have suffered considerable loss, but have entered upon a fruitless enterprise, the enemy not only having the advantage of the eminence from the banks, but being able at any moment to choose their own point of attack, and retire at pleasure, until another favourable opportunity might be presented, when perhaps the boats, turning round a bend of the river, might be met by a galling fire from some thick jungle or from behind some wall or embankment.

After different plans were proposed and rejected, according to instructions received from Brigadier-General Macgregor, it was finally decided that the troops intended for the escort should be placed under the command of Captain Sotheby, R.N. They consisted of 145 seamen and marines, 100 Gurkhas, and 50 Sikhs, with one 12-pounder howitzer, in addition to the steamer *Jumna* with two small guns. It was supposed that sailors would then be in their element, and in the event of getting into a difficulty, would, no doubt, be well able to get out of it. The defective knowledge as to the strength of the forts on the river invested the expedition with some degree of peril; but it was of the utmost importance that it should be carried out with the least possible delay, that the bridging of the river might be completed in order to facilitate the transit of the Gurkhas to the siege of Lucknow.

About eight o'clock in the afternoon of the 13th of February, the troops for the escort duty left Seekregunge for Raibundpore Ghat, the place of embarkation, where they arrived about eleven o'clock at night, after a wearisome march across a country without roads. Here they pitched two small tents, their rations of rum were served out, and no persuasion was required to retire to rest. On the 16th, the headquarters, under Colonel Rowcroft, marched to a place called Chupra Ghat, on the Gogra, where a brigade of Gurkhas had been sent by the orders of Jung Bahadoor to render any necessary assistance in the advance of the fleet; but being completely bound down by the orders of their chief, the European officers in military charge had little control over them, and were utterly unable to force them to yield their aid in the manner most required and most serviceable, rendering their assistance of little value.

The following day one regiment of Gurkhas, with two guns, was persuaded to march in the direction of Chanderpore, a strong fort on the right bank of the Gogra, but, in obedience to Jung's orders, they refused to cross the river, except in company with the whole force, and the only advantage derived from their presence was, that they were present as spectators of the capture of the fort from the opposite bank.

After the escort reached Raibundpore Ghat, on the night of the

13th, it was detained there until next morning, when, after the embarkation in the steamer and some of the boats, there was considerable delay by means of a strong wind blowing down the river; but after ceaseless energy and perseverance, notwithstanding the obstacles of wind, current, the absence of a pilot, and clouds of sand, the boats constantly running foul of each other, and sometimes creating the utmost confusion, and notwithstanding the absence of both chart and pilot, the fleet advanced on the 17th as far as the strong fort of Chanderpore, on the right bank, at ten o'clock in the morning.

Captain Sotheby landed about two miles below the fort, with 130 of the Naval Brigade, 35 Sikhs, and 60 Gurkhas. This fort, like many others in Oudh, which are now happily either destroyed or in the process of being destroyed, might, with a few brave defenders, have made a most successful resistance against a very superior force. It was constructed with a deep ditch and high embankment on all sides, except on that facing the river, where the height and precipitous nature of the embankments affording it sufficient strength, rendered a ditch unnecessary. Inside were rifle-pits and loopholed breastworks, approached by a zigzag path terminating with gates leading to a second set. It was also defended by strong bastions and a parapet, as well as substantial buildings in the centre, all loopholed.

And, in addition to this, it was surrounded by a thick jungle of prickly bamboo, so close set as to be almost impenetrable. This latter defence, which, in the hands of brave soldiers, might be turned to good account, is used by these renowned warriors, the Rajpoots of Oudh, for the purpose of cover in making their escape. In their own intestine feuds it was[1] regarded a disgrace to run without making some appearance of a stand, and, therefore, they would resist the besiegers for a day or two with unconquerable bravery, in a place in which they were perfectly secure, until, according to their view of chivalry, they could retire from the strife, during the darkness of the night, under cover of the jungle, without any stain being cast on their gallantry, or slur on their military honour.

But on this occasion, having Europeans to contend with, they did not think it judicious to remain so long. After Captain Sotheby had disembarked his men, the line being formed by the seamen, they advanced with a twelve-pounder mountain-train howitzer under Lieutenant Turnour, R.N. A body of marines and seamen skirmishers, with

---

1. This is written in the past tense, as it is hoped these feudal wars are past and gone forever in India.

support of Sikhs under Captain Weston, 36th Regiment Native Infantry (the marines and seamen being in charge of Mr. Ingles, mate, R.N., and the Sikhs under Lieutenant Burlton), were pushed forward; and having passed through the village, which was found to be deserted, the skirmishers were received with a heavy fire of musketry and guns from the rebels concealed in the rifle-pits and fort.

Captain Weston gallantly dashed forward, and was as gallantly followed; but in trying to force the gate, was severely wounded by a man inside, and immediately carried to the rear. The gun was then brought up within a hundred yards of the entrance, and under cover of a house, fired several rounds. At the same time. Captain Sotheby sent orders to Mr. Fowler, R.N., to advance in the steamer *Jumna*, and throw in a few rounds of grape and shot, which rattled through the bamboo; while at the same time the Gurkhas threatening their right, the defenders being afraid lest their retreat should be cut off, fled with all speed through the jungle in the rear, as the marines and Sikhs entered in the front.

There was much valuable property found in the fort, of which the Sikhs, as usually happens, laid hands on the lion's share. Two guns were taken, one six-pounder, and one four-pounder, with limbers, and one spare ammunition-wagon. The enemy were supposed to be about 300; their loss most probably was trifling, by reason of the thick cover under which they found shelter. The casualty list on our side was, two severely wounded, and two or three slightly, their firing being, as usual, too high—the bullets passed over the heads of our men. Having no cavalry, pursuit was impossible; and the object being attained, the adjacent buildings in the fort were burned, the piquets were withdrawn, and the men re-embarked.

Brigadier-General Macgregor, in his letter to the Secretary to Government, thus speaks of this affair:

I would beg to bring to the notice of his Lordship in Council the gallant and spirited conduct of all the officers and men engaged on this occasion, and particularly that of Captain Sotheby, R.N., whose performance of the very arduous duty of escorting that large fleet up so rapid and difficult a river, with one bank crowned with forts, manned by the enemy, has been such as to merit the very best acknowledgments that I can bestow. The crowning exploit of attacking and capturing the strongest fort on the river with his handful of men, will recommend itself

59

at once to the notice of his Lordship in Council.

After taking Chanderpore, the fleet proceeded up the river as far as Nourainie Ghat, where it arrived on the evening of the 19th. Here there was another fort, and 4000 or 5000 rebels in the vicinity. Four or five miles further on, Jung Bahadoor was encamped near Gai Ghat, with 8000 or 9000 troops and artillery. A fruitless attempt had been made by the *maharajah* to effect a lodgement of troops across the river, prior to the arrival of our force; but, owing to some mismanagement, which brought down the fire of the enemy from the opposite bank, terrifying and scaring the workmen employed at the rafts, the attempt was abandoned. It was therefore thought advisable to cross that night without delay, lest the enemy, hearing of the arrival of the fleet, should come down in force, and give serious opposition.

At nine, p.m., the boats were ready, and all arrangements were made for the crossing, and by ten o'clock the men of the Naval Brigade, who had formed the escort, with two twelve-pounder howitzers, five companies of Gurkhas, and the detachment of Sikhs, landed on the opposite bank. The other two guns of the naval artillery were brought down to the left bank of the river, a little below the fort, to cover the landing party; and notwithstanding a long march that day of twenty miles under a burning sun, and the men having this fatiguing duty of pulling the guns along a heavy sandbank, and wading up to their waists in water, they performed it with their usual good spirit and zeal; and about midnight the village and fort were seized and occupied. Arising from the difficulty of getting accurate information, it was quite impossible to ascertain the strength of the garrison; and therefore the fort was approached with all the caution that would be required with a formidable enemy in the entrenchments.

On approaching the fort a still and solemn silence prevailed throughout the ranks. Not a word was heard. They crept from the adjacent woods into the bamboo jungle which usually surrounds these Oudh forts. Slow and cautious was the advance. Next the rifle-pits were passed. A fire was found in front of the gate, and a native asleep on a charpoy (native bed). He was seized by the throat and passed to the rear before he was allowed to speak. The inner entrance was then found, and being open, the troops passed up the narrow causeway which led to the interior of the fort; and not until then was the discovery made that it had been abandoned by the rebels. If this had been known previously, the landing might have been effected without any delay, and the combatants would have been saved the disappointment of having no one to encounter. With the sod for a bed, and the trees for a canopy, the troops waited for the events of the ensuing day.

Early in the morning of the 20th the remainder of the force crossed the river, and every exertion was made to ferry over spare ammunition and other stores with the utmost speed, under the indefatigable energy of Lieutenant Grant, R.N. And in the forenoon the Sarun field force was augmented by a brigade of Gurkhas with six guns. About noon a few musket-shots were heard, which causing an alarm, the assembly was sounded. The men were formed into line, and the gunners stood to their guns. Upon inquiry it was found that the men of the advanced piquet fired upon what they imagined to be a reconnoitring party of the enemy; but turning out to be a false alarm, the troops, who had been greatly fatigued from marching and want of rest, retired to the shelter of the *tope* until the afternoon, when they were again ordered under arms.

About two o'clock, the force, including the Naval Brigade and four guns, with Royal Marines, 190 men, 44 Sikhs, and 1300 Gurkhas with six guns, attached to which were European artillery sergeants, left the camp, and marched six or seven miles to attack the rebels at the village of Phoolpore, three companies of Gurkhas and a few men of the Naval Brigade having been left to protect the baggage. Notwithstanding the fatigue of the previous day, and the absence of rest the previous night, still the men marched cheerfully and willingly to meet the enemy for the second time on the soil of Oudh. With this prospect before them, all fatigue and want of rest was forgotten.

By the order of Colonel Rowcroft, the line was formed about half a mile beyond our camping-ground: the Ramdhul regiment of Gurkhas was on the left of the line, the Naval Brigade with four guns was in the centre, and the other Gurkhas, with a light field-battery of six guns, were on the right. The Gurkhas were commanded by their own regimental officers; but to each regiment there was one or more European officer in military charge, who held a very anomalous and by no means agreeable position, not being able to give orders, and being obliged often to submit to much inconvenience from their resistless determination to have their own way.

The line then advanced, a detachment of Royal Marines under Lieutenant Pym, and Sikhs under Lieutenant Burlton, being pushed forward on the right, in skirmishing order, and two companies of Gurkhas on the left. Having passed several *topes* and hamlets without meeting with the insurgents, the line continued advancing as far as the village of Phoolpore; which being left on our right rear, and coming within range of their guns, a sharp and sudden cannonade from the rebels soon pointed out their position. They were posted, as usual, near and in a wood, with broken ground and some high crops in front, while their left rested on the river.

The enemy kept up a very heavy fire for some time from four or five guns, which was quickly responded to by the naval artillery under Lieutenant Turnour and by the guns of the Nepalese; but among the Gurkhas no little confusion ensued. It is said to be their custom in action to rally round their guns. This probably arises from the fact that they place more confidence in their long range than in the close quarters required for the use of the bayonet. Without pretending to account for the fact with any degree of accuracy, it is, however, quite certain that in a short time after the commencement of the action few of them were to be seen in the line—in fact, they disappeared. Those on the left went over to the right, where the Gurkha brigadier was commanding; and after the first violence of the fire had a little abated, they might be seen returning stealthily to their ranks.

The scene among the elephants which carried the spare ammunition might be regarded as amusing, if it had occurred on another less serious occasion. They roared and snorted, blowing with their great proboscis, the *mahouts*, or drivers, using every effort to bring back and quiet them. They kicked them behind the ears as they sat astride on their necks, and hammered them violently on the skull with a great iron spike to bring them to a sense of duty; they abused them, calling them insulting epithets, and by turns coaxed them with endearing terms—but all in vain; two, after a little time, between the influence of alternate abuse and entreaty, became quieted and accustomed to the noise of the cannon, while the third ran off the field, and no exertion could induce him to return.

The enemy were supposed to be about 2000 or 2500, with a few troops of cavalry and five guns, under the command of Gholam Hossein and Ali Hyder, of whom the latter was wounded in the action. After an hour the infantry gave way, and the cavalry were not long in following. The marines and Sikhs on the right pushed on in skirmishing order, advancing with such rapidity and daring, that upon coming sufficiently close to the enemy at their guns to be recognised, they cried out, "*Gora log*," (white people)! and ran, leaving their guns on the field, which the marines, under command of Lieutenant Pym, immediately captured, passing by the first, and then coming up with the second, which was abandoned and burst; the explosion of which, as well as its tumbril, probably gave rise to the idea that it was destroyed by a shot from a gun directed by Jung Bahadoor.

They then crept round, concealed by the bank of the river, nearing the enemy unobserved, until they came within a hundred yards; when a Gurkha officer ran up, violently vociferating that they were firing on the Gurkhas, and using threatening gestures to a marine who had just discharged his rifle. But, on getting rid of this troublesome messenger. Sergeant Butler and the marines rushed at the gun, taking it, it may be said, almost at the point of the bayonet, the enemy sticking tenaciously to their post, the last man not having retired ten yards, when they ran up breathless, and gallantly turning it against the former possessors, fired several rounds of grape on the flying foe. One of the Sikhs instantly struck a light, and the limber supplied a port-fire. The Gurkhas then quickly coming up, laid claim to the credit of capturing the guns which the marines and Sikhs left behind, and triumphantly paraded them in camp the following day.

The marines by this time got far in advance on the right in the pursuit, well supported by the detachment of Sikhs, who never held back when there was an enemy in front. The seamen likewise on the left pushed forward, leaving the Gurkha Brigade, with their artillery, in the rear; while the Ramdhul regiment of Gurkhas, which had, after four months' intercourse, fostered a degree of intimacy with our men, kept up well, and in company with the naval artillery and seamen under Captain Sotheby, R.N., pursued the enemy until the shades of evening rendered further pursuit impossible. We then returned to the *tope* about a mile in advance of the village of Phoolpore, where the Gurkha Brigade, not willing to march back to camp, seven miles distant, settled down to bivouac for the night, lighting their fires and making themselves as happy as the circumstances would allow.

The Naval Brigade returned to camp at ten o'clock at night, where the tents were ready pitched to receive them. Several of the enemy were killed, but the number could not be accurately ascertained, while our casualty list was very small. There were only a few of the Europeans wounded, and of the Gurkhas only one was killed, and very few wounded. In addition to those of the enemy found on the field after the action, their comrades were seen to be assiduous in picking up their wounded men, putting them in carts, and carrying them off the field in their flight; some of them, it was reported, were subsequently found dead on the road.

The steadiness and coolness of the seamen under Lieutenant Radcliffe, while the fire was hottest, and round shot falling about, and
tearing up the ground in every direction, were admirable; and the
only way to account for the small number of casualties, was the rapid
advance, by which the enemy lost their range; they finding it to their
advantage to play at long balls, while our men found the nearer they
got to the enemy the safer they were.

Thus ended the action at Phoolpore, in which, after a contest of
an hour, the rebels, who had occupied the right bank of the Gogra
for some days, in the presence of Jung Bahadoor's army, were over-
thrown and dispersed. Three guns were taken, and camp equipage was
destroyed, and "by the skilful dispositions that were made, and the
admirable manner in which they were carried out,"[2] complete success
followed, and the passage of the river was secured.

This was the only action in which I have seen the Gurkhas make a
"*Kookrie* charge." The *kookrie* is a crooked-bladed knife, varying from
twelve to fifteen inches long, and from being sharp at the point, it
spreads out towards the centre of the blade, perhaps to two or two-
and-a-half inches broad. It is a considerable weight, and with it they
who are expert in its use can deal a deadly blow. It is protected by a
scabbard, and worn at the side, in the *kamarband*, or girdle. They place
implicit confidence in its use, and can, it is said, sever the head from
the body of an ox with a single blow. And from being the national
arms of Nepaul, their greatest chiefs wear them, mounted either with
gold or silver, and sometimes splendidly adorned with jewels. When
preparing for the charge, the line forms in open order, either two or
four deep, and with a fierce yell, brandishing their formidable weapons
high in mid air, they rush wildly on.

After the first sharp volley was over, and the enemy had retired to
a little distance, our line advanced, and the Ramdhul regiment was
persuaded to try the effect of a charge through some thick crops and
a *tope* where it was possible a few of the enemy might have loitered
behind; but on dashing on, brandishing their *kookries*, and uttering
piercing yells, they approached the wood, fired their muskets, and entered, but found the enemy had gone.

For two days following the action, the seamen and marines of
the Naval Brigade were employed in constructing a bridge of boats;
but, on its completion, instead of being permitted to proceed with

2. Brigadier Macgregor's despatch.

the Nepalese troops to the siege of the capital, they were the first to cross it, making a retrograde movement into the district of Goruck-pore. This naturally produced much disappointment among the men, which was not altogether allayed by the assurance that was given that the post of honour was, on this occasion, in the rear, for that 37,000 rebels were reported to be in the vicinity of Fyzabad, while there were not 1500 troops left behind to meet them. If disparity of numbers is calculated to render a post honourable, so great a disproportion has a fair claim to distinction.

There was, however, to meet the odds, that "moral force which constitutes two-thirds of the strength of armies," augmenting the influence of the few, and magnifying their indomitable courage. Much correspondence had been kept up regarding the destinies of the Naval Brigade. At one time it was intended that it should go to Lucknow, and share the honour of its fall; but, as was justly remarked, it is impossible for every corps to be in the front, no matter how much they may desire it; some must be left behind, and, in addition to this inevitable necessity, there was another difficulty arising from the inconvenience of parading European troops, especially so small a force, with a large Nepalese army. Their prejudice against the slaying of the ox is very strong; I have heard, and have every reason to believe it true, that the officers in military charge with Jung's army never had beef on their mess table while in his camp.

Their food was confined to fowls and mutton, and even for the few days that we were together, disputes arose, notwithstanding the excessive caution invariably used. A serious quarrel was more than once imminent. When only two regiments were with us, there was little difficulty in keeping the peace; but on the arrival of the *maharajah's* army, with his still larger body of camp followers, it became troublesome work. Several frivolous complaints were made with reference to the killing of oxen for food for our men, and on one occasion our noble allies cut adrift the oxen which were crossing the river for the force, suspecting that they were intended for food; and one of them in a fury drew his *kookrie* in a most threatening manner on one of our men. Consequently, all things considered, it might have been injudicious to have gone with such troublesome allies on a long march.

CHAPTER 6

The Attack on Belwa

February 24th.—The Naval Brigade recrossed the river and encamped on the left bank. In the afternoon the Maharajah Jung Bahadoor held a *durbar*, or levee, which many of the officers attended. His Excellency's tent was in a small courtyard formed by a wall of canvas (if canvas can receive that name). His reception was most polite, and his manner gracious. His personal appearance was attractive for an Eastern. His features were small, his complexion sallow, and his expression shrewd and intelligent. He was attended by his principal officers, who, as well as himself, were richly attired. His costume was plain white—not a Parisian, but an Eastern fashion; and on his head he wore a magnificent tiara of diamonds and emeralds of great value. His brothers, who were present, were dressed in gaudy splendour, presenting a striking contrast to the simple magnificence of his own costume; their coats were not only embroidered, but the breast and collar appeared to be a mass of wrought gold. Others seemed to be richly attired according to their rank. One of them wore trousers, not, as is sometimes seen in Europe, with a gold stripe, but entirely covered or interwoven with gold. Their tiaras, with a bird-of paradise plume waving in front, varied in the degree of their magnificence; but none of them was equal to their chief's.

On coming out to meet us after entering the courtyard, each was introduced, and in a truly English style greeted us by shaking hands. On being conveyed to his tent, the fashion at his *durbar*, we were informed, was neither to uncover the head, nor to take off the shoes. The chief sat at the upper end of the tent; and along one side sat his general officers, while on the side opposite sat the officers who came to make their salaams, and whose plain campaigning uniform could not compete with the splendour of the Nepalese. After having sat for a short time, and among other topics making some inquiries about the Baltic and Black Sea, and the war in the Crimea, with which Jung seemed to be tolerably acquainted, we all rose up to retire. The conversation was of course confined to the senior officers, and those also who could speak Hindostanee; nor was it of long duration or very varied: the other officers of his court not offering any remark. On our departure the *maharajah* escorted us to the door of his enclosed courtyard, and shaking hands, we bade him farewell. It is not at all improbable that both he and his companions washed their hands after intercourse with the *Feringhee* allies. Next day, the 25th, the force marched from Gai Ghat, and in three marches arrived at Kuptangunge, which was only two marches from Fyzabad.

The first intention was to halt at the village of Bustee, which being in a central position, and only forty-four miles from the town of Goruckpore, relief might be given to that town if attacked. On further consideration it was deemed more desirable to make two marches in advance of this position, that the peaceable might be inspired with confidence, and the rebelliously disposed with a salutary fear, and thus the district in some degree becoming settled, the hands of the civil authorities might be strengthened.

The field force still consisted of the Naval Brigade and two regiments of Gurkhas 500 strong each; but, unfortunately, the Ramdhul regiment, which had been with us for some months, and upon which some dependence could be placed, was exchanged for one composed of raw recruits which had never seen a shot fired.

On the 2nd of March the force marched to Amorha, distant twelve or thirteen miles from Fyzabad, and pitched the camp in an open *maidan*, or plain. The country here is very much the same as that throughout Goruckpore; perfectly level, like the surface of a lake. Not a rise is to be seen in any direction, except where a tank has been sunk for the reception of water, and the clay which has been excavated forms an embankment of a few feet high.

Small villages and hamlets are scattered here and there, attached to the house of a *zamindar*, which is somewhat superior to the others in structure and size; while *topes* of mango-trees, a quarter or half a mile apart, give an air of luxuriance and greenness in the hot season, when, after the crops are cut, the arable land looks brown and barren until the first shower again converts it into verdure and productiveness. In some villages may be seen the house of a *rajah*, or *ranee*, i.e., the reigning widow of a *rajah*, which, from its size, and perhaps from an attempt at bastions and earthworks, gives the idea that it contains some articles of value to defend.

It is a religious act among the Hindoos to plant a *tope*, and dig a well. The inventor of that superstition acted on the soundest principles of worldly wisdom; for the former, in the fruit season, yields support to multitudes of the poor, while its foliage gives shelter to travellers from the broiling heat of the sun; and the latter being the source of productiveness in the irrigation of the fields, are easily sunk in every direction; and the ground being saturated by the deluges that fall during the rains, water is procured near the surface in the dry season, and is conveyed by little canals over every yard of ground.

On the arrival of the field force at Amorha, a messenger was sent to Colonel Rowcroft to say that the fort at Belwa, seven miles further on, was occupied by the enemy; and hearing that they were not numerous, urging him to send a party at once to take it before the garrison was reinforced. Belwa is only seven or eight miles distant from Fyzabad, which was once the seat of government of Oudh, and still, in importance, is a city, second only to Lucknow. The rebels occupied this city in great force, improving, by order of the *begum*, the old fortifications by which it was surrounded. After the Nepalese army had taken possession of, and passed through Goruckpore, one of their brigades was ordered in advance to the village of Belwa, as a sort of corps of observation; but, by reason of the proximity to Fyzabad, it was found necessary to throw up earthworks, and construct an entrenched camp in such an advanced and exposed position, and in the presence of a numerous enemy.

Earthworks were immediately thrown up, and a deep ditch was dug all round, under the superintendence of a skilful European engineer officer, who no doubt selected the best and most defensible ground; and in a short time a fort, with a strong and spacious *pucca* building in the centre, rose into view. It was occupied by the Gurkhas only a very short time, until Jung's army was on the point of crossing the Gogra. He then sent orders to his brigadier to march forthwith to join him. A large quantity of grain and supplies was in the fort at the time, for which there was no means of obtaining carriage in such haste.

The Bengal Yeomanry Cavalry were some miles distant, and in six hours could have come to take possession of the fort and supplies, which they could have held until reinforcements arrived; but Jung's orders were urgent—there was not sufficient time to destroy the entrenchments—his officers have too great a regard for their heads

68

to make any delay in obeying his orders, and the European officers in military charge do not seem to have had much influence in making any alteration in the movement. Finally, the camp was struck; the works were left intact; they marched to join Jung: and scarcely had it been evacuated two hours, when a body of the rebels, who had all along been hovering about like vultures round a carcase, entered into undisputed possession of the fort and grain. The earthworks were strengthened, four guns were planted in position on the bastions, and on the approach of the cavalry, the first intimation of the presence of an enemy was a shot from one of their guns.

This information being communicated as the force arrived on the camping ground at Amorha, and the number of the enemy being reported only 200, the best course to pursue seemed to be an immediate attack before reinforcements could arrive to strengthen the garrison. One hundred and sixty-eight men of the Naval Brigade, with four guns, and 24-pounder rockets, thirty-five Sikhs, and a regiment of Gurkhas, were ordered by Colonel Rowcroft to proceed in the afternoon to Belwa, where they were joined by the Bengal Yeomanry Cavalry,[1] 250 strong. Then three hearty cheers were raised by the new comrades, which were quickly, and with the best of good will, responded to by the jolly tars, who now, for the first time since their military career in India commenced, fell in with troops of their own country and colour. Right well did they know how to appreciate their presence and admire their bravery; and with the best of good will were they encamped together, and in many an action did they meet the enemy side by side during two arduous and trying campaigns.

After the long march of the morning, most of the men of the Naval Brigade got a lift on elephants, and by four o'clock in the afternoon were within a mile of Belwa. A plan of the fort had not been left with the colonel commanding our force, and consequently the nature of the entrenchment and ground was unknown. The number of our Europeans being small, considerable caution and circumspection was required, as any rash or unsuccessful attack, which should place many of our men *hors de combat* might be the means of paralysing our right arm at a time when there was not a European soldier within a hundred miles of us. On nearing Belwa the day was drawing to a close,

---

1. Men of the Mutiny by John Tulloch Nash & Henry Metcalfe - Two Accounts of the Great Indian Mutiny of 1857 - Fighting with the Bengal Yeomanry Cavalry by John Tulloch Nash and Private Metcalfe at Lucknow by Henry Metcalfe also published by Leonaur.

affording but little hope for active operations.

Five o'clock struck before our guns opened fire. It was reconnoitred, and found much stronger than what had been represented; while the defenders turned out to be much more numerous than had been reported. The naval guns threw in shell with great precision for some time; but being only 12-pounder howitzers it would be impossible to make a breach in earthworks with that weight of metal. It was now becoming dark, and to storm it with so small a number of Europeans might result in weakening the only reliable force, especially as our allies did not seem disposed to take part in such an enterprise. Darkness coming on, the force was obliged to retire, and took up their quarters that night in the camp of their new companions in arms, the Bengal Yeoman Cavalry. Next morning, in company with this valiant corps of volunteers, we returned to the camp at Amorha to await the tide of events.

That night and the following day the rebels received large reinforcements. Fyzabad was emptied of them. They flowed in from Nawabgunge, Gondah, and the adjoining districts. They flocked to the green standard, fortunately without having any very clear idea who waved it, or any spirit of cohesion to cement them together in a common cause.

CHAPTER 7

Battle of Amorha

On the 4th of March authentic reports were brought in of the many thousands that were gathering, and of fourteen guns that were ready for action. Their leaders interpreted the return from Belwa to the camp on the 2nd, not only as a retreat but as a defeat, and, like a drowning man catching at a straw, made the best use of it to raise the hopes of the supporters of a bad cause, and inspire among the *sepoys* and disaffected visions of future triumph. It required little to excite them to action, and they seldom seemed to be downcast after a defeat. They took it quite as a matter of course, and were ready for another attempt a few days afterwards notwithstanding the certainty of a similar result. But on this occasion they rejoiced in a fine chance. They knew well that our entire force, including sick, did not amount to more than 1500; and therefore with more confidence they assembled their hosts to the battle.

This part of the country was utterly disaffected. It was visible in the look and demeanour of every villager; they were nearly all tinged with rebellion, and the reward that was held out to our force for not obtaining permission to march to the scene of action in the front at Lucknow, on the ground that the rear would be the post of honour, that there the rebels would be numerous, seemed now on the point of being realized.

Considering the multitudes that could be collected from the adjacent frontier of Oudh and the paucity of the Sarun Field Force, there was much peril in this isolated position. There was not a European soldier within a hundred miles of us or more, and if a rising had been effected in our rear, and the ammunition and supplies which were on the road had been cut off, the force would not have been in an enviable position; but by excellent arrangements these contingencies were provided for and guarded against. A rifle-pit was dug round the camp, which had been pitched in an open plain. A thick jungle in our front was cut down, and a village cleared away, the walls of which were knocked down by a dozen of elephants, who expeditiously performed the work of demolition.

The obedience and docility of these animals is surprising. The walls of the houses were two or two and a half feet thick, and built of strong, tenacious, and compact mud. At the bidding of the *mahout* the elephant would push it with his ponderous forehead, throwing the weight of his body into the shove. Sometimes, if this failed, he would open his wide mouth and bite the top of the wall and pull down loosened and detached pieces with his trunk, and then, with the wall thus mutilated and weakened, he would try the pressure of his skull again, levelling a village with marvellous rapidity. These and other arrangements being made, we waited the advance of the enemy.

The camp was struck at two o'clock next morning, the 5th; the tents were packed and the baggage-carts were loaded, so as to put all the *impedimenta* into as small a space as possible, for protection in a neighbouring village, and that as few troops as possible might be required for a guard, lest the main body should be weakened.

The rebels' spies informed them that we were in full retreat, and on hearing tidings so flattering to their hopes, their courage rose several degrees, and prepared for a speedy pursuit. About seven o'clock, after a wearisome and tedious delay, the troops having been under arms for five hours, and at work nearly all night, a report was brought in by the *corindar* of a *ranee* who resided about a mile from our camp, that the enemy was going to attack Mhaun Sing, that he had just returned from their camp at Belwa, and that they had no intention of coming down on us that day. A report coming from so respectable an authority as the *ranee's* head man, gained implicit credence, and orders were issued to repitch the camp, which were on the point of being carried out, when another report came in of a contradictory character.

A patrol of cavalry was sent out to reconnoitre, and returning with tidings that the enemy was advancing. Colonel Rowcroft doubled the strength of the patrol, and ordered the officer in command to obtain further information. All hands stood to their arms. The force moved out of camp about seven o'clock, and having taken up a position about half a mile to the west of the village of Amorha, formed line . The Naval Brigade and four guns were in the centre across the road, under the command of Captain Sotheby, R.N. The two Gurkha regiments were on the right and left of the Naval Brigade, in military charge of Captains Brooks, Berkley, and Macgregor. The Sikh detachment under Lieutenant Burlton, was on the left of the Gurkhas; and the Bengal Yeomanry Cavalry, one squadron on the right of the line under Captain Chapman, and the other on the left under Major Richardson, covering both flanks.

It was at first conjectured that the report might have its origin from a party of the enemy being sent out to plunder the neighbouring villages; but soon their bugle-calls were heard, first sounding the halt and then the advance, which put it beyond all doubt that they were approaching. Our line remained steady in position, anxiously awaiting the moment when the enemy should come within range. Their bugle-calls were heard nearer and nearer, and they soon showed themselves in great force. They deployed into line, extending right and left to a great distance, probably a mile or more each way, overlapping our flanks, and threatening to overwhelm our small force. They pushed forward a cloud of skirmishers; there was no lack of drilled troops; they came on in admirable order, as if confident of success. Looking on these advancing masses from the rear of the line, our troops appeared a handful of men compared with this approaching wave crested with bayonets.

The naval guns under Lieutenant Turnour opened fire from the centre, and the enemy with ten guns commenced a heavy and furious cannonade on our line. This was kept up obstinately on both sides for some time. The skirmishers were thrown out, and the order was given, "The line will advance;" an order that was never rescinded, and that was promptly carried out, until the whole force was driven off the field. Their line was so extended, that when their centre was driven back they seemed, on their extreme right, to be quite unconscious of the fact, and marched down deliberately and leisurely towards our camp. This movement being observed, Colonel Rowcroft sent orders to Major Richardson, commanding the left squadron, to detach a troop, or, if necessary, with the squadron, to charge and clear out the enemy. This was gallantly and effectually carried out by Major Richardson, well supported by Captain Brooks of the 1st Light Cavalry, with two companies of Gurkhas.

The cavalry, in their impetuosity, dashed forward at a hand-gallop, riding through a *jheel* (a shallow lake, or sheet of water), no impediment retarding their advance or assuaging their ardour. They soon came upon the enemy, driving them back, cutting up and killing a

73

number of them, and dispersing them thoroughly. Several horses were shot or wounded, but fortunately no trooper received any serious injury, some having received slight wounds or a hair-breadth escape. Many a hand-to-hand fight might be described, when a *sepoy*, despairing of his chance of escape, turned round, stood his ground, and fought fiercely with his mounted antagonist, using either his bayonet or butt-end of his musket, as best suited his taste; and sometimes he would make a cut at the horses' legs with his *tulwar* as he passed, which was a favourite trick with those who were unable to make a defence.

After the first fierce cannonade was over, the roar of the artillery began to subside. They then seemed to consider, they then halted— then wavered. It is fatal to delay under such circumstances; when it comes to that, a dash is sure to gain the day. From the first moment they were observed to waver, no time was to be lost; a rapid and decisive blow was to be struck then or never, if complete success was to be ensured. Colonel Rowcroft immediately ordered a party of Naval Riflemen to reinforce the Royal Marine skirmishers, while he ordered Captain Chapman with his squadron to advance, inclining to the right, and charge the enemy's *sowars* and infantry: at the same time orders were sent to the Gorucknath regiment of Gurkhas to advance at the charge.

All this time the first order issued was attended to by the Naval Brigade, which continued advancing upon the multitudes in front, and never halted to draw breath except when they came within easy range for a discharge of grape. Then they unlimbered the guns, fired as many rounds as the retreating multitude would wait to receive; then limbering up, would gallop the guns more like horse than foot artillery, and when within range, would again unlimber and discharge as many rounds as the time admitted; limbered up and galloped on, chasing them with a speed, and working their guns with an activity, truly surprising.

Among the number of guns that were taken, one, from its proximity to the enemy, afforded a peculiar opportunity to be turned against themselves. Lieutenant Grant, Mr. Shearman the engineer, a seaman named Jesse Ward, another seaman, and Lord Charles Scott, midshipman, rushed forward, captured the gun, and loaded it from the contents of its own limber; but having no portfire, a rifle was discharged with the muzzle to the vent, which answered the purpose, giving the enemy the benefit of grape out of their own piece of ordnance.

Captain Chapman, in the meantime, with his squadron made a

most gallant charge, routing the left wing, and scattering the multitude. The enemy now no longer hesitated; their centre was driven back, and both wings shaken; the *sowars* (Native Cavalry) were in rapid retreat, and the infantry soon followed. The combined movement of the troops, the formidable charge of the cavalry, the steady advance of the Naval Brigade, soon shattered the whole line of the enemy. They abandoned eight guns, which were left unspiked, seven were taken on the field, one could not be found. They varied in size from an 18-pounder to a 9-pounder, 6-pounders, and guns of smaller calibre, with gun-carriages and seven limbers complete, well stored with ammunition, and drawn by bullocks, which were also left on the field, as well as a cart with 25,000 musket-balls.

The pursuit now commenced. For six miles the rebels were driven from *tope* to *tope*, and from village to village. Wherever they took shelter, from thence they were speedily expelled, until our horses and men, completely worn out with fatigue, and exhausted with heat, were obliged to halt. Once they made a short stand, keeping up a fire from the only two guns that they succeeded in carrying off, and discharging, as they did from the commencement of the engagement, a perfect hailstorm of musket-balls. Here we lost an officer of the Naval Brigade, Mr. Fowler, and one Gurkha, a private; but the effective fire of the guns, the steady advance of the line, and the right squadron moving forward, threatening another charge, soon drove them out of sight.

Considering the small number of European troops[1] which were available to meet such an overwhelming force, no doubt our position was that of considerable danger; but, as British seamen and soldiers always do, they faced it with a daring and determination adequate to dispel the danger; they gallantly dashed forward, amidst showers of ball, and after pushing forward two or three miles farther, they began to suffer so much from fatigue and heat, that they were obliged to halt. Having been up nearly the whole previous night, and during the action marching through heavy ground and thick cultivation, they halted for a short time to rest, and then returned to the camp.

The action commenced at half-past eight in the morning, and was terminated at half-past twelve. In four hours the enemy, who were reported to be 4000 *sepoys*, 10,000 irregular troops, 300 *sowars*, and ten guns, were completely defeated and routed by 1261 men and

---

1. Gurkhas, 850; Bengal Yeomanry Cavalry, 200; marines, 32; naval column, 140; 4 naval guns; 39 Sikhs. Total, 1261.

four guns, with a severe loss, in killed and wounded, of about 500. The *sepoys* were of the 1st, 10th, 53rd, and 56th Regiments of Native Infantry, 5th Regiment Gwalior Contingent, and 2nd Oudh Police Force. The Nazim Mahomed Hussein, and the Rajahs of Gondah and Churdah, and other chiefs, were present on elephants, but were said to have left early in the action. On the return of the force it was found that the few men who could be spared to guard the captured guns, had brought them into camp; and, to our no small satisfaction, we saw them safely parked, and among the spoils were limbers in good serviceable condition, which formerly were the property of the Honourable East India Company.

Thus the teeth of the tiger were drawn for that time, as the natives of India without guns venture to do but little, the noise of their cannon considerably raising their courage. In half an hour the camp was repitched, and the troops got rest and refreshment. By striking the tents and packing the baggage, the eyes of the rebels were completely blinded. Their spies told them we were retreating; and thus, being prepared for a pursuit and a speedy victory, they came on full of confidence, until, to their no small surprise and chagrin, never expecting to see so small a force showing so bold a front, they found a little phalanx that never gave way ready to receive them. It was marvellous to see so great a host chased away as if panic-stricken by the audacity of such a handful, facing about when they expected to see them turn right about face, and marching away. Some of the seamen would jocularly say to their comrades, as they were "bolting" off, "What are these rascals bolting away for? If they would only come on with sticks, they must have beat us."

But they were deficient in true patriotism, they were deficient in *esprit de corps*, and their foul deeds deprived them of the favour of the Ruler of armies. An educated Hindoo, who was too wise and far-seeing to sympathise with the *sepoys*, remarked to me that "God fought for us, and would fight for us again;" and his providence and intervention in our favour was duly acknowledged next morning, when, at a parade of the troops, thanksgivings were offered to the "Giver of all victories" for this great and signal success, and his providential care in permitting so little loss to be sustained on our side compared with that of the enemy.

Of the Naval Brigade we had to lament the loss of one officer killed; fourteen or fifteen men were wounded; of the Gurkhas, one was killed, and several were wounded; the cavalry had two horses

76

killed, and several were wounded; several troopers also were wounded, but none were killed; many, as may easily be imagined, had narrow escapes. The naval guns would naturally be a mark for the enemy to shoot at; and therefore would have a fair share of their attention. Every gun or limber was struck, once or oftener, by grape or round shot, but fortunately none were disabled. Some of the Jacks, seeing the balls falling about, striking their guns or their limbers without wounding a man, said, in their own phraseology, acknowledging a superhuman Providence, "Well, Bill, this almost makes me superstitious." The shot fell fast and thick, ricocheting along the ground in every direction. A heavy fire of musketry was constantly kept up; but fortunately the failing of the *sepoys* in firing too high was again our safety.

It was soon found that the nearer to the enemy, the greater was the security, the balls passing clear over the heads of the troops in the line, their whiz being the only inconvenience. Notwithstanding, it was evident, from the manner in which they retreated, that they were trained soldiers. This was not altogether proved by their uniform, however, which was rather "the worse for the wear." Some of them had cross-belts and red jackets, muskets, and bayonets; some had the uniform jacket without the trousers, and some the trousers without the jacket; some wore the jacket with the regulation musket, and some were reduced to the necessity of using native arms and dispense with uniform altogether. In fact, their tailors evidently did not supply them with the latest military cut.

Taking into consideration the comparative numbers, this battle was singularly successful, and may justly be regarded as having saved the rich fertile plains "of Goruckpore from a second inundation"[2] of rapacious harpies, who, no doubt, would have been aided by numerous local *baboos* and *zamindars*, if they had succeeded in their plans.

By the excellent arrangements that were made the numbers of our men appeared to be greater than they really were; so that when their leaders urged the *sepoys* to try the fortune of war again, they replied that they had been deceived already by being told that the European troops were only 400, while in the field they met the "*Gora log*" on the right flank, on the left flank, in the centre, and everywhere; thus paying a compliment to the activity with which our force moved, magnifying their numbers, and giving them a ubiquitous appearance. On their return to Fyzabad their friends laughed at them for being beaten by so small a force, and they were shamed into making promises (as

2. Brigadier Rowcroft's despatch.

we learned from the reports of the spies) to retrieve their character—promises which were never fulfilled; and gave out that they had bound themselves by an oath to attack the *Feringhees* and not to run away. They were resolved, however, to make someone suffer for the defeat, and consequently they hung their spy who told them that our force was retiring, and next day, the spy that told us a similar story about them, met a similar fate. He was convicted of a peculiarly aggravated offence: he was a *corindar* in the employment of a *ranee*, who, living close to our camp, was professedly on friendly terms with our government; he brought information that he had just come from the enemy's camp, and that they had not the least intention of attacking us that day, but were going in an opposite direction to punish Maun Sing.

And this intelligence he conveyed in order to put us off our guard at the very hour that he knew they were marching down towards our camp. He was accordingly convicted, and paid the penalty with death, which he met with perfect indifference, adjusting the noose round his neck with his own hands, and leaping from the back of the elephant on which he had been conveyed to the place of execution. Among the Gurkhas who were wounded, one was disabled for life by the loss of his leg; and becoming unfit for service, he was at once struck off the rolls of his regiment without receiving pay or pension. No care was bestowed on him, and he would have been left houseless and unable to earn a livelihood in a country far from his home, if a subscription had not been raised for him in camp to defray his expenses to Nepaul, and supply him with food by the way.

It is not a matter of surprise when men are compelled to serve, and being wounded or disabled, are cast off by the government of their country, that they should shun the risk which accompanies bravery, and keep out of harm's way as much as they can. And this failing seemed to attach as much to their officers as to their men; the higher they rise in rank being supposed to do the least; exertion, which is incompatible with the dignity of the senior, being confined to the junior. The detachment of Sikhs were as forward as usual, but their natural instinct for plunder is surprisingly strong.

At Lucknow they are reputed to have got the lion's share. They seemed to have been a privileged class in that way; at any rate, their great success kept them in a good humour, and no doubt rendered them well satisfied with our service. There are numerous stories about our men picking up some article of trifling value in many places which have been taken, perhaps emerging from a house with a clock under his arm, or a few silk handkerchiefs, or a brass *lota*; while the Sikhs, looking on perfectly regardless would wait until they had finished, and then go systematically to work in quest of *rupees* and gold *mohurs*. They knew the native's habit of hiding treasure, either built up in a wall or buried under the floor; and by sprinkling water about, discovered the spot where it dried up the quickest, and then speedily disentombed cash and other valuables.

On the fifth, as they were in pursuit of the fugitive rebels, some of them could not resist their favourite propensity. It is not sanctioned by the service, but it is a difficult matter to stop it. One was seen with a small bundle on his back as he marched through the high standing crops. By degrees it got bigger and bigger. He would lay it down now and again, fire off his musket, and renew his load. At last he got a lump on his back like a camel. The protuberance that was small in the beginning, by means of the articles accumulated in the route, had swollen to a considerable bulk, like an evil rumour, which increases in size every time it is rehearsed.

Never until now had the Naval Artillery an opportunity of being thoroughly equipped. Limbers and spare ammunition-wagons being captured in abundance, a selection might be made to meet the requirements of the battery. By the incessant industry of Mr. Burton, the ship's carpenter, the battery which took the field in the first action, labouring under the disadvantages of a very inefficient equipment, soon presented the appearance of one efficient for any service.

The Gurkhas seemed quite proud of their achievements in the action, and said that the brigadier had a lucky star, and that when they went into action with him, victory was the sure result, that their loss was trifling, and their casualties few.

During the time these two regiments were brigaded with the *Pearl's* men they were on excellent terms, and Brigadier Rowcroft, when acknowledging their services, returned thanks at the same time to Captain Sotheby, the officers and men, "who, with their guns," he said, "were his mainstay in the action, and most valuable to him at all times;" a compliment which was again repeated by the commander-in-chief, Sir Colin Campbell, who, in his letter of thanks, noticed more particularly the "gallantry of the Bengal Yeomanry Cavalry, and the bravery and steadiness of the Naval Brigade."

CHAPTER 8

Action near Tilga

For several days after the combat, the force was constantly on the alert, expecting to be attacked again. On the following Thursday and Tuesday, being regarded by them as "lucky days," they were more especially expected. The Gurkhas also have their "lucky days." On the 5th instant they were confident of success, even those on the sick list strained a point to bear arms. Their lucky days, however, passed away, and no *sepoys* appeared. Probably if this action had been less successful, or if fewer guns had been captured, they might have tried it again.

It was well known to the experienced East India officers that a bold front was the best security for success; and being convinced of the danger of the slightest appearance of weakness, the trench which had been dug round our camp was filled up, and the camp was pitched in the open plain. However, it was thought advisable to construct a small fort, in which the sick, the spare ammunition, and the baggage might be safely lodged, and requiring only a small guard, the greater part of the force might be free to take the field.

A fort was constructed taking in a small village and the Theseel, which being a strong brick building, made an excellent hospital. On the bastions three of the guns taken from the enemy on the 5th were mounted, rendering it perfectly secure, with a small guard, in the temporary absence of the force.

Their threats were repeated from week to week, more especially on their lucky days. The *fakir*, or priest, would urge them to an encounter, and the troops were continually harassed by false alarms, which were as vexatious as a real attack, causing them to be kept out under arms in the sun half the day. Sometimes from an early hour in the morning they would be ordered to stand to their arms, the tents and baggage being packed and lodged in the fort; and forming line in front of the camping ground, they would await an enemy who never appeared. At last, becoming accustomed to these reports, the striking of tents and the packing of baggage were dispensed with; but the men would return from the field in a bad humour at the *sepoys* not giving them a chance of exchanging a few shots.

The country in our rear was tranquil; fortunately for us, they were void of enterprise. A few thousands might have been detached from the main body, and making a circuit to our rear, have aroused the country into turbulence and confusion; but luckily the rebels managed with singular sagacity to collect a large army without procuring a general, and entertained a disposition to do much more mischief than they knew how to carry out. It was like a body without a head, and having no principle of cohesion, would naturally fall to pieces under a severe blow. They had, however, wonderful vitality, which did not arise from any settled government, but from being like the troubled sea that cannot rest. Beat them in twenty fights, and the shattered carcase of an army would again reappear, the pieces being collected together, and, like a ghost or dissolving view, would vanish at the first advance of our troops. After two or three engagements, in which they were well beaten, it became a matter of certainty in every subsequent encounter that they would run, and, therefore, the chief object was how to surprise and catch them.

The false alarms continued until the end of April, with two exceptions, when the enemy made their appearance. But it may be asked why the field force remained quiet so long within seven miles of their entrenchments without making some efforts to expel them? This is answered by the fact that our guns, being only 12-pounder howitzers, were not adapted to make a breach in a mud fort; and, secondly, there was a general order that forts should not be attacked without having guns of heavier metal.

The ensign was no sooner unfurled in Lucknow than regiments of fugitives flocked to the standard of the chiefs at Fyzabad, bringing with them cavalry and guns. For some time they hovered around our camp, but evidently reluctant to come to close quarters. The left wing of H.M.'s 13th Light Infantry, 300 strong, under Major Cox, joined our force on the 26th of March, and one Gurkha regiment was sent to Goruckpore. Thus reinforced, the brigade, though numerically weaker, taking into consideration the value of European troops and Enfield rifles, was virtually stronger.

The weather was now becoming exceedingly hot and oppressive, the sun striking fiercely through the tents. The usual routine of camp-life begun to assume a dull chronic form, and was remarkable only for its sameness. At daybreak the reveille sounded, a general rubbing of eyes and movement of languid limbs ensued, then the assembly sounded, and all hands appeared on the parade-ground in front of the camp. After parade came daily prayers, for the men of the Naval Brigade, which lasted about ten minutes. This custom not being unusual on board a "man-of-war," was continued throughout the campaign. Ball practice or light-infantry drill for an hour or more succeeded, until the sun gave convincing proofs that the men should keep close to their tents during the fiery heat of the day. Nearly all hands began to employ native *punca wallas* to fan them, and keep the flies at a respectable distance, as well as *kitmutgars* to wait on them at table; in fact, Jack was a gentleman, "every inch of him."

In order to render our abodes somewhat cooler, the soil under our tents was dug out, and a pit was excavated, three or four feet deep, the superfluous soil being manufactured into a mud wall; and these pits, resembling a sort of mausoleum for the living, although slightly damp, possessed the advantage of a temperature a few degrees cooler.

It would be difficult to say how valuable time was now spent. Sleep was probably the most general and innoxious amusement. Books were a rare commodity. Most of those which were brought up country having disappeared off the face of the earth; and newspapers not being numerous among the men, were regarded as a delicacy. Meal hours were tolerably regular, except when an alarm produced a change in the arrangements. Shortly after the dawn of day, a cup of tea and piece of toast, brought in by the *kitmutgar*, was presented to the recumbent Sahib with one eye shut, and the other scarcely open, who, overcome with heat and the fatigue of having nothing to do, would mechanically put forth his hand and take hold of the viands, which are called "*chota hazri*," *i.e.*, little breakfast.

Having gone through the duties of the morning, if he should be prone to great exertion, he would take a short walk, or, mounting his horse, would ride for an hour, until common prudence compelled him to take shelter; and then the operations of the day commence. After the toilet is made (with reference to which campaigners are not very particular), breakfast, or "*burra hazri*," is served up, at hours varying from nine o'clock until eleven or twelve o'clock; the former hour best suiting the demands of a brisk ride on horseback, while the latter would suit those whose exertions were not so violent, and who indulge in the more easy kind of horizontal exercise, in the shape of a stretch on a *charpoy*.

After breakfast a serious difficulty arises how to pass the day. To go outside the tent is to be grilled; to remain inside, is to be baked. A newspaper arrives by post, which meets with its quantum of abuse for telling nothing new; and if it does contain anything out of the common, it is not believed—it is read, it is abused for its emptiness, it is thrown down, and the worn-out reader falls back exhausted on his couch; perhaps he sleeps, perhaps he only shuts his eyes, trying to lull himself into the belief that he is asleep, until exhausted nature calls again for some support. After the lapse of a few hours, *tiffin* is announced, and after that there is a general relapse into the former state of temporary inactivity, until the long shadows from the trees are the harbingers of a temperature reduced from 108° to 90° or 95°.

Then, recovering from the fatigue of the day, one would mount his horse for a ride, another would walk a mile, or perhaps two. When *puncas* could not be rigged up in the tents, a native with a huge fan might be seen looking sleek and shining, frightening away the hosts of flies, the plague of which was very great, and producing a breath of artificial air. The attentive *punca walla* looking as if he needed a cooling himself as much as the *sahib*; with this difference, that his wardrobe consisted of only a yard or two of calico, the heat of which gave but little inconvenience.

Darkness having decidedly set in, dinner is announced by the faithful *kitmutgar*, who coming up with his two hands closed together, and raised in a supplicatory posture, says "*kana tayar, hai*," dinner is ready. This being concluded, it is followed by tea or coffee, pipes or cigars, winding up with *matériel* of a little stronger nature. After all the affairs of the day are duly discussed—after it is decided that all the rumours of the enemy's attack on the ensuing day is false—after the spies are all voted to be liars—after some argument is warmly kept up by two or more contending belligerents—and after both parties have succeeded in convincing themselves that his opponent is wrong, and that he himself is in the right,—they retire quite satisfied, and turn in for the night.

And thus the time is passed until the return of another day brings with it similar cares; and the attentive bearer[1] approaches respectfully, often lending his aid, by holding the hand of his *sahib*, and raising him up from a reclining, to a sitting posture, and, as if to relieve him of all

---

1. A valet.

possible exertion, the faithful slave (*"gulam"*), as the bearer humbly styles himself, having lighted the pipe of his master, would carefully place it in his mouth, and thus relieve him of the trying exertion of lifting his hand for the purpose. It is difficult for anyone who has not experienced it, to conceive the *ennui* and irksomeness that takes possession of men who pass the hot season in tents in India. The excessive heat, the close confinement to the cotton hut, the difficulty of getting books in camp during these troublous times; the proximity of the enemy, which prevented the possibility of making excursions to a distance, or riding further from camp than a mile or two; the hot winds, which carried clouds of broiling dust; the swarm of flies which crawl about, being too lazy to use their wings except when forcibly compelled, add to the inconvenience and monotony of a tent life at this season of the year.

On the 2nd of April information was received that the rebels at Belwa had been reinforced by 1500 men, and a horsed battery (four 9-pounders, and two 24-pounder howitzers). An attack being probable, there was a sharp look out, and cavalry patrols went reconnoitring. A villager gave information regarding their movements, and among other things he mentioned that, having gathered in all his grain, the produce of his land, the rebels not only took possession of it, but compelled him to bring it to their camp, and then, giving him a beating as a recompense, told him to come next morning if he wanted any more pay. In this way the rebels obtained from their countrymen the sinews of war.

Several thousand of the Lucknow *sepoys* having augmented the number of the insurgents about Fyzabad, one of their chiefs whom our force met in many an encounter, Mahomed Hossein, tried to persuade them to join his standard. To whom they replied that they had had fighting enough with the English already, and dispersed. It was reported that he offered them three months pay if they would beat our force out of the district; but they were unwilling to make the agreement except the pay was given beforehand. Information was also given that some others took him into custody for a week, on account of the arrears that were due; and that subsequently he did not trust himself to their tender mercies, but encamped among his own followers.

At this time sanguine hopes were entertained that another battery of artillery and more troops would be sent to relieve the Naval Brigade and enable them to return to the ship; but the rebels beleaguering Azimghur, detained the troops that were expected to advance into Goruckpore, and thus we were destined to continue in this out-of-the-way corner of the country, isolated from all the rest of the army.

April 17th.—A villager who probably got tired of having his grain looted, brought intelligence that a strong party of insurgents had entered a village not more than three and a half miles from our camp. A cavalry patrol was sent out to reconnoitre, and soon returned, corroborating the report. A detachment was immediately ordered under arms, 100 of the 13th Light Infantry, Captain Chapman's squadron of the Bengal Yeomanry Cavalry, and 200 Gurkhas under the command of Major Cox, and 100 men and two guns of the Naval Brigade, under the command of Captain Sotheby, R.N., left the camp about nine o'clock, a.m., and came up with the rebels near the village of Tilga. The cavalry, by making a circuit to their rear, took them by surprise, and discovered that their numbers were more than what was represented, having received reinforcements from Belwa, and four guns.

The cavalry went sufficiently close to occupy their attention until the infantry and guns arrived. By this time they numbered about 2000 *sepoys*, besides 1000 *budmashes*, a few *sowars*, and four guns. Shot and shell were soon sent among them; but the detachment was not sufficiently strong to drive them out of the village. A message was sent to Brigadier Rowcroft for more troops; and in the meantime Major Cox, well knowing the character of John Pandy, managed to draw them out of their hiding-place by a manoeuvre which soon had the desired effect. The detachment feigned a retreat; they imagining that the troops were running away, came out yelling and bellowing as if to inflate each other's courage, and seemed disposed to make a desperate effort to drive our party back to camp.

But when once out from under cover, the detachment halted, and gave them such a warm reception with rifles and shell, that they soon found themselves safer behind mud walls. The Rajah of Gondah's *pundit*[2] here lost his life. On seeing the detachment retire, he discovered that it was one of their "lucky days." He came out of the village, urging the rebels on, and telling them that his predictions were now about to be fulfilled. While thus trying to encourage his people, a stray shot cut him off in the midst of his exhortations, and showed the *rajah* the value of his predictions.

Having kept this numerous body of rebels at bay for upwards of

---

2. A wise man, or a sort of soothsayer.

an hour, Brigadier Rowcroft came out with the rest of the force, and making a detour of a mile and a half to the right, turned the left flank of the enemy. On perceiving the movement, fearing lest their retreat should be cut off, and putting more confidence in the activity of their legs than the precision of their fire, the rebels suddenly retreated, and were pursued by the cavalry.

But, in passing by a village, Major Richardson, with a troop of Bengal Yeomanry Cavalry, observed about 300 of the enemy, with one gun, collected under the cover of the houses. The contents of the gun and a volley of musketry were discharged at them; giving the order to charge, he bore down at a gallop, captured the gun, and scattered the rebels. Each *sepoy* defended himself as best he could, knowing there was no quarter, and that not his days only, but his minutes were numbered; and therefore resolved to sell his life as dearly as he could, and do his utmost to destroy at least one *Feringhee*. One would bend on one knee and meet the charge with his bayonet; another would reserve the contents of his musket until the trooper was almost sufficiently close to the muzzle that the flash could set his clothes on fire; another would lie down and make a cut at the legs of the horses as they passed; in fact, they stood as well as despair could make them stand.

Fifty or sixty of the rebels were cut down, and the nature of the affair may be guessed from the fact that, out of fifty-four, which was the number of the troop, fifteen or sixteen were either killed or wounded. Five horses were killed, five were missing, and seven wounded. Mr. Troup, a cornet, and Brown, a trooper, were killed on the spot; and the Adjutant, Mr. Bridgman, was dangerously wounded; and several others were severely wounded. One gun was taken, and the wheel of another was said to have been destroyed by a shell; but they managed to hide it in a *nullah* until next morning, when it was conveyed away. The rebels were under the command of a *corundar*, a sort of premier, of the Rajah of Gondah. They acknowledged to have lost 200 in killed and wounded—upwards of 80 were known to have been killed. Among the latter was a *sepoy* who had a few weeks before killed a trooper of the Bengal Yeomanry Cavalry with his own sword. He had been taken prisoner by the trooper, and while bringing him into camp, the *sepoy* made a grasp at his sword and despatched him; now he was in turn killed, and the sword recovered on the field.

After this action, the little remaining courage of the *sepoys* cooled down. They made their approaches with marked caution and circumspection. No doubt, in this affair, their chief object was loot. Their looting party bringing out our first detachment, and then the enemy being reinforced, brought out the remainder of the troops, and a general action was the result. The Naval Brigade under Captain Sotheby, and the infantry under Major Cox, attacking them in front, when the flank movement under Brigadier Rowcroft finally obliged them to retire.

It was a most unsatisfactory day for an action; the westerly winds which prevail in some parts of India becoming heated by passing over many hundreds of miles of roasted soil, which has become arid and parched by a burning sun; and while whisking a searching and unbearable dust into every crevice of the human face, added to the fiery rays which are shot from the luminary above, augmented by those reflected by the bleached verdureless soil over which the troops had to march, roasting their eyes, and toasting their skin, may give some idea of the atmosphere, which has been compared to a blast from a furnace, in which an army in the field has to live and fight at this season in India; but the old proverb, "*It is an ill wind that blows nobody good,*" is *à propos* in this case. It is made to produce a refreshingly low temperature in the bungalows of Europeans during the hot season, so that to permanent residents it may be considered an advantage. A kind of door called a tatty, is made of the *kus-kus*, a root which bears a resemblance to dry grass; and being placed in the doorway facing the west, is perpetually kept wet by a *cooley* throwing water over it; and the hot wind blowing through, produces a cool and refreshing air within, often reducing the thermometer from 100° to 70°.

CHAPTER 9

Fatiguing March from Amorha

On the 25th of April, the rebels again moved out of Belwa, and came towards our camp in three columns. The day was as hot and sultry as an April day can be in these parts. They seemed to know, at any rate, what was the best means of weakening European troops; if they failed in doing it by the sword, they adopted a very shrewd method in trying to do it by the climate.

After breakfast a trooper rode in from the advanced cavalry piquet, stating that the enemy were in sight. The bugle sounded to arms, and the horses were yoked to the guns; and a little after eleven o'clock the force marched out to meet them. The line being formed in front of the camp, Brigadier Rowcroft ordered the advance. After proceeding two miles, near the village of Jamoulee, one column of the enemy appeared on our left flank, one in front, and one on the right. The enemy numbered about 4000 men, with four guns. Our line then separated. The left wing, under the command of Major Cox, of H.M. 13th Light Infantry, consisted of a squadron of the Bengal Yeomanry Cavalry, a company and a half of the 13th, and 200 Gurkhas: with two guns, and 100 men of the Naval Brigade under Captain Sotheby.

The right wing, under Brigadier Rowcroft, consisted of about an equal number of cavalry and infantry, with two guns and a 24-pound rocket, under Lieutenant Tumour, R.N. The enemy opened fire with shell on the left wing, which, pushing on, caused them to retire; they then moved off more to the left, being still rapidly pursued. The guns under Captain Sotheby, firing with their usual precision, well supported by the rifles of the seamen under Mr. Ingles, mate, R.N., and the 13th Light Infantry, ably commanded by Major Cox, forced them to retire; but in doing so they inclined towards our left rear, while at the same time the right wing advancing, was unable to get closer to the rebels in front than 1500 yards: 24-pounder rockets, in charge of Lieutenant Grant, were then fired upon them; and these had the desired effect in dispersing the column, which took up a position in a mango-*tope*. The natives have a salutary dread of the rocket, which they call "*Bhan*," occasioned probably by a tradition, of which I have heard, attributing the death of the brother of their god *Ram* to this cause; for, on advancing, we were informed by a villager, that the *subedar* in command was the first to "bolt," saying that they could do nothing against *Bhan*. The others of course soon followed his example.

After a short halt to rest the troops, the brigadier moved over to the left, and joined Major Cox, who was still engaged with another column, which stood their ground in two villages; but by the time the force was again united, the rascals who had run away came on again in front, and on. our extreme right, apparently with the intention of threatening our camp. The right wing was obliged to retrace their steps, and when within 1200 yards, the rebels opened fire with shot and shell from a horsed battery, which they kept at a great distance, not wishing to run the risk of losing it at close quarters.

Having thus doubled back to the former position, they seemed disposed to keep up a game of long balls. They would not close, or permit our force to close with them; the line advanced, but, as it advanced, they retreated; it pushed on as fast as possible, but the sun was so fierce that the heat was melting. The horses were obliged to drag the guns over very bad, rough ground, enough to destroy more axles and gun-carriages than could easily be replaced; and between marching back and forward, and hunting them from one place to another, from eleven o'clock in the morning until five in the afternoon, the men and horses were so fagged and worn out, that many, both Gurkhas and Europeans, fell down on the road, so that the line was obliged to halt.

This was the most fatiguing day and most unsatisfactory "affair" the Goruckpore field force had engaged in up to this time. The insurgents so distributed their forces as to divide our attention; and keeping at such a distance, that it was quite impossible to get at them; a few were killed by the shell at a very long range; and on our side, although their practice with shot and shell was very good, there was no loss. The shell burst over the heads of the cavalry, and the balls rolled along past the line to the rear among the *dhoolee* bearers and camp followers, showing that their battery was managed by experienced gunners; no doubt trained for the service of the Honourable East India Company.

It can scarcely be said that they made an attack: all their manoeuvres seemed intended to harass our men, and keep at a sufficient distance to make their escape when closely pressed. When urged to the attack by their leaders telling them that our "guns were small," they remarked that the "spice (shot and shell) was very strong," and thought it safer to keep at a civil distance. If they only desired to allure our men into the sun, and thus weaken the force, the attempt was well managed: but even in this they were disappointed, few of our men suffering much after a night's rest, although the thermometer was up to 105°.

The villagers brought out vessels of water, and seemed disposed to be friendly; but not much reliance can be placed on their sincerity—very probably they performed the same office for the rebels half an hour before. The *bhisties*, or water-carriers attached to the camp, had also plenty to do. These indefatigable servants carry the water in the skin of a sheep turned inside out, called a *mussuck*, which is placed across their back. The skin is taken off entire without making a longitudinal incision, as is usual in performing this operation. The apertures occasioned by the legs are closed by the skin of each leg being tied tight; and the neck answers for a spout, through which the *mussuck* is filled, and from which the water is poured out, a greater or less quantity escaping according as it is distended or compressed.

On the following day, April 26th, news was brought in that during the affair of the previous day a body of rebels had started up twenty-two miles in our rear, and had taken up a position near Bustee. A small force, consisting of 200 Gurkhas and 50 of the 4th Madras Cavalry, under Captain Clarke, had attacked and beaten 400 of them; but it was discovered that this was only the advanced guard, and that a much larger force was coming down upon the town. In this skirmish the detachment of Gurkhas formed line and advanced boldly, but after a few shots were fired, their line was resembled by an eyewitness to a "flock of geese," that is, "end on."

The Madrasses here, under Captain Clarke, behaved gallantly, charging the enemy and disposing of thirty or forty, including their leader, one of the numerous family of "Sing," who are as well known as the Smiths of London. Captain Clarke then thought it necessary to retire from Bustee to Kuptangunge; but upon the force under Brigadier Rowcroft marching upon that place the same day, he was ordered to return and reoccupy the town.

The rebels seemed now to have completely surrounded us. Three or four thousand were still at Belwa in front; another column in our rear; 3000 or 4000 at Tandah, on the opposite side of the Gogra, on our left flank, threatening a move to our rear; while another body were not many miles from the town of Goruckpore. Under these circumstances it was thought advisable to retire that night with all speed to attack and disperse those near Bustee. At nine o'clock that night the camp was struck, the baggage was packed and sent off under a guard, while a number of *cooleys* or *bildars* were employed for three hours pulling down the walls and bastions of the small fort which had been constructed for the sick and baggage.

The fort being pretty well defaced, the remainder of the force had cleared off the ground by ten o'clock that night. The roads were very bad, and the difficulty of procuring sufficient conveyance for commissariat stores was so great that we did not arrive at Kuptangunge (twelve miles distant) until seven o'clock next morning. It was a most wearisome march, rendered particularly so by the sultriness of the night and the constant delays occasioned by the baggage. Either the *hackeries* must have been loaded more than usual, or the bullocks conspired not to work when urgently required. Sometimes they would rush frantically out of their frail yokes and scamper facetiously into a neighbouring field or village, giving a run to some unhappy driver.

As luck would have it, the moon shed her benign rays on us, enlivening the scene a little, and after a space of nine hours, a march of twelve miles was performed. On one or two occasions, where more than ordinary obstinacy of the draft-bullocks caused a delay, a few managed to steal a sleep on the roadside, spreading a rug or greatcoat and laying their heads on a lump of dry mud for a pillow.

A *syce*,[1] with a very valuable charger belonging to Major Richardson, went too far beyond the camping ground in company with his other servants and baggage. A party of the rebels being on the road at the time, captured him, to the great inconvenience of the owner, who lost at the same time all his clothes, letters, papers, and books. The *syce* and another servant were murdered, but the rest escaped. Others had a narrow escape that same night, by getting in advance of the advanced guard, and going too far from the column. After this surprise the camp-followers entertained a wholesome fear of going too far from the tents.

About 1000 rebels were found to be in possession of the fort of Nuggur, seven miles distant from our encampment, and another larger

1. A groom.

91

force, with artillery, was expected daily to join them from the other side of the river. On the 29th a detachment,[2] under the command of Major Cox, left the camp a little after noon, and having made a march of seven miles, took the enemy by surprise at half-past two o'clock, p.m. Approaching the jungle, which extends for a mile before reaching the village of Nuggur, and the old fort, which was surrounded by a high embankment and dry ditch, by the command of Major Cox the force made a detour, keeping the jungle half a mile to the right.

On getting within 500 yards of the village, the detachment was received with a heavy fire of musketry from the jungle and from behind the earthworks. Skirmishers of the 13th Light Infantry, the Sikhs, and Royal Marines, were sent in to drive them out from their hiding-place, and from the rifle-pits with which it was intersected. The two naval guns and rocket under Lieutenant Grant, R.N., were ordered to take up a position on a slight rise and open fire on that part of the village where the enemy seemed to be most numerous. Here they were well peppered with shell; and the 24-pounder rockets pitching into the village, set it on fire, and, as well as the guns, aided to silence the musketry of the enemy.

The Royal Marine and seamen skirmishers on the right, under Lieutenant Pym, Royal Marine Light Infantry, and a detachment of the 13th Light Infantry, under Captain Kerr, on the left, by a simultaneous movement, rushed into the village, and drove out the rebels, who made their escape through the jungle and across a *jheel* which bordered the village. They formed upon the opposite side; but, owing to the nature of the ground, it was impossible for the cavalry to charge; consequently they effected their escape, leaving behind their baggage, tents, oxen, ponies, and large stores of grain, all of which was saved that escaped the conflagration. A sergeant of the 13th, collecting about a dozen men, pursued the enemy, and one of them, along with a Sikh, succeeded in capturing the rebels' colours as they escaped, disposing of the man who carried them with his rifle. Major Richardson's horse, which had been taken off a few days before, was now recaptured. His baggage, uniform, also books and clothes, which had been lost, were now found scattered in various places; no doubt distributed and subdivided by the captors.

A man, who probably was on the point of walking off with the

2. 156 officers and men of Her Majesty's Light Infantry, 96 of the Naval Brigade, with two guns and a 24-pounder rocket-tube, 65 of the Bengal Yeomanry Cavalry, 292 Gurkhas, and 47 Sikhs.

prize, was found killed by the bursting of a shell near the horse, so that he had a narrow escape from both causes. Thirty or forty of the rebels were killed, but the chief portion of them escaped; of our men only three or four were wounded. A *kitmutgar* of one of the officers was attacked by a *budmash*; but, although unarmed, he had more "pluck" than his opponent, and managing to deprive him of his *tulwar*, tied his hands behind his back, and triumphantly delivered him up to the magistrate.

Owing to the admirable arrangements that were made by Major Cox, the bold advance and sudden rush into the fort and village, the action was brought to a speedy and successful issue, with but a very trifling loss; and in the evening the detachment returned to camp, many of those who went out in the morning infantry having returned cavalry, being mounted on the ponies which were captured from the insurgents.

On crossing the *jheel*, the rebels retreated with the utmost speed in the direction of Tandah, to join the other column which had been daily expected to make an inroad into the district. This sudden check, however, relieved it from any immediate prospect of such an incubus. And, further, it may be observed, that the field force left Amorha in the nick of time to save Bustee, and perhaps Goruckpore, from a second inundation.

CHAPTER 10

The Rebels beaten at Hurreah

By this time Jung Bahadoor's army was at Fyzabad, *en route* for Nepaul, where there was some little delay, owing to the rebels at Belwa occupying the left bank of the river. By them they soon ceased to be molested: some said that there was a private understanding on the subject. For this I cannot positively vouch; at any rate, they crossed the Gogra without meeting with any opposition, and on the 10th of May, with unwonted celerity, the advanced guard surprised us by marching into Bustee. The whole force shortly after arrived, bringing in their train an amount of baggage borne on elephants, camels, *hackeries*, and ponies, one-tenth of which no one ever believed came from Nepaul; in fact, they returned rich in the spoils of Lucknow. No doubt they had much which would be regarded by Europeans as lumber; but in their estimation would be articles of value, and perhaps articles of *virtu*. The remaining Gurkha regiments, which had been with us so long, were now ordered home, and our force became diminished to about 730, out of which the number of the sick was alarming.

On the 7th of May the fort at Nuggur was destroyed, and on the following day the force marched to Bustee, which, being a central position, was made the headquarters, and huts were ordered to be built for our men, instead of living in tents during the rains. A bungalow which had escaped the devastating genius of the *sepoys*, on their previous occupation of this village, was converted into a hospital, and in a very short time became crowded to excess. The climate now began to tell seriously on our men; almost all hands complained, more or less. The effects of living in a hothouse, with the thermometer ranging from 100° to 110°, varied with the unpleasantness of a dismal dust-storm, which obscured the light of the sun himself, was enough to make anyone feel something more than "*ennui*," and cast a shadow of dullness over the force.

Even the nights became so oppressive, that to expect relief even then was a vain hope. Day after day someone was cut off in the strength of his days, in a strange land, far from home, and without a relative to close his eyes. One day it was an officer, another day a non-commissioned officer, and sometimes a private; there was neither immunity nor precedence given to rank or age, when the cold hand of the last enemy clutched with an iron grasp.

Occasionally a dead or mutilated *tusseeldar*, or other government officer, would appear in camp, upon whom a party of rebels made a dash, marching an amazing distance, and escaping again in one night. It was a brutalising war, in which quarter was neither given or received. No European that fell into their hands could expect anything but a most cruel death, aggravated with great indignities, and therefore prisoners were not taken; for, if taken, it would only be to suffer execution in another form. Even to their own countrymen in the employment of government, they showed no mercy, sometimes even increasing in boldness and daring, making a fell swoop, from a distance, on some *theseel*, or village, not many miles from our camp, and escaping before tidings could be conveyed of their approach.

By the middle of June the huts were finished, and on the 13th instant the Naval Brigade shifted billet into them from their tents. This was a great change for the better. The quarters were lofty and airy, the roof was made of straw, and sufficiently thick to repel the sun's rays, as well as to keep out the rain. *Puncas* were rigged up, and pulled all day by native *punca wallas*; added to which, the rains setting in, cooled the air, enabling the men to breathe. The sick list then began to fluctuate, and at last showed a diminution.

The season now became quite changed; an occasional thunderstorm was quite a variety, not an agreeable one, it must be acknowledged, to those who had the misfortune to be in tents, and were obliged to paddle in water; but when well housed, the country presented a different appearance, and the climate was by no means so oppressive as when the soil was parched and dry. The camp routine was as dull as usual. The drills were relaxed, the season not being suitable for that exercise, and all hands relapsed into reading or sleeping on a *charpoy*; a state which lasted for a longer or shorter period according to the state of the weather. No orders having arrived that the brigade should return to the ship, all hands settled down with the prospect of another campaign, and several kinds of amusements were got up for the men.

Books were sent for, a reading-room was established, which, afterwards, when the force took the field, became a portable library, for which a tent was especially set apart. No sooner was the camp pitched after a march, than the reading-room tent, with the periodicals and daily papers, might be seen holding a conspicuous place. During the intervals of fine weather, divers athletic sports were got up for the men; jumping, racing, throwing shot for prizes, hurdle-racing, leaping and hopping. Sometimes it would be varied by a pony race, a *dhooley*[1] race, or an *ecka* race,[2] and occasionally the amusements of the day would be finished off as a great treat by an elephant race, or interrupted by a race between two or three Jacks dressed up in the costume of ladies of the last century, riding on donkeys with their feet touching the ground; and sometimes the grand finale would be a scamper, with loud shouts and vociferous cheering, after an unfortunate pig with his tail shaved.

In addition to these diurnal recreations there were theatricals in camp in the evening, or an occasional alarm in the night to keep up the excitement. There were bodies of insurgents constantly on the move, tossed about between one force and another, not knowing where to go, having much more reason to fear than to be feared; however, not knowing what desperate thing they might be tempted to do, it was always necessary to be on the "*qui vive*" whenever they were expected in the neighbourhood.

At this time tawny wolves from the adjacent jungles paid periodical visits to the camp, and one fine night, when some of the camp-followers were up later than usual, cooking their supper, some of these hungry visitors considered they had a better right to the meal than the cooks, and coming unpleasantly close, the strangers scared the servants, who ran screaming, and causing such an alarm throughout the camp, that the sentries turned out the guard, and in less than ten minutes the brigade was under arms, and the guns were manned ready for action. On discovering their mistake, the men returned to their tents to have their legitimate residue of rest.

Not more than a fortnight afterwards, a jackal began to play his tricks, producing a still more alarming disturbance. He entered one of the men's huts late at night, and commenced a voyage of discovery among the mess-traps in quest of provender; he was driven away again and again, but not being offended at the repulse, exhibited a

---

1. A kind of *palanquin* for the sick or wounded, carried on men's shoulders.
2. A small cart drawn by a pony. It is the Jarvey of India.

manifest reluctance to take his departure. He caught a pet monkey by the head, intending to make a meal off him in lieu of a better dish; but the pet was rescued, and the jackal ignominiously expelled from the hut. But not being bashful, he returned in a couple of hours, and began to make free with the limbs of one of the inmates of the hut, which caused the recipient of his attentions to leap out of bed and shout vociferously.

Another messmate caught the infection, and jumped up half-asleep and half-awake, and, without having a very clear notion why, he laid hold of his neighbour violently, and both exerted their lungs to the utmost pitch. The other inmates of the tent were soon aroused by the noise, and an attempt was made to kill the invader, who managed in the confusion to make his escape. The men in the other huts were awakened from their peaceful slumbers by the "row," and ran out to discover what it was all about. A sentry seeing the men rushing from their huts, fired his musket; another sentry followed his example, giving the alarm; and in an incredibly short space of time the whole force was on the alert. The cavalry patrol came in at a gallop to see what was the matter, and more than one distinguished officer was seen emerging from his quarters in his shirt sleeves, with his sword in one hand and a revolver in the other; while some faithful bearer might be seen running with similar weapons of defence after his waking *sahib*. In less than ten minutes there were men running in every direction to "see what was up;" while the jackal, no doubt, leisurely walked away, to wait for a more convenient opportunity to loot his dinner when the alarm had subsided.

After the taking of Lucknow, when flying columns had been sent after the rebels by the commander-in-chief, traversing Oudh in different directions, they became split up into many detached forces, and when driven from one place would reappear a few days afterwards in another; until at last they took refuge on the north side of the Gogra, having much fewer troops there to molest them than in Oudh. With the increase of 300 of the 6th Madras Cavalry, under Colonel Byng, the Goruckpore field force at Bustee amounted to about 1000 men. Even with so small a force it was necessary so to dispose them that the insurgents should get no rest; but being hunted down wherever they appeared, should never be permitted to take root in any particular locality. For this purpose the force was split up into small detachments, and sent to scour all parts of the district.

This was anything but a pleasant duty during the rains. When a *dour* of this kind was made, the dry hut and comfortable quarters were left behind at Bustee, and at the end of a long and wearisome march, the tents would be pitched where the ground was wet under foot, and with rain falling over head, the whole country was either a sheet of water or a muddy marsh, adding the appearance of dreariness to the experience of discomfort.

The first of these *dours* was commenced on the 23rd of May, when a detachment of two guns, and a 24-pounder rocket-tube of the Naval Artillery, with two troops of the Bengal Yeomanry Cavalry, marched to Kuptangunge to hold it as an outpost; and after a halt of a few days proceeded to Hurreah. On the 31st of the same month, one of these wandering bodies of rebels attacked, looted, and burned the village of Kuptangunge. The *theseeldar* and inhabitants fled to Bustee with all speed to give the alarm; but before assistance could be rendered all the mischief was done, and they were off.

On the 7th of June another detachment, consisting of twenty of the Royal Marine Light Infantry, and thirty-two of H.M.'s 13th Light Infantry, under Lieutenant Pym, Royal Marine Light Infantry, marched from Bustee at nine o'clock at night, and by three o'clock next morning arrived at Kuptangunge, where other troops were drawn up on the road ready to march. They then proceeded to Hurreah, where another small detachment had just arrived under Major Cox, who had left Bustee on the 30th of May, and after taking a circuitous route, and scouring the district in another direction, arrived here in time to take the command. The tents were pitched, and the troops, some of whom had completed a twenty-two miles march, lay down to rest for a few hours, until six o'clock the same day, when the tents were struck, and the baggage packed.

At two o'clock next morning, they[3] marched in the direction of Amorha in two columns, one under the command of Major Richardson, consisting of a detachment of Royal Marines, 13th Light Infantry, and a few Sikhs, with one troop of cavalry and two guns. While this column proceeded along the road, the other, led by Major Cox, went across country to attack the enemy, strongly posted in the house of a *ranee* near Amorha. At daylight the force arrived at a *nullah* in the rear of the house and village, from behind which the rebels opened fire on the cavalry. The Royal Marines coming up, were thrown out in

---

3. *Pearl's* Naval Brigade, 53; two 12-pounder howitzers, and one 24-pounder rocket-tube; 200 of the 13th Light Infantry; two troops of the 6th Madras Cavalry, two troops of the Bengal Yeomanry Cavalry, and 20 Sikhs.

skirmishing order, and returned the fire; the guns, under Lieutenant Turnour, R.N., were galloped up, and threw shot and shell among the main body, which after a quarter of an hour retreated into the house and adjacent buildings.

The force then forded the *nullah*, and throwing out skirmishers, Major Cox, with his usual skill and bravery, forced them to evacuate their position, and drove them towards Belwa. Several were killed in the retreat; our loss was inconsiderable. After a short halt, the force returned to Hurreah, and *bildars* were employed to destroy the fort which they had rebuilt at Amorha. The Royal Marines continued their march to Bustee, an attack being expected there from another quarter.

It is painful to be obliged to call to mind that the graves of those who fell in action, or died from disease, during the time we were encamped at Amorha, were torn open by the rebels after we left it; such was their savage barbarity, that even the bones of the dead were not allowed to rest in peace. The graves were then restored, and the damage was rectified before leaving the place. On the return of the force to Bustee, the rebels came on again with imperturbable pertinacity, and returning to Hurreah, seemed disposed to take up their quarters there during the rains, commencing to throw up earthworks and build huts. But on the 16th of June, another *dour* was made in the same direction. At seven o'clock in the evening, eighty seamen and marines under Captain Sotheby, one troop of Bengal Yeomanry Cavalry, and half a troop of Madras Cavalry, left Bustee, and by half past ten at night, arriving near Kuptangunge, they lay down on the road to rest until daybreak, intending to take the enemy by surprise at Hurreah.

But as they were about to push on, a fearful thunder-storm broke over their heads; rain fell in torrents; no tents were pitched to give shelter, the land was flooded, the road was turned into a river, and all hands were well drenched. A dram of rum was issued to the men, and they managed to get as far as the camping ground. The land being a sheet of water, was not in a very good condition for the working of guns. The attack was consequently postponed until the following day (the 18th), when, at three o'clock in the morning, having joined another detachment which had been sent out previously under Lieutenant-Colonel Byng of the 6th Madras Cavalry, the force[4] left Kuptan-

---

4. *Pearl's* Naval Brigade, 111; two 12-pounder howitzers, and one 24-pounder rocket-tube, under Captain Sotheby; 135 of the 13th Light Infantry; 50 Sikhs; 130 Bengal Yeomanry Cavalry; 100 of the 6th Madras Cavalry; one 9-pounder and one 24-pounder howitzer, Bengal Artillery.

gunge to attack the insurgents under Mahomed Hussein, who were posted and entrenched in the village of Hurreah, eight miles in front.

At midnight 150 of the Bengal Yeomanry Cavalry and 6th Madras Cavalry, under the command of Captain Mulcaster, went across country by a circuitous route, and after a fatiguing march of sixteen miles, took up a position in the rear of the enemy, masked by a *tope* of trees, with a view of cutting off their retreat, and if possible capture their chief, with his guns and elephants. About three o'clock in the morning of the 18th, the remainder of the force marched to meet the enemy in front.

The Nazim Mahomed Hussein had taken up a position with about 4000 or 5000 men, including 900 *sepoys* and six guns, in the villages of Sirsaie and Hurreah, On the right flank were two thick bamboo jungles and a village in the possession of the enemy, and on the left flank a *nullah*, a village, and a strong brick house, besides a *tope* of trees also occupied by them.

Captain Mulcaster and Captain Chapman continued to watch the enemy's movements until a little after sunrise, when the action commenced. Skirmishers were thrown out, and the guns were brought up to the front and opened fire. The enemy stood firm until the troops began to close; then, under the influence of the artillery and the steady advance of the riflemen driving them across the river, which, the skirmishers of the 13th, under Lieutenant Everett, the Royal Marines and seamen under Mr. Ingles, mate, immediately fording, they retired from the bridge. Captain Sotheby galloped up the naval guns, and finding the right in close collision with the enemy's left, who obstinately held the jungle, opened a destructive fire with shot and shell. All this time the cavalry were exposed to a continued and heavy fire from the enemy's rifles and infantry, who were in a position inaccessible to cavalry. Captain Chapman with his troop took a wide sweep, to cut off the elephants and baggage, which were at some distance; but being in a position inaccessible to cavalry, the movement had only the effect of causing some of it to be abandoned.

The two guns of the Bengal Artillery and the remainder of the 13th having been, with Lieutenant-Colonel Byng, engaged on the left, now advanced, took up a position on the road, and shelled the rebels out of the jungle; and the two naval guns, galloping over the bridge, found the enemy in great force. On the right, at a distance of 300 yards, a small mud battery was thrown up, with well-made embrasures, in order to command the bridge, and another in a *tope* about double the distance off. From the former they were soon cleared out by the howitzers; and as they were retreating from the latter, where they appeared to be a strong column of 1500 men, their movements were accelerated by the same agency. The naval guns here coming up with the skirmishers and the Bengal Yeomanry Cavalry at the same time, they were pursued until the infantry, from fatigue and intolerable heat, were obliged to halt.

The enemy, who were evidently trained soldiers, retired in good order, receiving protection from the numerous *topes* and small villages on their route. The action lasted four hours, and they are reported to have lost about seventy. Our casualty list was small, only seven or eight men, and several horses wounded. The naval guns under Lieutenant Turnour, assisted, by Mr. Maquay, mate, R.N., were remarked to have moved with great rapidity, and to have fired with great precision. There was only one of the enemy's captured, with some of their baggage and ammunition. That part of the district was, however, cleared for the present, and the Nazim effected his escape, and that but narrowly; he was obliged to retire into the jungle, there to take up his quarters in an old fort, with a few trusty followers.

The force did not long remain at Hurreah, and two days afterwards had the benefit of another thunderstorm, which caused the men in tents to be "all afloat;" a circumstance by no means conducive to the well-being of the troops, or calculated to restore to health those who had lately been suffering from fever or dysentery. But these inconveniences never produced discontent whenever there was active service to be carried out; let the weather be ever so trying, or the heat ever so oppressive, the men were at all times ready, forward, and even impatient to leave the sick list before the time.

CHAPTER 11

The Enemy Beaten at Amorha

On the 29th of August a detachment of the Naval Brigade under Lieutenant Fawkes, R.N., took part in an action near Lumptee. The force,[1] under the command of Captain Garrard of the 27th Regiment, Native Infantry, repelled, with unshaken steadiness and promptitude, an attack of the enemy under the Rajah of Gondah, consisting of 150 *sowars*, 300 *sepoys*, and 1900 irregular troops, with four guns. By the time the enemy's advanced guard got within two miles of the entrenchments, the detachment of Her Majesty's 13th Light Infantry was ordered to take up a position on the left of the road in a *tope*, and the detachment of the 27th Madras Native Infantry on the right, under cover of a village. The seamen and guns took ground in the centre, in another village. The enemy advanced in three columns, and attacked the left and centre several times, but were repelled by the steady firing of the rifles and the effective precision of the shells. The attack was kept up until about four o'clock, p.m., when they attempted to turn the flank of the position taken up by Captain Garrard; but failing in this, they retired, and the force followed them up, the guns and cavalry pursuing, until they halted and recommenced the firing.

The naval guns then advanced rapidly, and silenced their battery, forcing them to retreat. After a pursuit of three or four miles, the force returned to Amorha. The loss of the enemy was about fifty; our detachment suffered very slightly.

On the same day, about half-past five in the evening, another attack was made by the rebels on another outpost at Hurreah, eight miles distant. They were about 800 strong, with a force in reserve, and three

---

1. *Pearl's* Naval Brigade, 50, with two guns; 50 of Her Majesty's 13th Light Infantry; 50 Sikhs; 350 of the 27th Madras Native Infantry; one troop of the 6th Madras Cavalry.

guns. Intelligence of the fact was immediately sent to headquarters at Bustee, and at ten o'clock that night a force[2] was sent out with the utmost rapidity under Major Cox, of the 13th Light Infantry. They had been repelled by Captain Vine with his small detachment; but on the approach of the reinforcement from Bustee, and on the arrival of the cavalry in advance at two o'clock next morning, they lost no time in retiring.

Major Cox immediately pushed on to Debreah, where he again came up with them on the 1st of September. They numbered about 1000 infantry, fifty *sowars*, and three guns. After a fatiguing march, he attacked, defeated, and routed them, Major Cox himself leading a party of the 13th to a charge against a body of the rebels concealed behind the embankment of a tank, clearing them out, and with the whole detachment pursued them up close, until they retired with a loss of about ninety in killed and wounded; the detachment at the same time suffering much from bad roads, oppressive heat, and heavy ground; but they went through it with their usual cheerfulness and steadiness, inspired by the intrepidity of their leader with a confidence of success.

On the evening of the 6th of September another *dour* was made by a detachment under the command of Commander Grant, R.N., at a season of the year most trying to the strongest constitution and most undaunted perseverance; but was conducted with a zeal and judgment which deservedly gained the highest commendation from the brigadier in command. The force consisted of two 12-pounder howitzers, and a 24-pounder rocket-tube, with seventy-three seamen and marines, and seventy non-commissioned officers, rank and file, of Her Majesty's 18th Light Infantry, under Lieutenant Gillett. The object was to relieve Bansee, a town in the northern part of the district of Goruckpore, which belonged to a friendly *rajah*; the small garrison of Sikhs who held the place, being hard pressed by the rebels, a prompt and speedy march of a sufficient force was the only chance for its safety.

On reaching Gontah, twelve miles distant from the place. Captain Mulcaster joined the detachment with a squadron of cavalry, and assuming the command, pushed on with all speed, and arrived at Bansee on the 8th, after a march of fifty miles, in thirty-nine hours.

The roads were in a deplorable state after the rains. The guns were

---

2. 350 of Her Majesty's 13th Light Infantry; two guns of Naval Brigade under Lieutenant Tumour; one troop of Bengal Yeomanry Cavalry.

carried on elephants. The men were sometimes marching up to their knees in mud, and sometimes up to their waist in water, Jack suggesting that a boat would be more suitable. In one place they waded for nearly three miles, besides having forded two *nullahs* and crossed another in a boat, which with some difficulty was procured for the purpose. In addition to the difficulties under foot, the sun, as usual, poured down his rays of fire, which was most harassing to the men, who, nevertheless, pushed on, and the enemy, on hearing of their approach, retired. Then the Raptee, a river deep and rapid at that season of the year, was crossed by a portion of the force, and the cavalry pursuing the fugitives cut up several.

Havildar Narain Sing, of the Sikh battalion, leaving his corps, galloped on, and having cut down two of the enemy, returned to his men; and on a subsequent occasion this same native Sikh officer, on the retreat of the enemy across a river, threw off his clothes, and taking his sword between his teeth, swam across and cut down five of the rebels.

On arriving at the house of the *rajah*, which was converted into a sort of fortress, it was found that the ammunition of the Sikh garrison had run so short, that only three rounds of percussion-caps remained per man. Here the Europeans got shelter from the sun; but having out-marched the commissariat, were without provisions until nine o'clock at night. The Sikhs, to stay the cravings of hunger, commenced to make *chupatties* (a sort of thin native cake baked in a pan), which were very acceptable under the circumstances; but Jack gave it as his opinion that they had the flavour of baked sawdust.

Brigadier Fischer, of the Madras Native Infantry, joined the force on the 10th, and on the 12th marched from Bansee, a few men having been left behind who were thoroughly "done up" with fatigue, heat, and exposure. The rest of the force, losing no time, reached Doomureahgunge on the 13th, when the advanced guard was fired upon by a body of rebels from a line of earthworks commanding the road. The naval guns (12-pr mountain-train howitzers) having been taken off the backs of the elephants, and the horses being yoked to them, were speedily galloped to the front; the marines and seamen, under Lieutenant Ingles, advanced at the double to cover their guns. The infantry forming line advanced steadily to the front, waded over fields flooded with water, and on coming within range, the guns opened fire, throwing shell into their entrenched camp and on the main body, until they were obliged to retire.

Next day, with indomitable perseverance, the force crossed the river, and marched northward towards Intwa, expecting to catch the enemy in a village where they had taken up their quarters; but the road, being quite impassable without swimming, they were obliged to return and recross the river. The object of the expedition being accomplished, they marched back to Bustee, which was reached on the 17th; and the following morning the sick, who were left behind, also arrived at headquarters.

A similar expedition, if possible, more harassing, was subsequently made by another detachment[3] of the Naval Brigade under Lieutenant Ingles, which left Bustee on the 27th of the same month, and arriving at Bansee by forced marches, crossed the Raptee and came up with the rear-guard of the rebels at Mowee. The cavalry and guns quickly dispersed them, driving them into the jungle; and after a pursuit of five or six miles, the force returned, having suffered greatly from a hard day's work, wading through water, and scouring through thick jungle.

The rebels, driven from Oudh, were daily increasing on the north of the Grogra, and the Goruckpore field force was obliged to do the work of double their number. It was split up into small detachments, which were continually despatched to drive off wandering bands of insurgents, who were becoming more and more audacious in their approaches, from having no spot of ground which they could calculate on as a safe retreat. Sometimes they would make a dash at some village, mutilating or killing the *theseeldar* or some unfortunate Burkundazee, and then looting the neighbourhood, would make their escape. The movements of these flying columns were so rapid, that it was quite impossible to get timely intelligence of their approach, and equally impossible to calculate where they intended to go, or what turning they were next likely to take.

One of these wandering clouds passed within ten miles of Bustee, and killed two Madras *syces* (grooms) which they met on the road. Captain Sotheby, in company with Commander Tumour, had a narrow escape, having ridden along the road only half an hour before they crossed. The same day the Naval Brigade was in danger of suffering a severe loss in its commanding officer from another cause. He was much injured by a bad fall from his horse, but fortunately the injury

---

3. *Pearl's* Naval Brigade, two 12-pounder howitzers, 30 men and 2 officers, under Lieutenant Ingles, R.N.; 72 of Her Majesty's 13th Light Infantry, under Colonel Twynan, and 27 of the Bengal Yeomanry Cavalry.

turned out not to be so severe as was anticipated, and after a temporary indisposition, Captain Sotheby was again restored to duty. Such are the many chances that flutter about in time of war.

While the proceedings just narrated were carrying out in the north of the district, another affair took place in the west of it towards Fyzabad. The detachment which held the outpost at Amorha, was attacked on October 1st about noon. The villagers reported that the enemy, numbering about 1200, with two guns, were advancing in three columns, their usual order, one on the centre, and one on each flank. Captain Garrard, of the 27th Native Infantry, was in command. The detachment[4] moved out, and took up a position at a distance of about 800 yards in front of the camp. The seamen and Sikhs took ground in the centre, and a small body of infantry were thrown out on both flanks.

About two o'clock in the afternoon, the enemy commenced the attack on both flanks and centre, which was renewed several times; but being repulsed each time by the rifles and shell, towards evening they commenced a retreat, when they were hotly pursued by the horsed guns, supported by the cavalry and Sikhs. The cavalry charging on the left, and the guns directed by Lieutenant Maquay, pursuing them with unexpected speed, came within a short distance of several of the retreating mutineers. A few of the cavalry advanced, intending to charge, but on approaching too near, the *sepoys* went through threatening motions with their muskets, causing either the horses or their riders to turn about.

An attempt was made more than once to bring them to the point, but the *sepoys* kept them at bay. Four of the seamen at the gun were ordered to charge; an order which they gallantly obeyed. Lee, Williams, Rayfield, and Simmonds, dashed forward, and came up with a few that still had not made their escape; after a short encounter, the clash of swords being but for a moment, and they were despatched. Lee received a severe sword-cut in the arm, Rayfield a slight contusion in the arm, which was said to have been a bite from the *sepoy* when deprived of his other weapon, and Williams only a very slight wound. The affair being thus brought to a termination, the detachment returned to camp.

On the 23rd of October, another *dour* was made to Bansee, the

---

4. Fifty of the *Pearl's* Naval Brigade and two 12-pounder howitzers under Lieutenant Fawkes; 50 of the 13th Light Infantry; 50 Sikhs; 70 Madras Infantry, and one troop of Madras Cavalry.

rebels again coming down to that neighbourhood. The force consisted of a detachment of the Bengal Yeomanry Cavalry, two naval guns, and a company of H.M.'s 13th Light Infantry; and having had a brush with the enemy, returned to headquarters. On the 26th of the same month, an attack was made by a detachment under the command of Colonel Lord Mark Kerr, 13th Light Infantry, on Jugdespore, a fort in the jungle, lying about twenty-five miles north-west from Bustee, which being more strongly garrisoned than had been expected, his lordship drew off his men in good order, and retired. This movement gave rise to reports that the Naval Brigade guns were taken; and many amusing letters on the subject were written in the Indian papers by the seamen, in which they indignantly repelled the charge, expressing their astonishment that the public were ignorant of the fact that there are two things Jack never loses, and these are "his grog and his guns."

The outlying detachments having been called in, the whole field force marched from Bustee, on the 24th of November, towards the north of the district. The rebels by this time having been routed out of Oudh and the Dooab, congregated along the belt of jungle which separates our territory from Nepaul. A field hospital was established at Bustee, and small detachments from the different corps left as a guard, Lieutenant-Colonel Whistler, of the 6th Madras Cavalry, being in command. A siege train also arriving at Bustee, the same day, was ordered to join the force, and subsequently was turned over to the *Pearl's* Naval Brigade.

On the 25th the force marched to Bhanpore, and was there joined by a Madras battery, under the command of Captain Cadell, and next day moved on to Doomureahgunge, which is situated on the right bank of the Raptee. When within two miles of the village, a native brought information that our bugle-calls on the line of march were heard by the advanced piquet of the rebels, and that they were preparing to retreat. The brigade soon after halted, on the enemy being seen on the left, not more than a mile distant. *Sowars* were observed riding up and down, in front of the infantry, which had taken up a position in a mango-*tope*. A detachment was sent out under Lieutenant-Colonel Cox, of the 13th Light Infantry, consisting of 200 Sikhs of the Ferozepore regiment, under Lieutenant-Colonel Brazier, 200 of the 13th Light Infantry, and two guns of Captain Cadell's battery, with a troop of cavalry.

While Colonel Cox attacked the insurgents on the left of the road, the remainder of the force, under Brigadier Rowcroft, consisting of the rest of the 13th, the Sikhs, the Naval Brigade and artillery, advanced along the road towards the village, in order to cut off any possibility of escape in that direction. As soon as the Madras Artillery got within range. Captain Cadell opened fire with his guns, and soon drove them out of the *tope*. The detachment still pressed on, driving them before them as they went, until they "shoved" them up into the bend of a *nullah*, out of which they could not extricate themselves without either fighting or swimming; the latter course they preferred.

The cavalry charged down the bank of the *nullah*, and drove them into the water; not, however, without the loss of their brave leader, Captain Gifford, and a trooper, who were killed, and several others wounded. A scene then was acted which could not be witnessed in a warfare between two civilized European nations. The war in India was a war of extermination, without any shadow of doubt; the crime not only of the *sepoys* who mutinied and killed their officers, but of the other rebels, who, unprovoked, took a savage delight in the blood of Europeans, was such that the universal feeling which prevailed was "death" to the perpetrators. It was utterly impossible to discover the men among the multitudes who had done the deeds, and therefore all who bore arms against the government were regarded as being implicated. In this state of things few ever went through the empty formality of making prisoners.

Many of the *sepoys* who escaped the sabres of the cavalry, were drowned in the *nullah*, when making an attempt to escape; and many others appeared with only their black heads above water, making the last vain effort to save life, either by wading or swimming. It is only when there is no chance of escape that the natives of India exhibit great courage, or rather indifference, at meeting death. When an opportunity offers to get away, they show no greater contempt for life than other people. The heads of the fugitives dotted about then became marks to fire at, until all disappeared, except one or two, who, escaping among a shower of balls, crawled up the opposite bank, and hid among the high crops.

One, in particular, was standing up to his chin in the water, unable to swim across, and submitting to the annoyance of being the object of many "pot shots," for nearly half an hour. An officer's servant, his fellow countryman, showing his zeal for the "Company Bahadoor," commenced firing missiles, in the form of lumps of hard clay, which were the first to take effect. An officer standing by charged him with the folly of being a rebel, and told him that he was going that day to receive the reward of his deeds in the other world; stating it in plainer language than I have thought it necessary to write. He replied with a volley of abuse, in no measured or choice language, and told him it was no business of his. A torrent of foul epithets ensued: but in this kind of warfare it is hopeless for a European to compete with a native of India. Their language abounds in such a choice collection of insulting terms, that it is incomparably rich in untranslateable slang. In fact I have heard of men in the bazaars who would not object to attack any one with lingo for a very small remuneration. Whether this individual was a member of that profession or not, it was impossible to ascertain; at any rate his time was drawing to a close, for a trooper then coming up, fired, and the wretched man made one struggle—for a moment the water was disturbed—but the next minute and the circling ripples subsided; he sunk to rise no more, and all was as calm above as if nothing had happened.

One small gun and limber was taken, and the force retired. But on halting for a short time to rest the troops, an officer going into a field of *dhall*, was saluted by a *sepoy* in full uniform, with a Punjab medal on his breast, who presented his musket, but did not fire. Being only armed with a sword, he called a soldier of the 13th, who despatched him, and as he retired, boasting how well he had done it, a more experienced campaigner immediately proceeded to denude him of the medal, and investigate the contents of his *kamerband*, in which was discovered a large deposit of Company's *rupees*. It was considered scarcely equitable that another should step in and capture the proceeds of his prize.

To rifle the slain for the gold *mohurs* or Company's *rupees*, became of such usual occurrence, the *sepoys* carrying their property in their *kamerband*, or turban, that the man who made the "bag" (a sporting expression in common use) had a vested interest in his antagonist. There was a halt at Doomureahgunge for some days, while a bridge of boats was constructing across the Raptee. Balla Rao, a brother, as some call him, or some other near relative of the Nana, as others say, occupied the opposite side with several thousand men and a strong force of artillery. He continued collecting revenue at the rate of about 5000 *rupees* per day, and report said that he sent his *salaams* to the *begum*, offering her cash, and informing her of his successes. The former she is said to have declined, not being in any immediate want of subsidies, but as to the latter she congratulated him.

On the evening of the 2nd, Brigadier Rowcroft received intelligence that the force under the Nazim Mahomed Hossein, of about 2000 or 3000 men, with six guns, had left his fort at Bungaon, and with the utmost effrontery encamped only six or eight miles distant from our camp higher up the river, evidently with a view of crossing over and joining Balla Rao.

On the 3rd of December, a portion of the force under the command of Brigadier Rowcroft, went out to attack him. Two guns and fifty men of the Naval Brigade, under Captain Sotheby, C.B., 350 of H.M.'s 13th Light Infantry, a detachment of Sikhs, the Bengal Yeomanry Cavalry, a detachment of the 27th Madras Native Infantry, with four guns of Captain Cadell's battery—about 850 men of all arms—went out about half-past five in the morning, and about eight o'clock found the enemy protected behind mud walls and earthworks, in the village of Bururiah, and in two large woods with a thick forest and jungle to retire to behind. There was some broken ground in front, a difficulty which was soon overcome.

The enemy opened fire with three guns and musketry, when Captain Sotheby's two guns in the centre, and two of Captain Cadell's on the left, with two others in charge of Captain Highmoor on the right, quickly responded. The enemy at first stood their ground more firmly than usual, the naval guns and Madras battery playing upon them with round-shot, shell, and grape. They held to their trenches obstinately, until the steady and resistless advance shook their resolution. The seamen and marines went close up to their works in front in skirmishing order, under a heavy fire, while the Sikhs and a company of the 13th skirted the jungle to the left; the enemy then finding themselves threatened on the flank, relinquished their position and commenced a retreat. And being favoured by the woods and thick cover, they managed to get their guns over a small river where there was a ford, and into the forest, where they were driven after a two hours' combat, having been expelled from the woods and villages.

The rebel force becoming scattered, there were several parties who seemed to go "on their own hook" as they expressed it, and took a few "pot shots" at any stray *sowars* who might be fluttering about. On any of them making their appearance, "*crack*," "*crack*," quickly followed, and his retreat was either hastened, or he fell. The loss of the enemy was reckoned to be between thirty and forty; two seamen were wounded, and of the other corps, there were about twelve wounded. The number of hair-breadth escapes were about the same as usual on these occasions, such as a bullet through some part of the clothes, or having a badge taken off a helmet, or some trifle of that sort. After a short halt, the force returned to camp, fatigued and hungry, at three o'clock in the afternoon.

CHAPTER 12

Battle of Toolseepore

On the 5th of December, the bridge of boats was complete, and the Naval Brigade crossed to the north side of the river. The sick and wounded were sent to Bustee, to the field hospital, and now Brigadier Rowcroft's column was moving northward inclining to the west so as to enclose the shattered forces of the *begum*, which were hemmed in on all sides in the northern district of Oudh. The commander-in-chief, Lord Clyde, was moving down upon them from the westward. Sir Hope Grant, with a large force of cavalry, was moving up from the south, and Brigadier Rowcroft's column was drawing round from the east, while the Nepaul jungles were on the north. Here the last grand smash was to take place of those marauding mutineers who had made many a home sad for the previous two years. And with this grand finale, the *Pearl's* Naval Brigade wound up their two campaigns in India. The arrangements were admirably made.

The southern districts of Oudh had been cleared by the numerous flying columns which had traversed it in every direction, and they were all hunted up into this one corner of the country. The queen's well-timed proclamation had been read, and many availed themselves of the royal clemency; but all those who could not convince themselves that any government could be so merciful as to extend the golden sceptre of favour after all that had been perpetrated, or still clinging to the last hope in a failing cause, fled to the north, expecting, when unable to stand in the open field, to be able to take shelter in the jungles of Nepaul.

After crossing the river, the force marched to Intwa, leaving a detachment at Doomureahgunge to guard the bridge of boats and *ghat*. The camping ground was an open plain, where we halted for several days, and the siege train, which was handed over to the Naval Brigade, was here parked in front of our camp.

The field force now began to muster strong, consisting of the Ferozpore regiment of Sikhs, about 600 men; H.M's 13th Light Infantry, nearly an equal number; 300 of the 6th Madras Cavalry, a Madras battery, the Bengal Yeomanry Cavalry, and the Naval Brigade. The several corps were daily drilled in front of the lines, and the band played in the evening for the benefit of those who attended the promenade; the weather at this season is delightful, but it lasts only two or three months. The days are not unpleasantly warm, and the nights are cool, in fact sometimes they are biting cold; and on going outside the tents soon after sunrise a noble view of the snowy range of the Himalayas can be seen lifting up to heaven their white crests tinted with a roseate hue, as they glitter in the beams of the rising sun.

On the 18th the siege train arrived from Doomureahgunge—two 18-pounders, one 8-inch howitzer, and two 8- inch mortars; these, in addition to two 5½-inch mortars, were turned over to the *Pearl's* Naval Brigade. Every seaman and marine was now attached to the siege train, with the exception of those who manned the light field battery of four 12-pounder howitzers and two 9-pounders. The men had become sufficiently acquainted with the management of horses, bullocks, and elephants to feel quite at home among them. One elephant became quite a pet among the men—rather a clumsy one, we must admit, becoming so tame that he paid a daily visit to the several tents to receive donations, in the form of bread, and on his arrival announced himself with the sniff of his proboscis, or a touch of a tent rope. The elephants that are used for beasts of burden are caught in the jungle, and soon become domesticated, but do not breed in a tame state. They are wonderful animals—so powerful, and yet so gentle, so clumsy, and apparently so void of intelligence, yet so docile; they are so capable of resisting, so violent and untameable when they become infuriated, perfectly regardless whom they tread down in their blind rage, and yet generally so obedient to command.

When the *mahout* speaks, he seems to understand. When he tells him what to do, he obeys. Occasionally he is brought to the river to bathe; the *mahout* standing on his back drives him into the deep water, where he flounders about for some time, projecting the extremity of his trunk above the surface to breathe. He is then brought to the shallow water, where he lies down on one side, while he is rubbed and washed, and then is turned on the other for the same operation; all this time paying the utmost deference to the orders of the *mahout*. He rolls about like a huge monster, and after playing for some time and apparently enjoying the bath, returns to his "moorings," where he is attached to a tree by a chain round his hind leg.

Captain Sotheby had now got the command of a formidable armament, and it would have been difficult, if not impossible, to have procured artillerymen at so short a notice so well trained, or better fitted to manage heavy guns. The four mortars were in the charge of Lieutenant Pym, R.M., Light Infantry, and his detachment of Royal Marines, and Marine Artillery.

It was expected that the rebels would make a last dying struggle at the fortress of Toolseepore in the north of Oudh, and in order to finish off the campaign with as little delay as possible, these heavy guns were sent on with the force. Toolseepore was one of the last that held out when Oudh was annexed, and being of great strength it was impossible to say that its owner, who belonged to the insurgent party, might not resist to the last.

On the morning of the 20th, the force marched from Intwa to Biskohur on the Oudh frontier: the boundary line between Goruckpore and that kingdom being marked by small pillars two or three hundred yard» apart, ran through our camp, so that some of the force were in Goruckpore and some in Oudh. The morning was as dismal as both tradition and experience combine to prove a December morning to be. The road was wretchedly bad, owing to heavy rains that usually fall at this season of the year; a thick mist enveloped everything, and through it the sun made sundry abortive efforts to shine. The cold, early in the morning, was intense, and the damp mist rendered it still more so.

The horses sunk in the mud up to their knees, and many of the baggage-carts did not arrive on the camping ground until late that night; the bullocks being unable to drag them along with their wheels becoming embedded in the tenacious liquid mud. When the tents were pitched, rain threatened, and a small trench was dug round the frail tenement to catch the water, and a little embankment was thrown up all around to keep it out; and on the 22nd, the force marched to Goolereah Ghat, and encamped on the bank of the Boora Raptee, not more than five miles from Toolseepore, where the enemy were assembled in great force.

Brigadier Rowcroft had an interview with Sir Hope Grant the same day, from whom orders were received to attack the rebels on the following morning. The brigadier suffered a severe loss this day in the departure of the 1st Punjab Cavalry, which went *en route* for the commander-in-chief's camp, and being on the eve of a battle, if their services had been secured for one day longer, the success would have been much more complete and satisfactory. They are a noble corps, well mounted, and a fine race of men; they go by the name of Hughes' Horse, and are an irregular regiment, a sort of yeomanry; the troopers belonging to a respectable class in their own country, supplying their own horses, and being paid a liberal monthly allowance. In lieu of them H.M's 53rd regiment was sent to join our forces, and arrived that night, and although a regiment of veterans than whom none could do their work better, a cavalry regiment was much more required at that time.

23rd of December.—Having had an early breakfast this morning, at half-past six o'clock the tents were struck, and the baggage was packed, so as to be ready to follow at the conclusion of the action. The force forded the river between nine and ten o'clock; the siege train from its cumbrousness occupying some time, but considering the steepness of the banks, and the nature of the soil, was transported with more speed than would have been anticipated. The large guns were drawn by elephants, and the mortars by twenty-four bullocks. When the whole force had crossed, the line was formed, and, under the orders of Brigadier Rowcroft, advanced towards the enemy, who were seen about two miles distant on an extensive open plain, with a few villages scattered here and there, which they turned to account by occupying them with a party of infantry and guns. They were, as usual, well aware how to make use of every available position, which was as expeditiously relinquished when hard pressed, as it was originally well chosen.

H.M's 13th Light Infantry, under the command of Lord Mark Kerr, took ground on the extreme right; on their left was the Madras battery of four guns, under Captain Cadell, and the Bengal Yeomanry Cavalry (200 sabres); on the extreme left of the line were a body of the 27th Madras Native Infantry, and between 200 and 300 of the 6th Madras Cavalry; next on their right was H.M.'s 53rd regiment, under Colonel English, and between the 53rd and the Ferozpore regiment of Sikhs, under Colonel Brazier, were the four naval guns and two 24-lb. rocket tubes under the command of Commander Turnour, R.N. Lieutenant Maquay and Mr. C. Foot, midshipman, being also attached to the battery. The Naval Brigade and siege train, under the command of Captain Sotheby, C.B., kept as close to the line as the nature of the ground, which was intersected with small watercourses, would admit.

All the men, both seamen and marines, were now turned into gunners; so that, with the exception of the four 12-pr howitzers and rockets, there was little opportunity for the others to take part in the action; these, with which Captain Sotheby was ever present, pushed on to the front, and notwithstanding the rough character of the ground, were conspicuous for the rapidity of their movements, and the speed of their advance in close proximity to the skirmishers of the 53rd, as they pursued and routed the enemy. "Come on, boys," said some of the soldiers, and Jack limbered up, vowed he would go anywhere, and on he dashed, managing the horses and guns with such activity and readiness, that some of them said, using an expletive better suppressed, "Well, I'll believe anything about sailors after this."

On the right, the 18th attacked a village, where a large body of rebels with a gun had taken up a position under cover of the mud walls; as they advanced the enemy kept up a heavy fire of shot and musketry, but the soldiers entered it with a rush, took one gun at the point of the bayonet, and bayoneted the gunner who persisted in sticking to his idol[1] to the last. Another gunner was found with his brains blown out, apparently with his own hand, seeing no chance of escape. On the left, the 53rd, the Sikhs, the four naval guns, and the two 24-lb. rocket tubes, were pushed rapidly forward. The rebels here seem to have stood their ground much better than usual. They waited under cover of a bank of a *nullah* until the troops came within 150 yards of them, and reserving their fire until they thought themselves sure of the object, discharged a volley, and then fled before the undaunted advance of the 53rd.

This regiment then charged a body of rebels, who were drawn up in support of a gun, and almost came up with them, but being completely "blown" by the distance they were obliged to run, were unable to get to close quarters with men whose agility is proverbial; the enemy soon made their escape, and succeeded in getting their gun off also. It is in such cases as this that the loss of cavalry has so often been felt; infantry doing all that infantry can do, but being quite unable to do the work of cavalry into the bargain. The siege train in charge of Commander Grant, R.N., kept up close in rear of the line, but had only an opportunity of firing one or two rounds on a village held by a party of the insurgents on our left rear.

---

1. The natives almost, if not altogether, worship their guns.

In an hour and a half, the rebels being completely routed and driven back, the Ferozpore regiment of Sikhs, a noble corps, pushed on well in front, and were the first (after the rebel army had retired) to enter the fort of Toolseepore, which was found deserted. The rebels, numbering about 300 cavalry, 12,000 infantry, and several guns, came down in three columns, and after having deployed into line, extended to a great distance on the left and right. *Sowars* were galloping up and down in front of their line, probably encouraging them to exterminate the *Feringhees*; but their resistance was of short duration, and their cavalry never ventured to charge.

One gun was taken by H.M.'s 13th Light Infantry, and one by H.M's 53rd, which was left behind when the line advanced, and on returning in search of it, it could not be found. Our force of all arms in the field was about 2,500 men, and our loss was four killed and several wounded, in addition to two or three *dhoolee* bearers, who were also killed. The loss of the enemy could not be easily ascertained, but must have been considerable, many were left on the field, besides many others who no doubt, were carried off when wounded.

On arriving about 1500 yards from the fort, the siege train halted, and a man was seen on the rampart hoisting something which in the distance looked like a flag. At first those attached to the siege train fancied that their turn had arrived, and were making preparations for action; but it soon appeared that the man was a Sikh who had entered the fort which the enemy had evacuated in the morning to give battle, and after the defeat thought it wiser not to re-enter. No doubt, as their information was generally better than ours, they heard of the heavy pieces of ordnance that were in the field, and the stalwart men that manned them. Whether the rumour that got afloat among them that seamen were little men, who carried these pieces of artillery under their arm, or not, it is impossible to say; but from the very absurd stories which were circulated among them by designing men, and which were implicitly believed, when to the prejudice of the Europeans or government, it may justly be argued that they would believe almost anything.

The fort was constructed in the form of a square, surrounded by a deep ditch, filled with water, and inside the ditch thick mud-walls and bastions; there were houses, a garden and magazine inside, and sufficiently extensive to contain a large force. The powder and arms were destroyed.

Two unhappy accidents occurred in the evening after the action.

The troops sat down on the ground to rest, and a private of the 53rd, when taking up his rifle, which he had left on full cock, thoughtlessly held the muzzle towards him, and a twig catching the trigger, caused it to go off, shooting him through the breast. Instantaneous death ensued. And in the evening a soldier of another regiment, under the effects of drink, fired off his rifle through a tent, shooting one Sikh, and wounding another. He was immediately put under arrest to await his trial. It fell to my lot the following morning to commit the remains of the Europeans that fell in action to a soldier's grave.

This was the last action in which the *Pearl's* Naval Brigade took a part, and it was the last general action that took place during the mutiny; the war being declared over on the first day of the new year, in the following week.

The rebels now held no place of any importance, but were scattered about, chiefly on the borders of the jungle skirting Nepaul. After the defeat they retired about six miles, but their position was quite untenable, being hemmed in on all sides, the only outlet being into Nepaul. Our camp, which had been struck and packed in the morning, was sent for and arrived late that evening; much of the baggage, owing to the nature of the ground and the total absence of roads, not coming up until the middle of the night or next day. The troops soon retired to snatch some rest, and prepare for a renewal of the action the following day; but the excessive rains rendering the ground a swamp, caused the movement to be postponed one day more, which brought us to the 25th; and, in spite of it being Christmas-day, all prospects of peace and quietness were banished. After an early breakfast the troops "got under way." A guard was left in the camp, but before marching half- a-mile, intelligence arrived that the rebel force had broken up; their leaders going off in different directions. The troops then returned to camp to prepare the Christmas dinner.

The town of Toolseepore now presented a most desolate appearance; it was burnt the day of the action, and the walls of the houses alone were standing; its streets were rather more regular than usual in native towns, and built in a cruciform shape, one street running at right angles to the other. There were evident signs of the scourge of war in every direction; in one place the ghastly corpse, which lay unburied, and what was still stranger, which had escaped the jackal and the vulture; in another place a pool of water mingled with blood, giving evidence of the resting-place of the slain which had been removed. Here and there miserable-looking mortals might be seen among the ruins, some, perhaps, camp-followers, looking for loot or concealed treasure; others, perhaps, the former owners in disguise, seeking to recover the imperishable metal from the general wreck; and some were wretched, decrepit, attenuated mendicants, to whom the streets may have been a patrimony, but now being left friendless, and having nothing apparently to live for, looked as if it was a matter of perfect indifference how soon they were called upon to die.

Such are the sad results of war. Well may it be regarded the heaviest scourge that can befall a nation. It not only renders many a wife a widow, and many a family fatherless, and many a house sad, and many a heart sick; but an invading army carries desolation wherever it goes, marching, perhaps, through richly cultivated land, where the crops of standing corn, which have been cultivated with care, and toil, and expense, are trodden down and destroyed by horses, by elephants, by oxen, by artillery and men; and in addition to this, its tendency to deaden the principles of religion, by often being obliged, in self-defence, to meet the enemy on days held sacred among Christian nations, and by accustoming men to regard life as of little value, and hardening instead of awakening them to a sense that they are beings destined to live forever.

CHAPTER 13

Voyage Home

The troops had no sooner settled down in camp than Sir Hope Grant arrived, having ridden over in the morning from his own force, which was posted more to the southward; and after a conference held with Brigadier Rowcroft, farther intelligence having, in the meantime, arrived, that the rebels were making all speed to get to the eastward along the Tarai,[1] orders were issued that the force should immediately follow in pursuit. The great object was to prevent them from escaping in that direction, lest they should again inundate Goruckpore and perhaps Bengal. The Christmas dinner, already in process of preparation, was completely "knocked on the head." The tents were struck, the baggage was packed, and the force started off to the northward, inclining towards the east, to intercept them in their line of march.

H.M's 53rd Regiment was left to hold Toolseepore, and prevent any escape in that direction, while the force under Brigadier Rowcroft commenced the march about noon, passing over a country without roads, fording *nullahs*, and crossing dykes. The baggage-carts were unfortunate in getting into holes, and ruts, and heavy ground. Occasionally one would capsize, and another would stick in a ditch, three feet deep in mud, obstinately obstructing the progress of all the others that followed. The siege train, composed of heavy guns and mortars, drawn by elephants and bullocks, was sometimes in a "regular fix," being completely stuck in the mud; but by patience and perseverance, and no small share of exertion on the part of the seamen and marines, it arrived at the camping-ground in the evening, the last of them being parked about ten o'clock p.m.

A strong reconnoitring party, under Lieutenant-Colonel Cox, had

---

1. A belt of jungle between British India and Nepaul.

been sent out after the enemy early in the day, and came up with their rear-guard; but darkness setting in, it was impossible to pursue further, and he returned to the camp. Very little baggage made its appearance until the following morning, and some unlucky ones did not see their carts for three consecutive days. Fortunately the tents were pitched a little before dark, and those who had no *charpoy*, retired to rest on a bed of straw scantily supplied, on wet ground. There was not much in the proceedings of the Christmas-day to remind campaigners of the peace and quietness that prevail at this season of the year in favoured lands. There was no reunion of friends, but a hot pursuit of enemies; the bell of the village church was not heard to toll, but the shrill notes of the bugle were frequently sounding; in fact, there was nothing to remind of "home."

The men breakfasted early that morning, and being ordered to strike the camp before dinner was ready, in addition to a wearisome march, they were obliged to fast until late at night. It fared a little better with the officers. The *kansama*, or head native steward of our mess, no sooner arrived on the camping-ground, than he lit a fire, and then having speared a turkey, a brace of geese, and a brace of fowls on a long iron spit, put them to roast horizontally in front, while a ham and other dinner appurtenances were deposited in their respective pots on the top of it. Having then spread rugs on the ground before a blazing fire, many, after a fatiguing day, lay stretched, getting the benefit of the heat, which was as acceptable as on a cold Christmas night in England. It was a misty, dark, and damp night. But campaigners must rough it and make themselves as comfortable, in spite of appearances, as the circumstances will admit.

British officers lying before the fire on one side, and a dozen of *kitmutgars* on the other, sitting down on their hunkers, shrunken with the nipping cold, formed a picture sufficiently grotesque for *Punch*— the whites *vis à vis* with the blacks, and a blazing wood fire extending longitudinally between them, lighting up their faces and forming a group of whom one party strongly contrasted with the other. After exercising a fair share of patience, at the fashionable hour of half-past ten o'clock, dinner was served up, and in the course of an hour all had retired to snatch a few hours' rest.

Next morning was charming, and the Himalayas rose to view in all their grandeur. We were not further distant from the nearest spur in the Nepaul territory than fifteen or sixteen miles, and notwithstanding that the highest range was probably sixty or seventy miles distant,

121

their great height and the pure atmosphere caused them to appear comparatively close. But it was not a time to indulge in a reverie on scenery. The rebels were fast getting to the eastward of us, skirting the jungle, and consequently the force marched with as much speed as a country without roads would permit a force to travel, which was encumbered with *hackeries* for the carriage of baggage and a siege train besides.

By sunset we arrived at Pepyrea, and encamped on ground which was almost in every direction a swamp, in consequence of the recent rains. At this season it is more agreeable to march during the day than at three o'clock in the morning, which is usual in India. The cold at that hour is bitter, but during the day the climate is a delightful temperature. The transition from heat to cold in the course of twenty-four hours may be trying to some constitutions, but taking all things into consideration, during the cold season it is very enjoyable.

On the following morning we recrossed the Boora Raptee, marched to Intwa, and pitched the tents on the old camping- ground. Here we found Sir Hope Grant encamped with his flying column, consisting of Hodson's Horse (Punjabees), a troop of Royal Horse Artillery; also the 9th Lancers, who, notwithstanding the rough life, looked in as good condition as if they had just been reviewed in Hyde Park. There were no *hackeries* drawn by bullocks allowed to march with this column. All the baggage was carried either on ponies or camels, in order that, at any moment, they might be able to go a great distance without impediment or delay. The multitude of camels employed was very great, and the amazing distance these animals can travel with a heavy load, and without food or water, renders them of enormous value in carrying baggage, and constitutes a flying column of great efficiency, at any moment being ready to start off and intercept the enemy when they least expect any opposition. It was by this means Sir Hope Grant was so successful in coming up with the rebels so frequently, and denuding them of such a multitude of guns.

On the 28th there was a halt to refresh man and beast, the cattle not having had an opportunity of being regularly fed for three days; while Sir Hope Grant with his flying column started off towards the north to intercept the rebels in their flight to the eastward. Brigadier Rowcroft's force followed next day, and came up with Sir H. Grant's encampment at Dhokohuree. No other stronghold being in the possession of the rebels, the siege train was no longer required; it was therefore left behind, and the Naval Brigade were relieved of the labour it incurred in dragging it over such a roadless region.

The light field-guns and rockets were the only artillery that was now manned by the seamen; and they returned to the ranks again to do the duty of light infantry. The men of the Naval Brigade were always on excellent terms with their companions in arms: they seldom were long in camp with any corps without leaving them as friends. Sometimes when a swell trooper commenced poking fun at Jack, he was always ready with his answer, giving as good a piece of humour as he received. Occasionally a little badinage was interchanged about Jack's costume or seat on horseback, which may not have been quite military, not being bestocked to the throat, or so trimly buttoned up to the chin. They were told they might chaff, when they could fire a broadside, or furl a sail in a gale of wind, as well as Jack "handled his guns and galloped his horses on shore."

It is no difficult matter to find a Briton inspired by bravery and ready to mount a horse and join in a charge on the enemy's ranks; but it is not every day that men are found who can manage a ship in a tornado, can rig or unrig her if required, can furl her sails in a storm, and weather the most boisterous tempest; and stepping off the plank to *terra firma*, can harness their horses and mount them; can lay down the boarding-pike, and take up the rifle; can make a gun-carriage, a limber and harness, and then come off victorious in upwards of twenty engagements.

On the 29th the force marched to Puchpurwah while Sir H. Grant made a sweep with his cavalry and horse artillery to scour the skirt of the Tarai. He came up with the thieves as they were cooking their dinner, a time when they have a decided objection to be disturbed, and when their "prejudices" are grossly "violated." On the general's approach they bolted into the jungle, which was quite impenetrable to cavalry, and in the evening he arrived in camp. There was a halt at Puchpurwah for some days. We here spent the last day of the year 1858, and on the 1st day of the New Year orders were received from the governor-general that the Naval Brigade should forthwith proceed to Calcutta. The war was declared over. They were well pleased to see the last of it, and, as may easily be imagined, there was a general rejoicing at the prospect of returning home, after serving two campaigns in India.

The three 12-pounder howitzers, ammunition, stores, horses, and ponies were made over to the Royal Horse Artillery, and in the evening of the 2nd of January, Brigadier Rowcroft, C.B., requested permission to address the men before leaving. A parade was ordered for the purpose, and the Brigadier expressed his regret at the Naval Brigade leaving the force under his command; while he said:

The successes we have gained are mainly due to your courage and gallantry. I have also observed the excellent discipline and conduct of your brigade, which reflects great credit on Captain Sotheby and the officers, as well as on yourselves; I therefore regret to lose your services, but am glad that, upon your departure, you are homeward-bound, which you all so much desire.

Three hearty cheers for the brigadier rent the air, and they were wound up with one cheer more. Next morning, the Naval Brigade left Puchpurwah, many of the officers and men, as well as the band of H.M.'s 13th Light Infantry, accompanying them and playing suitable tunes. When they halted to return to the camp, they gave the brigade three cheers, which was heartily returned, not forgetting a cheer for Lieutenant-Colonel Cox, and one for Lord Mark Kerr, the colonel of the 13th. They then bade farewell to their companions in arms, with whom they had so often served side by side, and turned their face towards home.

On arriving at Dhokohuree, we found the 6th Madras Cavalry, and H.M.'s 73rd Regiment encamped there; and next day proceeded en route for Allahabad, which was reached, by knocking two marches into one every day, on the 15th of January, and the camp was pitched close to the fort. We marched from the north to the south of Oudh, passing through Fyzabad, Ajjuddia, and Sultanpore; places which will ever be famous in Indian history. A line of forts are constructing at intervals along that road, which may serve as places of refuge for Europeans in the event of another revolt. On the 17th the men embarked in the steamer *Benares*, and on the 2nd of February arrived at Calcutta.

The high estimation in which the governor-general held the *Pearl's* Naval Brigade, was not more distinctly evinced by his repeated refusal to grant permission to return to the ship, notwithstanding the urgent requests that were continually sent to him on the subject, than by a Gazette "extraordinary," which was published by His Excellency's orders, dated:

Allahabad, Monday, January 17, 1859,
Military Department.
No. 653 of 1859.— His Excellency the Viceroy and Governor-General cannot allow the officers and men forming the Naval

Brigade of Her Majesty's ship *Pearl* to pass through Allahabad, on their return to their ship, without expressing his acknowledgment of the excellent service which they have rendered to the State. Disembarked on the 12th of September, 1857, they have for fifteen months formed a main part of the small force to which the security of the wide district of Goruckpore, and of the country adjoining it, has been entrusted, and which has held during that time important advanced posts, exposed to constant attack from the strongholds of the rebels.

The duty has been arduous and harassing, but it has been cheerfully and thoroughly performed, and the discipline of the *Pearl's* Brigade has been admirable. The Gazettes of the 9th and 23rd March, 27th April, 11th May, 22nd June, 6th and 13th July, 13th August, 12th and 19th October, 23rd and 26th November, 1858, and 11th January, 1859, have shown that when the Goruckpore Field Force has been engaged, the brigade has signally distinguished itself.

The Governor-General cordially thanks Captain Sotheby, C.B., and his brave officers and men, for the valuable assistance which they have given to the army in Bengal, and he is glad to think that they do not quit the scene of their services without the satisfaction of seeing peace restored to the rich districts which they have protected.

K. J. H. Birch, Major-General,
Secretary to the Government of
India with the Governor-General.

From the very first His Excellency clearly perceived the value of experienced artillery, that arm of the service being proverbially of paramount importance in Indian warfare; and knowing what a great augmentation the brigades of the *Shannon* and *Pearl* would be to the military forces, gladly accepted their services as soon as volunteered, and refused permission to their leaving the country at a time when troops were imperatively demanded to maintain our very existence in India. And thus a practical example was given how the navy can be turned to the best account in a great emergency; that seamen, from their pliability of character and habitual obedience to command, can easily adapt themselves to any circumstances; and, instead of spending their time at cutlass-drill or shifting topsails in a peaceable port by way of exercise, are ready at any moment, when there is no enemy to meet

Bulrampour
Bahaderpour
Balpoora
Kydrabad
Ratulah
H
R
A
I
T
C
H
D
Mahudya
Moolypour
Wholagunge
Bustee
Tilkapour
OUDE
FYZABAD
Beklabad
Acbarpour
Shahjehanpour
Chowarah
Jafingpour
D
E
G
Moradgunge

Gunduck R.

Soopour

S

Neaolya

Bowet Gaut

Bassa
Domba

Musurpatty

Luckya Gdid
Dumgonty

Ramp...

Luckya

Bangrapatty

Genera

Buzzah

Masear

Suragpour Bansigaut

Purrownali

Samamah

Jugdsopour
Burrahgong

Usmunah

Donreeah
Bogah

Ramcowly Juckerah

Sanderpour

Makaragey

Tiparah

Marostnu

Parisatty

Nongong...

GOORACPOUR

A Well

Demary

Ralanpour

Potronpour

Rampour

Boggaur

Badgeraty

Rampour

Beetly

Onoule

Bundarry

Bemykee

Searjun

Chandahpour Marpour

Bamacerl

Kerra

Burrar...

Naptau

Masaree

Oudi

Parrah

Discentpour

Deragh

Damara

Meercha

Buckentpour
Balluah

Chamtah

Mobarickpout
Oudmaore

Simpla
Hawoly
Dobey

Posra

Sunkammupour

Golenar

Piparurah

Peace

Tarowa

Satrolya

Manjawly

Garratto

Chandsky
Soanpour

Kynutte

Sellempour

Bucha or Keetty Lake

chmers or Keetty R.

Nonsuny

Morratteah

Marwareak

er

apour

OORA

EPUR

B

UR

Fort

on their own element, to man a battery or take the field, with un-daunted bravery in active service, as artillery, five hundred miles from their ships, and thereby render incalculable service to the State.

On the return of the seamen and marines to Calcutta, they were entertained by the inhabitants at a public banquet in the town hall, as an expression of their sense of the services they had performed. Cal-cutta had never witnessed anything of the kind before except once, when the men of the *Shannon*, on their return from the North-West-ern Provinces, were greeted by a similar entertainment. The hall of the building was decorated in a very effective and tasteful manner; on every column were flags, and standards, and streamers, their bright colours mingling with the softer hues of the flowers and evergreens, which hung in graceful festoons. The walls were adorned with trans-parencies, stars of arms, and other devices. There was much ingenuity displayed to add brilliancy and gracefulness to the decorations; the tables extended the whole length of the hall, in parallel rows; and in the centre was a circular one, around which the petty officers and non-commissioned officers assembled. The governor-general's band, and also the band of the 99th, were in attendance, enlivening the en-tertainment by their performances.

About six o'clock the men landed from the ship (two hundred and five in number), and, preceded by the band of the 99th, marched to the Town Hall, where they were loudly cheered by the assembled inhabitants of Calcutta, while the band played *Rule Britannia*; a nu-merous assemblage of ladies and gentlemen, among whom were some of the highest officials, waiting to receive them; and nothing could exceed the warmth of their reception; and nothing could be more cordial or complimentary than the expressions of those who bid them welcome. Among those present and foremost at the hospitable board, were Sir J. Colville, General Sir James Outram, and Mr. Ritchie.

The usual toasts were proposed after dinner by the petty officers and non-commissioned officers of the Royal Marines, and received with almost deafening bursts of cheering. First the Queen; then the Prince Consort and the Royal Family; then his Excellency the Gov-ernor-General; and next came Sir James Outram and the army. The gallant general was lavish of his compliments; and in recounting the deeds that had been done by the Naval Brigade, produced them as a proof that "British seamen would never disappoint the expectations of the British people."

After the community of Calcutta and their hospitable entertainers were proposed, and the toast duly honoured, it was responded to by Sir J. Colville, who congratulated the men, after conquering in many arduous struggles, in bringing back their intrepid commander; and pointed out how much more fortunate the *Pearl's* brigade was in that respect than the brigade of the *Shannon*, to the memory of whose gallant captain a just tribute of respect and honour was paid. He concluded his speech by proposing the health of Captain Sotheby, which the men received with rapturous cheering.

The petty officers by this time began to gain confidence, and one after another rose up to propose several other toasts, not forgetting their old companions-in-arms up the country, the Bengal Yeomanry Cavalry, Lord Mark Kerr, and Lieutenant-Colonel Cox, and H.M's 13th Light Infantry; also Brigadier Rowcroft, who led them on to victory in many an action. And about half-past nine o'clock the dinner party was broken up, and the men separated in an orderly manner, some returning on board the ship, and some preferring to remain on shore for the night.

But, among the many speeches that were made, perhaps a higher compliment was not paid by any than that by Mr. Ritchie, the advocate-general, who at a public meeting in Calcutta, assembled for the purpose of interesting the inhabitants to support a chaplain for the merchant-seamen, contrasted the general demeanour of the Naval Brigades composed of the seamen of the Royal and Indian navies, with those composed of merchant- seamen, who had not been brought under the restraints or moral training of religion. Speaking of the crews of the *Shannon* and *Pearl*, "names that will never be forgotten in Calcutta," he said:

It was not their prowess in the field to which I allude, though this has never been surpassed even by British sailors; but their admirable steadiness, good conduct, and humanity, throughout a most trying campaign, and under circumstances of great temptation.

And having given the merchant-seamen full credit for their bravery in the field during the mutinies, contrasted at the same time, the good conduct and discipline of the others, with the demeanour of those against whom charges for several offences had been brought officially before his notice.

On the 13th of February, 1859, the *Pearl* left Calcutta, and called in at Madras, where the officers were as hospitably entertained by the members of the Madras Club, as the men were at Calcutta. The banquet was nobly served, and the rooms were thronged with members who came, at an unavoidably short notice, to receive their guests. This *"feast of reason, and genuine flow of soul,"* went off as such a banquet should go off, indicative of goodwill and kindly feelings on the part of the entertainers and entertained; having met together as strangers, and having parted as friends. The *Pearl* was to sail on the 25th; but the hearty invitation from the members of the club was not to be put off, and consequently there was a delay until the following morning. The services that had been rendered by the Naval Brigades were not unknown at Madras. Their actions were often recounted, and "Peel and Sotheby" were chronicled in the leading journal "as household names."

In thus recording the actions of the past, and giving honour to whom honour is due, it would be unbecoming to pass over in silence the courtesy and consideration shown by the other services, from His Excellency the Governor-General, downwards. That great statesman, with a coolness undaunted by dangers, and with a firmness unshaken by alarms, steered a mighty empire through troubled waters, and brought her to an anchor in peace. And when so-called errors of judgment are hid under the shadow of an increased reputation, history will closely associate his name with some of the grandest achievements in the East.

Although our loss in action was trifling, yet the sum of those who were wounded, who died, or were killed in action, and were invalided in consequence of the effects of exposure or climate, amounted to about one- fourth of the number of men who formed the original force. Most of those who were invalided recovered, as well as the wounded, who were skilfully treated by Mr. J. W. Shone, the surgeon in charge, and whose attention to the sick was at all times unremitting.

It would be difficult to account for the small loss sustained in action, except it happened that the *sepoys*, like the Gurkhas, (and I have heard the same remark made of other Easterns, with what truth the reader may judge from the results), paid more attention to the distance the balls carried than to the taking of an accurate aim at the object. This may arise from the use of arms that do not kill point-blank at a greater distance than a hundred yards. The Gurkhas serving with the brigade have often been observed to point their muskets in the air and fire away. If the *sepoys* adopted the same plan, the difficulty would be accounted for. And again, when the rebels took up a position, it was their custom to wait to be attacked. When the attacking force arrived at a spot for which they had their guns laid (the range being known), they discharged a few rounds.

Sometimes their fire takes effect; but when the line pushes on, they lose their range, which, from their excitement, they seem never to regain; or, shall we not be willing to acknowledge the providence and protection of a higher power, who showed a favour unto us by crowning our arms with victory, by shielding our troops from harm, and reserving the great and rich empire of India to the sway of Britain for higher and nobler ends, calling upon us to do something more for that people than has ever yet been done, to give light among the benighted, and diffuse the knowledge of Christianity among nations and tribes who wander in darkness and in the land of the shadow of death?

The *Pearl* on her voyage home remained for several days at Trincomalee, and at the Cape of Good Hope, and touching for one day at St. Helena, on the 6th of June, after an absence of three years and one week, the circuit of the world being completed, the anchor was cast at Spithead. The following day she was ordered into Portsmouth harbour, and on the 16th of June was paid off. The conduct of the men in general was excellent, and punishments were few. The same discipline that prevailed throughout the commission prevailed to the end, and their demeanour during the time of being paid off reflected upon them much credit. The custom of paying-off dinners, which is nearly extinct, was brought to life, and the officers met together in the evening for the last time.

The names of the officers who formed the Naval Brigade were—

Captain Sotheby, who received the order of C.B., and was appointed extra *aide-de-camp* to the queen.

Lieutenant Pym, Royal Marine Light Infantry.

Lieutenant Turnour, R.N., Lieutenant Radcliffe, R.N., and Lieutenant Grant, R.N., who were promoted to the rank of commanders for service in the field.

Mr. Ingles, mate, and Mr. Maquay, mate, who were promoted to the rank of lieutenants, for service in the field.

Lord Charles Scott, who had been invalided in consequence of disease engendered by the climate, during the arduous service of the first campaign.

The Honourable Victor Montagu, midshipman, acting *aide-de-camp* to Brigadier Rowcroft.

Mr. Stephenson, midshipman, acting *aide-de-camp* to Captain Sotheby, C.B.

Mr. Foot, midshipman, who was attached to the light field-battery under the command of Commander Tumour.

Lieutenant Fawkes, R.N.

Mr. Edwards, midshipman.

Mr. Merewether, master's-assistant.

Mr. J. Fowler, who was killed in action on the 5th of March, 1858.

Mr. J. W. Shone, assistant-surgeon, who was promoted to the rank of surgeon.

Mr. Parkin, gunner.

Mr. Cooley, boatswain.

Mr. Burton, carpenter.

Mr. Shearman, assistant-engineer.

Mr. Bowling, clerk.

Rev. Edward A. Williams, M.A., chaplain, R.N.

And thus the services of the brigade were acknowledged by the Lords of the Admiralty, in the promotion of those officers who were eligible for promotion by means of length of service, the lieutenants being made commanders, and the mates lieutenants. The warrant-officers and assistant-engineer were each raised one step in rank; while the petty officers received warrants; and no doubt the midshipmen will be rewarded in due time.

The Shannon's Brigade in India

W. Peel

Contents

To the memory of
Sir William Peel
And to the
Officers and Blue Jackets of his Naval Brigade
Are dedicated
These recollections of our Indian Campaign

H.M.S. SHANNON AT CALCUTTA

Preface

In offering this book to the public, I do not profess to give a history of the Indian Mutiny, or even of a small portion of it. I can only write a description of the scenes witnessed by one individual of a large army, and give the reports of operations which he did *not* witness as they often reached him, some incorrectly, others perhaps utterly without foundation.

I cannot but feel that no small responsibility attaches to one who attempts to print an account, however crude, of the deeds of such a man as Sir William Peel, or of his blue jackets; but as, after a lapse of three years, none has yet appeared, I trust that my simple narrative may not be considered inappropriate as a slight memento of a portion of the last services of our lamented commander.

In preparing these pages for publication, I have adhered to the form of a journal, although, not considered the most readable style for a book, because they are compiled from letters and journals written at the time.

During our year's campaign in India, one feeling pervaded the minds of the officers of the Naval Brigade, which only strengthened as time went on, and an expression of which cannot possibly be omitted here. This was the obligation we all felt we were under to the whole army, from the commander-in-chief down to the naughty drummer-boy who (afraid of getting licked by his comrades) sounded the "advance" at Kallee-Nuddee without orders, for their unremitting consideration and civility to every officer or blue jacket of ours. Had a sentry orders only to admit a favoured few to the roof of the Dilkushah, he would stretch a point in favour of the crown and anchor button; were baggage-camels to be issued, the Naval Brigade were first served; did we want medical assistance, a surgeon from the staff was sent to us; we had only to ask for a thing to get it; and was one of our men a little "disguised" and in trouble—as even sailors will be sometimes—he was quietly handed over to his own officers to be settled with; and although thus openly favoured, in no instance did any feeling of jealously appear, but all seemed animated with a desire to show to blue jackets on land the civility and hospitality which I trust we always endeavour to show to red coats afloat.

I must not neglect this opportunity of tendering my sincere thanks to the *Shannon's* late chaplain, for his kindness in allowing me the use of his journal, and to Mrs. Verschoyle, the lady to whose kindness and skill I am indebted for the photograph of Sir William Peel, which does duty as frontispiece.

In sending these pages to the press, I cannot foresee whether they will be cast upon the already swollen heap of unread books, or be deemed worthy of a happier fate; but once launched into print, copies *may* be stranded on the shores where the scenes are laid, and I hope these lines may meet the eyes of those whose cordial hospitality and good-fellowship, to my brother officers and myself, have left recollections which I assure them will not easily be effaced. But deeper still, in my own mind, lies the remembrance of the affectionate kindness of those ultimate friends, in whose superior and elevating society were spent many successive Sundays or Friday evenings, and unmindful of whom I can never, in word or thought, refer to my year in India.

Claydon House:
Nov. 16, 1861.

CHAPTER 1

A Short Sketch of the Proceedings of H.M.S. Shannon

Her Majesty's screw steam frigate *Shannon*, of 51 guns, 600 horse-power, and 2667 tons, was commissioned by Captain William Peel at Portsmouth on the 13th of September, 1856. At this time she was the finest frigate afloat, being the first of a new and very powerful class, calculated to obtain great speed under sail or steam, and to carry very heavy metal. Her armament consisted of twenty 56 cwt. 32-prs. on the upper deck, one 95 cwt. 68-pr. on the forecastle, and thirty 65 cwt. 8-in. guns on the main deck, and she could steam twelve knots.

After she was fitted out she went round to Plymouth Sound, and, as if destined for adventure from the very commencement of her career, was nearly lost thereon the 3rd of January of the ensuing year. At about 6 a.m. a strong westerly gale sprung up, and it became necessary to veer cable, as the ship was lying at single anchor. In doing this the cable parted, and the other anchor was at once let go quickly, how-ever, though this was done, from the great force of the wind the ship had already gathered sternway, and, to everybody's consternation, the second cable also snapped.

There was but one other cable bent, the starboard sheet, and that anchor could not be let go at once. All hands were turned up to clear it away, and Captain Peel rushed on deck in his shirt and trowsers. In the meantime the ship was drifting rapidly to the eastward, with her broadside to the wind. Owing to the great personal exertions of the first lieutenant, Mr. Vaughan, the sheet anchor was presently cleared away and let go, and providentially it brought the ship up, or she must have left her bones on the rocks below Bovisand.

The *Shannon* was ordered to Lisbon; but on the 10th of January, off Ushant, in a strong westerly breeze, the step of the mainmast was discovered to be sprung, and the ship returned to Plymouth, where she remained for a long time in dock. When again ready for sea, she went for a cruise off Cape Clear, and returned to Spithead. She was now ordered to prepare for service in China, and left England on the 17th of March, 1857.

The *Shannon's* outward voyage was attended by no remarkable incident. Three times between England and the Cape a man fell overboard, and on each occasion her boats, fitted with Clifford's lowering apparatus, were manned and lowered with great celerity, and on two occasions the men were saved. The third case was that of Mr. J. Coaker, master's assistant, a most promising young Greenwich scholar, who fell off the fore-yard, but his head striking the fore-chains, he was killed before reaching the water. His body was picked up and brought on board, and in the evening was committed to the deep, sewn up in a hammock, with two 32-pr. shot at his feet, and covered by the Union Jack; the body was brought up on a grating with his cap and dirk placed over the breast. All the officers attended, the ship's company on the gangway, the marines on the quarter-deck, and the band playing the "*Dead March in Saul.*" The Rev. E. L. Bowman read the funeral service; and at the words "we therefore commit his body to the deep," the remains of poor young Coaker glanced over the side and plunged into the sea.

The *Shannon* anchored in Simon's Bay on the 7th of May, and sailed again on the 11th. About the 20th of the month, in a strong north-westerly gale, the speed of the ship under canvas was very remarkable; under double-reefed topsails, courses, and reefed fore-topmast studding-sail, the ship sometimes averaged fourteen and fifteen knots an hour; and, during one squall, when the log was hove by the officer of the watch, she was going 15.8.

On the 11th of June, the *Shannon* anchored off Singapore. On her arrival here the first intimation was received of the outbreak in India; and the *simoom*, arriving with troops for China, was ordered to return with them to Calcutta; so she steamed out, the military band on board playing "*You may go to Hong Kong for me.*" On the 23rd Lord Elgin embarked with his suite, and the *Shannon* sailed for Hong Kong, where she arrived on the 2nd of July.

On the 16th, hearing that affairs in India were assuming a very troublous aspect, the Earl of Elgin and suite re-embarked; and, taking on board a detachment of Royal Marines, and of the 90th Regiment, sailed for Calcutta, touching at Singapore *en route.*

On the 6th of August the *Shannon* arrived off the mouths of the Ganges. The water here is very shallow, and the low mud shore cannot be perceived from any distance, so the most careful navigation is requisite. Soundings were obtained, the ship put under easy sail, a gun fired, and a jack hoisted for a pilot. The Calcutta pilot service is a distinct service in itself, under martial law like the Royal Navy, and turns out many a good seaman and steady officer, and the pilots receive half-pay and retiring pensions after a certain term of service. At length a smart little brig came under the *Shannon's* stern, lowered a boat, and sent a pilot on board: and the frigate, furling sails, steamed through the dull and muddy waters to the mouth of the Hooghly.

The scenery of that part of the Delta formed by the mouths of the Ganges called the Sunderbunds, is anything but inviting: from the mast-head of a large ship, as far as the eye can reach, no rise of land is visible in any direction; at high water the sea is almost on a level with the tops of the innumerable mud islands, and which are uninhabited save by crocodiles and a few wild beasts; they are covered with a thick and almost impenetrable jungle, and there are seen the gigantic leaves and luxuriant vegetation of a tropical climate. This description of scenery continues to within a few miles of Calcutta itself, varied only by occasional mud flats, from which arise pestilential odours in the hot season.

On nearing Calcutta, the east bank of the river, called Garden Reach, is covered with villas and pleasure-grounds; here are the headquarters of the Peninsular and Oriental Company, while nearly opposite are the grey buildings of Bishop's College; on passing these, and the frowning batteries and green slopes of Port William, the *Shannon* was repeatedly cheered,— for at this time every English arm was cordially welcomed; and the opportune arrival of two men-of-war, the *Shannon* and *Pearl*, whose heavy guns could sweep the Maidan, gave confidence to the anxious hearts of India's rulers, and seemed to take a load off every European mind; and at 5 p. m., as the frigate's anchor dropped from her bows, and the governor-general's salute of nineteen guns thundered through the sultry air, echoing and re-echoing on the walls of Government House, it may have suggested a hint of England's might to the despot of Oude, now a captive in Fort William.

At Calcutta, Lord Elgin disembarked; he afterwards chartered the steamer *Ava*, and returned in her to China. In the meantime, Captain Peel offered to the governor-general the services of the blue jackets of the *Shannon*, with their ships' guns, to form a Naval Brigade, which were accepted, and preparations for service on shore immediately begun; the dress of the men was in no respect altered, but their straw hats were covered with white cotton, and provided with curtains to protect the back of the neck.

On the 12th of August, Dr. Wilson, Lord Bishop of Calcutta, visited the ship; after going all over her, the ship's company assembled on the quarter-deck, and he addressed them energetically, saying, that if he were not eighty-four years of age, he would go up to fight the *sepoys* himself. On the 13th, a large flat came alongside the *Shannon*, and was laden with ten 8-inch guns and two brass field-pieces, with a proportion of ammunition, and a supply of clothing and medical comforts for the men. The great rivers of India are its main arteries of commerce, which is carried on by means of steamers, or flats towed by them; these flats have great beam, but do not draw more than two foot, or two foot six; they are thatched over to keep out the burning sun, and are available for the navigation of the rivers at all seasons of the year.

On the 14th, the river-steamer *Chunar* came alongside the frigate, and Captain Peel embarked, with the following officers: Lieuts. Young, Wilson, Hay, and Salmon; Captain Gray and Lieut. Stirling, R.M.; Lieut. Lind, of Hageby, of the Swedish Navy; the Rev. E. L. Bowman; Dr. Flanagan; Mr. Comerford, assistant-paymaster; Messrs. M. Daniel, Garvey, E. Daniel, Lord Walter Kerr, Lord Arthur Clinton, and Mr. Church, midshipmen; Messrs. Brown, Bone, and Henri, engineers; Mr. Thompson, gunner; Mr. Bryce, carpenter; Mr. Stanton, assistant-clerk; and Messrs. Watson and Lascelles, naval cadets. Four hundred and fifty men, with their arms and ammunition, embarked in the flat, which was taken in tow by the *Chunar*. Captain Peel also took up a launch and cutter belonging to the *Shannon*. The ship was left under the command of Mr. Vaughan, the first lieutenant; and as the *Chunar* steamed away, three hearty cheers were exchanged.

From this time the officers left on board the *Shannon* were daily employed volunteering men from English merchant ships in the river; and in this manner one hundred men were raised, and immediately put through a course of drill.

On the 12th of September, Captain Sotheby, R.K, started for the interior, with one hundred and fifty-five of the ship's company of H.M.S. *Pearl*,—an account of whose proceedings has been published by her chaplain, the Rev. E. A. Williams, (published by Leonaur with this book).

On the morning of the 18th, the river steamer *Benares*, with a flat in tow, came alongside the *Shannon*, and Lieut. Vaughan embarked on board of her, with the following officers: Lieut. Wratislaw; Mr. Verney, mate; Mr. Way, midshipman; and Mr. Richards, naval cadet; one hundred and twenty men embarked in the flat, with their rifles and ammunition. As this reinforcement steamed away up the Hooghly, they gave the old ship three cheers, which were stoutly returned by the little party left on board. The frigate was left under the command of Mr. Waters, master, with about one hundred and forty men, moored close to the shore, and a brass gun was mounted in the main-top to sweep the Maiden in case of any disturbance in Calcutta.

The further proceedings of this detachment, afterwards called the first company, and a general sketch of the movements of the *Shannon's* Naval Brigade, are detailed in the pages of the following journal.

CHAPTER 2

Journey to Allahabad in the River Steamer Benares

September 18th.—This morning the steamer *Benares* with a flat in tow came alongside the *Shannon*, and receiving on board the second detachment of Naval Brigade proceeded up the Hooghly with her jolly-boat in tow.

September 21st.—Cutwa. This is the first station we have stopped at for coal: the town is situated at the point where the two rivers Bargarutti and Hadjee run into the Hooghly, the former of which we ascend tomorrow; we have come a hundred and twenty miles, and already find the weather cooler. Several passengers are going with us to Allahabad, amongst others the Rev. T. Moore, appointed chaplain of Cawnpore, Colonel Longden of H. M. 10th Regiment, and Captain Maxwell of the Bengal Artillery.

September 25th.—We are now above Berhampore where the steamer *River Bird* is on shore; we tried to tug her off, but in vain, so they will have to wait for the dry season, and then make a regular dock for her, as she is only about fifteen feet from the channel.
Captain Peel only went as far as Berhampore in the *Chunar*, here her engines proved so defective that he applied for another steamer, and the *River Bird* was sent to him: she went up as far as Dinapore, when it was found that she drew too much water to proceed any further: Captain Peel then went on in the steamer *Mirzapore*, which finally brought the flat up to Allahabad. The *River Bird* got on shore on her way down to Calcutta.

September 26th.—Above Berhampore. The day before yesterday, we saw a faint blue line rising above the horizon, and since then the Rajmahal range of hills has gradually risen to view: it is quite a novelty to be in a country so flat that one can uninterruptedly mark the approach to hills from a great distance: some of the green jungle scenery on the banks of the river is pretty: the current here is very strong, and we have been struggling with it all day.

September 27th.—We hear that the steamer *Chunar*, with Captain Sotheby of the *Pearl* on board, has stuck in the mud, and is now about twenty miles ahead of us; however, we hope that our good boat, the *Benares*, will take us all the way up to Allahabad without accident, as she draws less water.

September 29th.—We have been steaming along all day, as usual, and are now close to the Rajmahal hills, which are very pretty after the flat country through which we have been passing for so long: they are partly covered with woods, of which the trees are much less tall than those on the plains; the Ganges here attains its greatest size and strength, and the current is very powerful: there does not appear to be much cultivation, at any rate near the banks of the river; a few huts are to be seen, the natives being chiefly engaged in pastoral occupations. There is a remarkable race of Highlanders called the "Sonthals," who live amongst the wilds of the Rajmahal hills; they are very fierce, powerful, and athletic, they have never been subdued, and sometimes make incursions from their mountain fastnesses upon the helpless Hindoos. We just touched on a mud-bank this morning, but on the whole are making a good passage, wonderfully free from accidents, if not very rapid. In the forenoon we assisted an E. I. C. gun-boat which we found with both her anchors stuck fast in the mud.

September 30th.—We are now a little way below three rocks in the middle of the Ganges, called the Colgong rocks; they rise to the height of fifty or sixty feet from the water, and are much rent and torn, and in their ragged clefts grow most picturesque trees and shrubs; it is not very easy to pass these rocks as the current is so strong. We pass our days very pleasantly: in the morning at daylight we heave the anchor up, and as soon as we are fairly under weigh, all hands fall in for an hour's drill: then follows breakfast, and at about nine parade, with perhaps a quarter of an hour's drill: by this time it is too hot to do much, so the day is spent in reading and writing, listening to the sonorous but rather wearisome chant of the native leadsman, "*tien barni lâni,*" and shooting at birds and alligators until 5 p.m., when we have

147

another parade and about half an hour's drill; at six we dine, at sunset we anchor, and the evening is passed under the awning in reading, singing, and other amusements.

October 3rd.—Jehangeerah. Yesterday morning we landed all our men at Bhagulpore for drill. The river here is seven miles broad, and we are now steaming along with flat country on the starboard and hilly country on the port side.

JEHANGEERAH

October 4th.—Above Monghir. This morning we arrived at Monghir, and left again in the afternoon: it is a very pretty town surrounded by a semi-ruinous wall built by the Hindoos about a hundred years ago, when this place marked the British frontier: it is protected by a fort of great antiquity, built on a picturesque site on a rock jutting out into the river. The town wall is of very great extent, and encloses a space said to be larger than Fort William at Calcutta. This place is remarkable for the number of wooden folding-chairs made in it; also for its hammers with iron handles, which unscrew and disclose a knife, fork, and corkscrew, ingeniously but roughly made; also for small mats and hand-*punkahs* made of a particular sort of grass.

Here also are manufactured guns and rifles, bearing the names of celebrated English gunsmiths, and so skilfully imitated that one would not at first sight detect the deception; those, however, who are allured by their cheapness into buying them, generally find that bullets fired from them possess very erratic propensities, and they frequently burst after a few discharges. The country to the south of the Ganges still maintains its hilly character, while that to the north is flat and muddy. Today has been set apart by the governor-general, as a day of humili-

148

ation and prayer, and a fund is to be raised for the benefit of the wives and families of those who may fall in quelling the mutiny.

October 6th.—This morning, just before noon, our steamer grounded; it was the first time since leaving Calcutta, so that, on the whole, we may consider ourselves rather fortunate: it was 9 p.m. before we get her off, though our men worked hard all day, assisting the steamer's crew.

October 7th.—Twelve days hence we hope to reach Allahabad; the weather is already much cooler.

October 10th.—Yesterday afternoon we left the large military station of Dinapore, taking with us two small field-pieces for Captain Sotheby at Buxar. Dinapore seems to be the most civilised place that we have touched at on our journey from Calcutta: we heard there that Delhi was taken, its king captured, and his two sons shot; we heard also of the relief of Lucknow and death of General Neil; and that Captain Peel has arrived safely at Allahabad with all his men and guns. The hills that we used to see to the southward and eastward have disappeared; the country is flat on both sides, and the water very muddy, but the river not so broad. We pass many dead bodies, in various stages of decomposition, floating down the river; they are generally the bodies of natives which have been partly burnt on the banks of the sacred Ganges, and are sometimes brought from a considerable distance for this purpose, by their affectionate relatives: when the families are too poor to afford a funeral pyre, the body is simply cast into the water, food for the crows and vultures.

Every day we have several hours hard drill; we landed all hands twice at Dinapore, and we find that our men do very well at the manual and platoon exercises, at which they are of course well drilled on board, but they make occasional mistakes in marching and wheeling, for which there is not space on the deck of the flat. Perhaps the most difficult thing for sailors to learn is to keep such a distance when marching in file that they will fall into their right places in fronting. We never insist much on their keeping step; this will come in time.

When I was writing yesterday evening, an enormous locust with large wings, swooped down upon my desk, the wings then suddenly disappeared, and the creature began hopping about the table on its spider-like legs in a most grotesque manner. I threw my handkerchief over him and popped him into a bottle of gin; I examined him when he was dead, and found him to be of about the size of a small bat, but having the power of shutting up his large transparent wings into a kind of tape, and then rolling them up into a ball on the hinder part of his back; hence their sudden disappearance. I caught another shortly afterwards, and now they are both in a pickle bottle full of gin, ready to send down to the *Shannon* by the first opportunity.

October 11th.—Above Dinapore. The evenings now begin to get very cool, and last night so cold that I was glad of a blanket; but the days are still warm, the sun hot and the winds cool. We are beginning to make better progress; the current is not so strong above Dinapore, as there are fewer tributaries; we hope to reach Allahabad in about ten days, and very glad shall we be to rejoin our old shipmates.

October 12th.—Yesterday evening we arrived at Buxar, where we saw Captain Sotheby and his party; it is an old mud fort, built by the Hindoos; its chief strength consists in a very deep ditch by which it is surrounded, crossed in one place by a narrow drawbridge. There are at present only five or six small brass guns, but if there were a dozen larger ones it would be rather a strong place, and resist a considerable body of *sepoys*. The men and officers of the *Pearl* are all letting their beards and moustaches grow, but Captain Peel has given an order that his Naval Brigade are to continue to shave; however, we are not very particular about the beards.

October 13th.—Ten miles below Ghazeepore. A bar of sand here crosses the river, which is actually fordable; over this bar we are forcing our way, although there is only about four foot of water, and we draw four foot six. It is a most unusual occurrence for the river to be so broad and so shallow; in a short time it will have formed for itself a channel; just at present it spreads over a breadth of perhaps two miles; but the rains are now over, and the waters have fallen.

October 14th.—This Ganges is a wonderful river, its gigantic tributary streams, together with its own vast length through lands so fertile, and by cities so populous, ought to make India one of the first countries in the world. With reference to some remarks made in the House of Commons, suggesting that gun-boats should be sent out here for the protection of towns situated on the rivers, I believe that they would be invaluable; the gun-boats which were used in the last war mostly drew six or seven feet water; now I learn from Captain Elder who commands this steamer, a most intelligent and superior man, that for a gun-boat to be serviceable on the Ganges between Calcutta and

Allahabad, in the dry season, she must not draw more water than two foot six; and for a gun-boat to be serviceable between Calcutta and Dinapore only, she must not draw more than four foot six.

In the rainy season, a vessel drawing ten foot of water might go up as high as Allahabad, but in the dry season, a vessel drawing only two foot six when loaded with provisions, guns, coal, &c., would find some difficulty in getting up, although by heaving her over the mud, it might be done at all times of the year. Though the Ganges is so very shallow, there is generally plenty of breadth, so that gun-boats might be constructed of great beam, thirty feet at least, to enable them to draw so little water. There are many depots of coal along the river, so that a gun-boat would not require to have great stowage of fuel. The East India Company has a sort of gun-raft consisting of two boats decked over with a large paddle-wheel between them; this raft draws three foot water, and carries four 12-pr. brass howitzers; surely this might be improved upon.

It would not be a very great objection to gun-boats for the Ganges to have the engines above water-line; even if they *were* damaged in action, they might be rowed or even punted with poles in shallow water, where the current does not run too strong; in smooth water like the Ganges, an engagement would be quite a different thing to one on the open sea, where damage to the engines might be attended by the total loss of the boat. Last night we reached Ghazeepore, where we found H.M.'s 37th Regiment; it seems to be a large, straggling station with plenty of trees and open ground, and is notoriously healthy. We saw some Hindoos burning a body as we passed today, the odour from which was very sickening.

The river here is much narrower, but the country does not appear as if it was much flooded during the heavy rains; no hills are to be seen in any direction. The natives are very much surprised at the continuous flood of soldiers that are arriving, and want to know where they all come from; it is to be hoped it will produce a good moral effect on them. Tomorrow forenoon we hope to arrive at *Benares*. One man, who is now recovering from cholera, is the only serious case of illness that we have had since we left Calcutta, although many men are on the sick list with boils and sores from inflamed mosquito bites.

October 16th.—Last night we arrived at *Benares*, the Oxford of India and headquarters of Sanscrit scholarship: it is a very large Hindoo city of great antiquity, on the north bank of the Ganges, with many curious old specimens of architecture: the view from the water is one of the finest of its kind in India, as the river bends first towards and then from it; the water side is lined with magnificent nights of broad stone steps called *ghauts*, which are the daily lounge of the native population; here they undergo the process of washing in the sacred river, which is fortunately a religious ceremony, and then sit on the steps, smoking, or dozing, or besmearing themselves with the marks of their *caste* in yellow paint or sacred Ganges mud.

The houses of the native town are small, but there are numerous mosques, the peculiarly oriental gracefulness of whose swelling domes and tapering minarets attract and charm the eye, although in size they cannot compete with those of the headquarters of Islamism: here, as at Stamboul, the town does not improve on acquaintance; one finds on landing only steep, narrow, and ill-paved streets which will afford passage to no wheeled vehicle. Tomorrow we hope to arrive at Mirzapore.

October 17th.—Today we passed Chunar, one of the most picturesque fortresses in India, situated on a high sandstone rock on the south bank of the river, and completely commanding it: it is deservedly held in great estimation by the Hindoos, who have a tradition that it is under the direct protection of the Almighty, and cannot be captured: English troops, took it by assault some years ago, but that has not shaken their faith in the least.

October 18th.—Yesterday at about 1.30 p.m. we arrived at Mirzapore, which we left early this morning: it is the last station before we reach Allahabad, and a principal commercial city. We have today met with such a strong current that we have been obliged to anchor, and tomorrow it will be as much as we shall be able to do to stem it. I brought a letter of introduction to Mr. Venables, a merchant here, who distinguished himself very much in the mutiny, and he was so good as to invite me to dine with him in the evening at his bungalow about a mile from the *ghaut*.

Now a "*ghaut*" is a term applied equally to a mountain pass, or a landing-place; I believe that it means literally "a passage;" a "bungalow" is, properly speaking, "a summer country house;" most people in Bengal have offices and "go-downs" (storehouses) in town, and a bungalow in a "compound" a little way out of town. A "compound" is the enclosure in which a house is situated, and this one word includes what in England would-be called a yard, a park, a shrubbery, or grounds. Mirzapore is a large town, situated on the frontiers of the rebellious country; it is now garrisoned by a few Madras troops only, who openly say in the native bazaars that if the *sepoys* come, they will join them: "for" say they, "what could we do? We are not strong enough to overcome them, and we should only be cut to pieces by our own countrymen if we resisted:" so the Europeans living there go to bed every night with the happy consciousness that they may all find their throats cut in the morning.

From what I hear I believe that the natives of India do not, for the most part, side against us, except in Oude, where they bitterly hate us: there they are a very different race from the enervated Hindoo; they are bred to carry arms from their youth, and every one is a soldier from his childhood, both in feeling and carriage. We hear that the *sepoys* have assembled near Lucknow, that there is a good deal of fighting going on, and that our troops find it as much as they can do to repel the attacks: but reinforcements are daily pouring in, and I believe that the Naval Brigade is likely to be sent on immediately.

October 19th.—This evening we have anchored where we are not more than ten miles from Allahabad in a direct line, but very much farther by the river, We hope to arrive there tomorrow about mid-day,

October 20th.—This morning we landed, about half a mile from the Fort of Allahabad; the first detachment come down to meet us, and we all marched up to barracks together with the band playing.

CHAPTER 3

Relief of Lucknow and Engagements at Cawnpore

October 21st.—Today we have been busily employed bringing the tents and baggage up from the steamer *Benares*.

October 22nd.—Tomorrow the advanced guard and siege-train, in charge of Lieut. Vaughan, with one hundred men and four officers, start for the front. The officers are, Lieut. Salmon, Mr. M. Daniel, Lords W. Kerr and A. Clinton, midshipmen: Mr. E. Daniel, who received the Victoria Cross when serving under Captain Peel in the Crimea, has already been sent on to Cawnpore, as an artillery officer was telegraphed for. We have got very good quarters here, and have turned regular soldiers; officers patrol all night and mount guard', and our men drill far better than we could have expected. We have five parades and two drills daily; at the morning parade it is quite a sight to see our men fall in under the colonnades of the barracks: each one puts on a clean suit of clothes from head to foot daily, there being a proportion of "*dobies*" (washermen) to each company; every man wears shoes, which are well blacked and polished; and the mountings of the Minié or Enfield rifles glisten in the sun: the officers fall in, and such drill as can be performed in the shade is gone through.

October 24th.—Yesterday morning Lieut. Vaughan left with his detachment. Another party is now ordered to be ready to start, consisting of Lieuts. Young and Hay, Mr. Garvey, mate, and Mr. Church, midshipman. From what one hears of campaigning in India in time of peace, it seems to be generally little more than a picnic; tents are provided for the officers, lined with a sort of coarse, coloured chintz, carpeted, with blinds for the doors to keep the sun out. In peacetime, the march of a body of men averages twelve miles a day; and when they arrive at the end of their march, they find that the servants have pitched the tents, prepared a meal, and put out a change of linen; the *"bheestie"* is ready with a skin of water for a bath, and the *dobie* is waiting to wash the clothes they take off.

October 28th.—6 a.m. Exercised at light infantry and company drill. 10 a.m. Mustered by companies. Cleared lower barracks of slops, stores, &c, and placed them in an upper room. At 1.30 p.m. the second company of the Naval Brigade, under the command of Lieut. Hay, marched out with Captain Peel: the officers accompanying them are, Mr, Bowman, chaplain; Mr. Garvey, mate; Mr. Church, midshipman; and Messrs. Watson and Lascelles, *aides-de-camp* to the captain; besides these, he takes up two engineers, with the carpenter and artificers. There remain now to garrison this large fort about a hundred and fifty men of the Naval Brigade, including sick, band, and officers.

The officers remaining behind are, Lieut. Wilson, in command; Lieut. Wratislaw, commanding the first company, whose subalterns are Mr. Way, midshipman, and myself; Mr. Lind, of Hageby, a lieutenant in the Swedish navy, doing duty as a mate in our service, commanding the third company, whose subaltern is Mr. Richards, naval cadet; Mr. Thompson, gunner; Mr. Comerford, assistant-paymaster; and Mr. Staunton, assistant-clerk. We expect to follow the others very shortly. Yesterday I was doing duty as subaltern of the main guard, and this morning I turned out the guard to salute Captain Peel and his party as they passed out.

October 29th,—Sent ten men to hospital; total number of men sick, sixty-four. A fatigue-party of thirty men employed at the arsenal arranging stores; issued rifles to the band. Died in hospital, Henry Patt, bandsman. Seventeen officers and two hundred and sixty-seven men marched into barracks on the strength of the garrison.

October 30th.—Forty *coolies* employed hauling up the jolly-boat and cutter. The fortress of Allahabad is situated in the fork, made by the confluence of the Rivers Ganges and Jumna, and has always been regarded as a very strong and important military post; it can accommodate a large number of men in tents, but only six hundred in the barracks; it was built about two hundred years ago, but the land face has since been considerably modernised; the two river faces have not been much altered, and consist of imposing walls and massive bastions of red sandstone, pierced with the small embrasures and loopholes characteristic of the old days of Oriental chivalry; the fort contains the largest arsenal in this part of India: it is entered by three approaches, the Main, the Jumna, and the Ganges Gates,—the latter of these is bricked up, and no longer used, but the Main Gate, approached through the winding ways of modern fortification, is a handsome entrance, on each side of which are cells, reserved for State prisoners in close confinement.

About five hundred yards from the glacis, a permanent camp has been pitched, for the use of regiments passing up the country; near the fort is the town of Allahabad proper, which consists almost entirely of native huts; about two miles to the eastward of it are the cantonments, which were formerly the prettiest in this part of India; now only a few of the houses are habitable, and the rest are but half burnt ruins, looking most desolate in their deserted and abandoned gardens; the church too has been sacked and burned, but could be restored; the roads near the cantonments are very good, and the country is prettily wooded.

October 31st—4.30 a.m. Sent a fatigue-party of twenty men to the railway station to transport camel carts. Carpenters employed painting boats. Launched cutter to send for Lieut.-General Sir Colin Campbell, K.C.B., Commander-in-Chief. 9 p.m. Sent an escort of one officer and twenty-one men to meet Sir Colin Campbell at the bridge of boats over the Ganges. Sixty-seven men in hospital. On this day, the detachment of the Naval Brigade under Sir William Peel arrived at Futtehpore.

November 1st.—3 a.m. Sir Colin Campbell and suite arrived; and at sunrise the garrison fired a salute of seventeen guns. 10 a.m. Mustered by companies, and performed Divine service. Number of sick, seventy.

November 2nd.—7.30 a.m. Sir Colin Campbell and suite left the garrison, under a salute of seventeen guns. Exercised the band at rifle drill. Number of sick, sixty-three.

November 3rd.—A company of H.M. 82nd Regiment marched into barracks. Number of sick, sixty-one. Today we have heard of Captain Peel's engagement at Kudjwa, the following brief account of which is from the pen of our chaplain, Mr. Bowman:—

November 1st.—5.30 a.m. A force consisting of a hundred men and officers of the Naval Brigade, with Lieut. Hay, Mr. Garvey, Lieut. Stirling, R.M., and Mr. Bone, one company of Royal Engi-

156

neers, two companies of H. M. 53rd Regiment, and a detachment of sixty men of different regiments, afterwards joined by one company of H. M. 90th Highlanders, about five hundred and thirty men in all, the whole under command of Colonel Powell, G.B., started from Futtehpore in pursuit of a body of the mutineers: after marching twenty-four miles, at 3 p.m. they came within sight of the enemy, found them intrenched in a strong position behind some hillocks of sand, and driving their skirmishers out of a field of long corn, engaged and defeated them, capturing two guns and an ammunition waggon: the whole force of the enemy exceeded four thousand men, of whom about two thousand were *sepoys* and fought in uniform, many with medals on their breasts.

Their loss in the action was estimated at over four hundred killed, and included their commander and wounded. Colonel Powell was killed early in the action, when the command devolved on Captain Peel. The battle was fought near the village of Kudjwa, and lasted two hours and a half, the force encamping in the vicinity of a village called Binkee that evening. The following day, the force under Captain Peel returned to Futtehpore in high spirits, and was received with loud cheering. Lieut. Hay, R.N. was slightly wounded in the hand, and Lieut. Stirling, R.M. was severely wounded in the calf of the leg.[1]

November 4th.—A company of H.M. 82nd Regiment marched into barracks.

November 6th.— 9-30 p.m. Lieut. Wratislaw, with fifty men, left the garrison, by order of Brigadier Campbell, to protect the hospital. Some men were seen prowling round the walls of the fort the other night, and the brigadier ordered me out with a picquet to see what they were about; the men ran away, but our attention was thus drawn to some windows in the wall, open drains, and the arsenal, all of which were in a very unprotected state. As this fortress is not strongly garrisoned, great precautions are taken both by day and night; after gun-fire, the drawbridges are hauled up, and the gates locked, and there is neither ingress nor egress without written permission from the commandant; all the sentries are visited, guards turned out, and walls patrolled twice during the night, by the subaltern commanding the main guard, and once by the captain of the week; any person within or without the

---

1. See Appendix.

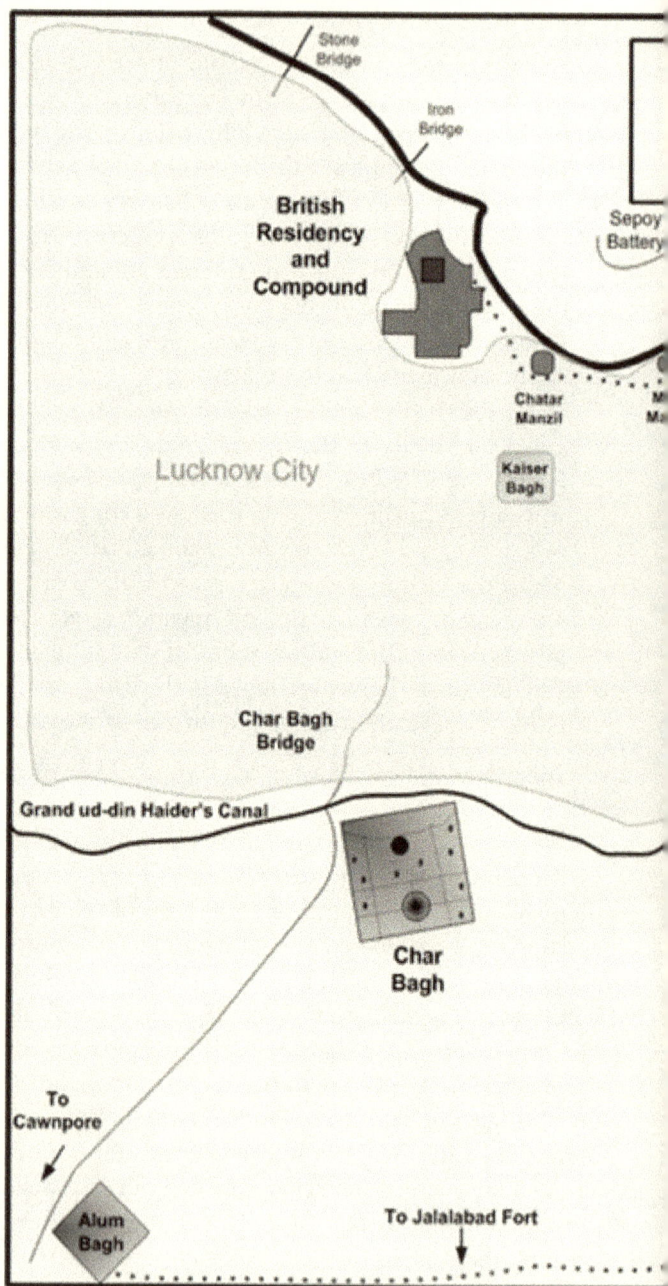

Stone
Bridge

Iron
Bridge

**British
Residency
and
Compound**

Sepoy
Battery

Chatar
Manzil

M
Ma

Kaiser
Bagh

Lucknow City

**Char Bagh
Bridge**

Grand ud-din Haider's Canal

**Char
Bagh**

To
Cawnpore

**Alum
Bagh**

To Jalalabad Fort

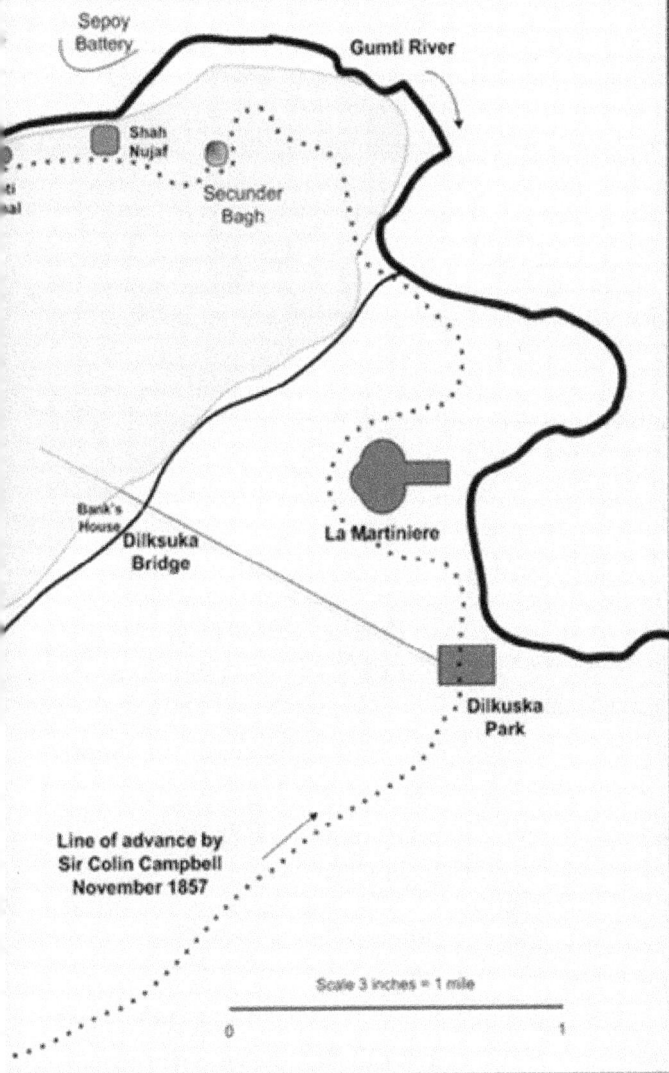

Sir Colin Campbell's Relief of Lucknow November 1857

North

Sepoy Battery

Gumti River

Shah Nujaf

Secunder Bagh

La Martiniere

Bank's House

Dilksuka Bridge

Dilkuska Park

Line of advance by Sir Colin Campbell November 1857

Scale 3 inches = 1 mile

0   1

fort not answering when hailed, is fired at by the sentry, and on hearing a shot fired all the guards turn out.

Some years ago, a very curious pillar, some fifty feet long, was found here, made of one solid piece of stone; the colonel then commanding the garrison had it set up in the middle of the parade-ground, with a comical-looking carved lion on the top. It goes by the name of Bheem Singh's Lat. A Calcutta magazine gives the following account of it:

It is one stone, 42 feet 7 inches in height, of which 7 feet 7 inches may be considered the base, which was probably buried to some extent in the ground, or in the masonry that supported it. The shaft, properly so called, is 3 feet in diameter at the base, diminishing to 2 feet 2 inches at the summit; the neck, immediately below the capital, represents with considerable purity the honeysuckle ornament of the Assyrians, which the Greeks borrowed from them with the Ionic order. The pillar at Allahabad lost its capital, but the deficiency was supplied from two of the Tirhoot examples which retain their capitals, with the lions which crowned the summits of all. This pillar is one of a group of monoliths set up by Asoka in the middle of the third century, B.C.; they were all alike in form, and all bore the same inscription, being four short edicts, containing the creed and principal doctrines of Buddhism, which he had recently embraced. Of these one is at Delhi, having been re-erected by Ferozeshah in his palace, as a monument of his victory over the Hindoos; three more are standing near the River Gunduck, in Tirhoot; a fragment of another was discovered near Delhi, and part of a seventh was used as a roller on the Benares road by a Company's engineer officer.

On this day, Captain Peel, with the first detachment of the Naval Brigade, arrived at Cawnpore.

November 7th.—6.30 a.m. Lieut. Wratislaw and party returned from the hospital. H. M. 82nd Regiment marched out of barracks. Carpenters employed painting boats. Died, Michael Shea, R.M. By order of the commandant, Brigadier Campbell, porter is now served out to our men.

November 8th.—6.30 a.m. Mustered by companies and marched to the garrison chapel. 5 p.m. Sent funeral party to inter the remains of Michael Shea, deceased. Number of sick, sixty-four.

November 12th.—The following account of the operations of the detachment of the Naval Brigade which accompanied Sir Colin Campbell to the relief of Lucknow, is from the journal of our chaplain: a list of the officers will be found in the last chapter.

November 12th.—The Naval Brigade arrived at the camping ground near the Alumbagh; a short time before their arrival, about two thousand of the enemy were observed on the left, about a thousand yards off, among corn and sugar-cane fields; our men immediately brought their great guns into position on the road, and the Horse Artillery, Highlanders and lancers, went in pursuit; after firing a few round shot, the enemy dispersed.

November 13th.—Last night, the wounded from the battle of Kudjwa arrived, and amongst them were Lieut. Stirling, R.M. and an officer of the 93rd of the name of Conyngham; both were wounded by a bullet in the calf of the leg.

November 14th.—The washermen knock our clothes to pieces terribly, but get them beautifully white and clean, far beyond anything I ever saw in England; this, however, is chiefly owing to the burning sun, which would bleach a chimney-sweep in about ten minutes, brushes and all. Our men have all sorts of pets: cats, dogs, goats, pigeons, monkeys, parrots, and even sheep and squirrels; every morning, about twenty men and monkeys go down to a covered bath in the ditch of the fort, adjoining which is a smaller one used by the officers. Every barrack-room has a small square hole in each of its four corners for ventilation, and what with the birds flying in at the windows and out through the ceiling, one's room is a perfect aviary.

November 14th.—(From Mr. Bowman's Journal.) The whole force got under weigh, and proceeded by a circuitous route to attack Lucknow; on the march, which was among cornfields and woods that would have afforded splendid cover for the enemy, the troops were several times engaged, and on one occasion some of the Highlanders were driven back, but being reinforced, compelled the enemy to retreat: on nearing Lucknow they made a stand, but were driven back with the loss of two guns. Two large buildings, or rather palaces were taken by our troops; one, called the Dilkushah, is a royal hunting-seat, situated on a hill overlooking Lucknow; the other, a European college called the Martinière, built by a Frenchman, General Martine, who was commander-in-chief of the Oude army many years ago, is situated a little below the Dilkushah.

We now all moved into a compound near the Martinière, but had hardly ocupied it when several round shot were fired right among us; at the same time a determined attack was made by the enemy with musketry, which soon obliged us all, men and guns, to evacuate the place. Our large guns were rapidly taken, under a heavy fire, into a position whence they might drive back the enemy, and some troops were also ordered to charge, the enemy were repulsed, and we then returned and bivouacked for the night.

We had a sad misfortune with one of our guns; it accidentally went off while being loaded, probably on account of not having been properly sponged, killed Francis Cassiday, captain of the maintop, severely wounded two other blue jackets, killed one Highlander, and severely wounded two others. The total loss of the army today has been upwards of twenty killed and wounded, and among the former are two officers of the Carabineers.

November 15th.—(From Mr. Bowman's Journal.) The army rested.

November 16th.—(From Mr. Bowman's Journal.) The 8th Regiment, Hodson's horse, and three guns of the Royal Artillery, under command of Lieut. Walker, the whole under command of Colonel Little, remained at the Dilkushah to guard the baggage, stores, sick and wounded: the remainder of the army proceeded to attack Lucknow. Presently the advanced guard was heard in conflict with the enemy; when the Naval Brigade guns came up to where the fighting was going on, they found that a sort of summer palace called the Secundra Bagh, was being attacked: it was full of *sepoys*, who kept up a killing fire from the roofs and neighbouring walls. The engagement was very severe, and an officer came rushing back along the line shouting for infantry, and hurrying up the heavy guns.

When the field hospital arrived at the scene of action, it took up its position under the walls of the Secundra Bagh, inside of which the fighting was still going on: this was the safest position that could be selected, but the shot, shell, and musket-balls were cutting the trees about in all directions, and falling among the wounded who were brought in rapidly; in a few hours the place was covered with *doolies* full of wounded, who were afterwards removed to beds placed along the wall. In the evening a report was spread that one of the adjacent towers contained a magazine; this caused a panic, and the whole of the wounded were removed into the open, where they remained for some time: afterwards the report was found to have been false; they were moved back again, and there they remained during the first awful night. Lieut. Salmon was brought in, wounded in the thigh by a musket-ball during the afternoon. Martin Abbot Daniel, midshipman, was killed by a round shot which tore away the right side of his head. In writing to his father, Captain Peel says:

> It was in the front of the Shah Najeef, and in command of an 8-in. howitzer, that your noble son was killed; the enemy's fire was very heavy, and I had just asked your son if his gun was ready; he replied "All ready, sir," when I said, "Fire the howitzer," and he was answering "Aye, aye," when a round shot in less than a moment deprived him of life. We buried him where he fell, our chaplain reading the service, and in laying him in his resting place we felt, captain, officers and men, that we had lost one of the best and noblest of the *Shannons*.

The firing slackened considerably during the night, and our troops advanced some distance towards the Residency, having stormed and taken the barracks and several bungalows. Twelve or thirteen of the Naval Brigade were brought in wounded, and three or four were killed.

November 17th.—(From Mr. Bowman's Journal.) On account of the unsafe position and exposed situation of the hospital, the sick were removed this morning to a village about a hundred and fifty yards off: this village was built, as are many in Oude, consisting of a square court, surrounded by mud cottages, whose doors and windows all open to the interior: on the outside are very thick blank mud walls, the whole forming rather a strong fortification. The sick had not been here long before the enemy had evidently received information of the move, for several round shot were sent into the court, the second of which killed two camels which were lying down in the centre of the square,

163

the third going right through the roof of the building in which Dr. Dickson and some of the staff were living.

The hospital was in a most precarious position, as it was open to the rear, a large breach having been made in the wall, and no sentries having been posted at the entry. During the night heavy firing was heard close to, probably the enemy engaging our picquets: a few men coming in might have massacred the whole of our sick and wounded; but the night passed without any attempt being made, although a general attack was expected, the bells ringing every half hour and the firing recommencing each time. Today, great cheering was heard all round, which announced the fact that communication had been opened with the Residency. Generals Havelock and Outram met Sir Colin Campbell, and the women and children were now considered out of danger.

November 20th.— The garrison saluted Major-General Dupuis, R.A., with thirteen guns, on his leaving the fork This evening we received intelligence that there were two thousand *sepoys* about three miles off: all the troops in the permanent camp were immediately got under arms, and everyone in the fort was on the *"qui-vive;"* but there was no attack, and all ended in smoke. A few nights ago, we sent out an advanced picquet of fifty men, and on another occasion, two field-pieces and a hundred men, but neither time did any *sepoys* appear; so either spies must have brought false intelligence, or the rebels taken alarm.

November 23rd.—(From Mr. Bowman's Journal,) Last night, the whole force retreated from Lucknow, and arrived at the Dilkushah. The retrograde movement was made in a most successful manner, without any pursuit or annoyance from the enemy. A large number of shot were necessarily left behind in the Residency, and also a few disabled guns,

November 24th.—(From Mr. Bowman's Journal.) The army started from the Dilkushah for the Alumbagh, leaving behind two of the Naval Brigade guns and two thousand men to cover the retreat, and follow on the succeeding day. General Havelock died this day at the Dilkushah, of dysentery: he will be buried tomorrow in the Alumbagh. A 24-pr. about a thousand yards off annoys the garrison of the Alumbagh very much, several shots having struck the tents, and a few natives having been

164

killed: this gun goes by the name of "Nancy Dawson." The *sepoy* commanders pay their men for every round shot or bullet they bring in: this affords very pretty practice for our picquets, as there are constantly several men out in the open, picking up shot that fell short.

November 26th.—Allahabad contains many valuable stores and is very strong, yet it has no standing garrison besides the Naval Brigade. I have had my room partitioned off with grass mats, to keep out the draughts; there is no sort of protection in these barracks from cold in winter, nothing has been thought of but how to keep them cool in summer. We hear that there is a party of *sepoys* between Cawnpore and Lucknow intercepting the post, which may account for our receiving no news from that direction.

November 28th.—(From Mr. Bowman's Journal.) Orders arrived early in the morning for the Naval Brigade to march at 7 a. m. Captain Peel took upon himself to ignore the order, and directed the men to get their breakfasts before starting; at noon they marched fifteen miles, and then received orders to bivouac for two hours, after this they again started and reached the camp of the main army, about three miles from Cawnpore, at 2 a.m. No tents were pitched, but the guns were kept ready for action.

We hear that the Gwalior Contingent attacked Cawnpore on the 26th, and General Wyndham hearing that they were approaching, went out to meet them with about fifteen hundred men: they fell in with a strong reconnoitring party of the enemy, attacked and defeated them, capturing three guns; they then returned and encamped about two miles from Cawnpore: the next day at 11.30 a.m. the alarm was sounded, and thirty-six blue jackets with two 24-prs. with Mr. Garvey, mate, under command of Lieut. Hay, advanced to meet the enemy, and after a short time came in sight of them.

The enemy fired the first shot from a gun on the road, but as soon as our guns replied, they opened fire with grape and canister from batteries on either side of it: our guns not being properly supported, and being in advance of the skirmishers, Lieut. Hay received orders from General Dupuis to retire and leave them, which he did, having spiked one: our blue jackets advanced again shortly afterwards with the Rifles and 88th, and

GUNNERS IN ACTION

brought them in: Lieut. Hay was struck in the stomach by a spent grape-shot, and carried to the rear. The retreat now became general, and our troops pursued by the enemy and harassed by musketry, reached the entrenched camp at about 5.30 p.m. with their guns. Mr. H. A. Lascelles, naval cadet, A.D.C. to Captain Peel, distinguished himself a good deal, seizing a rifle from a wounded man of the 88th, and charging with that regiment.

November 30th.—We were all much astonished this morning to see a post-captain in top-boots, spurs, and corduroys, come riding across the parade-ground; he wore a full-dress sword-belt, and a curious looking sword, very much curved, and broad, with a wooden hilt, an undress frock-coat with the three stripes, and a number of shiny leather accoutrements hanging about him by marvellously contrived straps; there was a drinking flask, a revolver case, a present-use pouch, a reserve pouch, and a telescope case, all made of black shiny leather; his saddle was quite new and white, with white holsters and bags hanging from it, white bridle, and white reins; this all turned out to be Captain Oliver Jones, an officer on half-pay, come up here for a *lark* as he told me.

CHAPTER 4

Recapture of Cawnpore

December 6th.—8-30 a.m. Received orders per electric telegraph for Lieut. Wilson, Mr. Verney, the band, and eighty men to proceed to Cawnpore.

December 7th.—Cheemee. Yesterday, at three hours' notice, we left Allahabad for Cawnpore, Since Captain Peel started, one thought has been uppermost in each mind, namely, the desire to follow him. When we left yesterday, the scene among our men ordered to remain was most extraordinary, old petty-officers and young seamen giving way to floods of tears at not being ordered to the front. This is the end of the railway at present, and we march this afternoon at one or two o'clock with bullock-waggons.

We have just met Lieuts. Hay and Salmon going to Allahabad wounded, with the women, children, and wounded relieved from Lucknow: Lieut. Salmon is shot through the thigh, and Lieut. Hay has received an internal wound, caused by a spent ball striking his sword-belt; Lieuts. Young and Salmon have been recommended for the Victoria Cross. I hear that at Cawnpore shot and shell are flying into the tents, Lieut. Young is at present in command of our men at that place.

Futtehpor. We hear that the road between this and Cawnpore is not safe, but that the rebels have been well thrashed. Our journey, even this far, has been full of adventures, an account of which in an idle moment (see April 22nd, 1858) might amuse; but as they chiefly consisted of carts breaking down, and oxen and waggons weaving themselves into a curious and writhing fabric.

(From Mr. Bowman's Journal.) Orders have come for the baggage to proceed immediately to the commander-in-chief's camp, about three miles off on the Calpee Road. The enemy deserted the city of Cawnpore at about three o'clock this morning; yesterday they had guns in position to play upon the Grand Trunk Road; when our guns went to attack them they appeared taken by surprise, and did not at first return the fire. After encountering rather a heavy fire for a short time, they retreated with our men full in pursuit. They made one stand behind an entrenchment, which was stormed and carried by the Royal Marines under Captain Gray, R.M., and the 53rd.

The enemy then fled down the Calpee Road, pursued by our troops, that being the only one open to them, as a two-gun battery commanded by Lord Walter Kerr was opposed to them on the Futtehpore Road. Seventeen guns were captured, also their camp, which contained a great portion of the things taken from the 88th, 90th, &c, on the occasion of General Wyndham's retreat. The cavalry pursued the enemy for about fifteen miles, cutting them to pieces, and our guns went down the road about nine miles: in the evening the troops returned with a great quantity of baggage and ammunition.

Our loss has been very trifling; two officers were killed—Lieut. Vincent of the 8th, and Lieut. Salmond of the Staff; the latter was found with his throat cut, a short distance down the Calpee Road. The loss of the Naval Brigade was two men slightly wounded.

KERR'S BATTERY, CAWNPORE.

December 9th.—Futtehpore. This day at noon we start; four of our men who were ordered to remain behind have smuggled themselves into our party. Yesterday we caught a *sepoy* with a large quantity of spoil, amongst which was a pair of cymbals, which the chief magistrate of the place kindly gave us, and they will be a great addition to our band.

December 10th.—Alas! we are detained at Futtehpore; however, there is no fighting going on now at Cawnpore, so matters might be much worse. This place is distant from Allahabad seventy miles, and from Cawnpore fifty.

December 13th.—Cawnpore. We marched in here yesterday at noon; on the road I purchased a bottle of brandy for one pound, thinking myself most fortunate in being able to do so: not half an hour afterwards Captain Oliver Jones rode up and presented me with another bottle; I do not remember to have ever received a more valuable present, or one for which I felt more gratitude. Now we have arrived we find that there are not tents for us, so we sleep in the tents of those who were here before, and spend the greater part of our time in the open air. Although I know that the opinion is not generally entertained, I give the result of my own short experience when I say that I find the natives of India tractable, and the better classes, such as servants, &c., grateful and honest. The English residents generally appear to me very prejudiced against the natives, and show this in their behaviour; for my own part, I must say that I receive many marks of attachment from my servants, in return for the trifling acts of kindness which I endeavour to do them.

Contrary to the advice which was given me, I have treated my *kitmagar* kindly, and have reposed confidence in him; I try to gain his goodwill, and he has amply repaid me by following me up here when he had a very bad foot; he said that I was a good master, and he knew I depended on his coming up, and would not disappoint me. As for the abject tillers of the soil, I fear they are so stupid, so ignorant, so wanting in the characteristics which distinguish the man from the brute, that I could quite understand instinct leading them to murder a sleeping man for the sake of the piece of bread in his hand. I think that a cause of the mutiny *may* be that in every British mind in India contempt for the natives is deeply rooted. When a kindness is done to a native by an Englishman, it is often accompanied by a contemptuous thought which appears only too clearly in the countenance; the terms in which I have heard even clergymen and others, who would desire to do good to the Hindoos, speak of them, convinces me that this is the case; it must be most trying to a people who consider us as outcasts.

December 14th.—Today we have shifted camp to a plain two miles further from Cawnpore.

December 15th.—Lieut. Vaughan and Lord Walter Kerr have started with a party of blue jackets for Bithoor, where Nana Sahib had his palace: they are gone to assist in pumping out some wells, at the bottom of which treasure is said to lie, as a silver cup was fished out of one with a spear.

December 18th.—Lieut. Vaughan returned with his party, but had been unsuccessful in making any head against the springs supplying the wells at Bithoor.

December 20th.—We are now encamped about three miles from Cawnpore. Ever since our arrival I have suffered from extreme lassitude attended with weakness, giddiness, and loss appetite, which renders me totally unequal to any exertion of mind or body, although up to the present time my name has not appeared on the sick list. I have been taking a mixture of quinine which has done me much good, and I hope it may now please God that I may recover. We have two pieces of news this morning; one is that all the rest of the Naval Brigade are coming up from Allahabad; the other that a large force of the rebels, with fifteen guns, refused to believe that Delhi had fallen, and advanced towards it; the British officer in command came out to meet them, utterly routed them and captured the fifteen guns.

The chaplain here, the Rev. T. Moore, who came up with us in the *Benares* to Allahabad is the most hard-working man possible: hospitable and generous almost to excess, he spends a great portion of his time, often twelve hours out of the twenty-four, among the sick in the hospitals: he is at present laid up from over-work, but I trust will be about again in a day or two: he has hired a large house which, with the exception of one room, he has turned into a private hospital for wounded officers: under fire he has proved himself among the coolest and the bravest; he is a man of about five and thirty, although he looks ten years younger.

December 22nd.—Lieut. Wratislaw arrived at Cawnpore with the last detachment of the Naval Brigade. We have a most facetious petty officer of the name of Devereux; he is a good seaman but given to talking very bad *French;* one day on the passage out, when apostrophising the afterguard with even less politeness than usual, Captain Peel overheard him, and knowing him for an old offender turned sharply round on him; "What's that you say, sir?" said the captain; the man looked up scratching his old red head, with a knowing look on his scarred and wrinkled face, and with a sly twinkle in his eye replied: "I was making the remark, sir, as 'ow it blows werry 'ard in the Chiny seas." Of course this has now passed into a proverb among the *Shannons*.

December 23rd.—7 a.m. Exercised the Naval Brigade together for the first time at company drill. 4 p.m. Exercised the first company at Light Infantry drill. A day or two ago I visited the "Yellow Bungalow," the house in which the barbarous massacres were committed; it is built in the form of a court; in the centre stands a tree, and all round is a verandah; I saw one of the rooms with its floors and walls covered with blood, although attempts had been made to whitewash the stains; from the beams of the verandah hung pieces of cord by which the children had been hung up, and stabbed by the *sepoys*: on the wall behind a door was written with a pin or some sharp instrument:

Countrymen and women, remember 15 July, 1857. Your wives and families are here in misery, and at the disposal of savages who has ravished both old and young, and then killed us; oh! oh! my child, my child! countrymen revenge, it.

Near the house is the well into which the murdered bodies were thrown, and which has since been filled up.

CHAPTER 5

Battle of the Kallee-Nuddee

December 24th.—6 am. Struck tents, and proceeded towards Futtegurh on the Grand Trunk Road. 1.30 p.m. Encamped, having marched thirteen miles.

December 25th.—Christmas Day. 8.30 a.m. General parade; performed divine service. We are now sixteen or seventeen miles from Cawnpore, where we have left seventy-eight men and Lord Arthur Clinton, under the command of Lord Walter Kerr, midshipman. I soon got knocked up yesterday, as we marched until nearly noon, and it was one before the tents were pitched; but my *syce* led my horse by my side, and I rode at least four or five miles. We chummed together for our Christmas dinners, in parties of five or six, each bringing what he could to the general stock, and so we spent as merry a day as possible under the circumstances.

Captain Peel has presented to the commander-in-chief, in the name of the Naval Brigade, as a Christmas present, a small brass *cohorn*, captured at Lucknow; it is mounted on a little carriage, with a suitable inscription, made by our engineers, assisted by the carpenters and stokers. Our engineers, Mr. Bone and Mr. Henri, have been of the greatest possible service, sighting our guns as accurately as rifles, and most zealously giving their whole energies to promoting the efficiency of our battery.

December 27th.—I have marched today the whole distance without mounting my horse; our march was only thirteen miles, so that an old stager would laugh at my considering it an achievement; but I do not think I could have marched much further. It is Sunday, but marching every day, it is difficult to make a difference between Sundays and week-days; there is the same routine of washing, feeding, and sleeping to be gone through, and it must be done on Sunday as well as on any other day. I find my horse most useful; he has such pluck that I know he would run as long as he could stand. Today we have halted at a place called Arrown; and yesterday we encamped at Poorah, about twenty-six miles from Cawnpore. Tomorrow General Wyndham is to march with a strong brigade to a fort about eight miles off; if it is defended, he is to capture and blow it up. Lieut. Young and Mr. Daniel, midshipman, go in charge of a gun, which will be sent with two gun's crews.

The country we are marching through is very flat, but generally well wooded, with a great deal of cultivation; and the roads are good but dusty. Yesterday when we halted, a number of camels went to graze in a field of young wheat; the owner of the wheat came out, and called down curses from heaven on the camel-drivers; they were so appalled at this, that in three minutes they had driven out every camel: such is the effect of superstition. I fear that many of the camels are very badly used, as I sometimes see their backs bleeding when the pack-saddles are taken off. Young camels are frequently born on the march, and their mammas have to carry them for several days, until they are able to run pretty well; then a little wooden toggle is passed through the infant's nose, a piece of string connects it with the maternal tail, and thus it commences its walk through life, following in its parent's footsteps.

A camel carries its supply of water in a large bladder; when thirsty, the animal has the power of bringing this up with a bubbling, gurgling sound, until it hangs down some eighteen inches below his mouth, and, having taken some of the water, he again swallows it; until one is accustomed to it, this is a most disagreeable and disgusting sight. When being laden he will give utterance to dismal moans, which become more piteous as his load increases; and if more is placed on his back than he approves of, he will start up; shake it all off and run "bobbery" through the camp, perhaps dragging after him, bumping and bounding over earth and stones, some valuable box, which has therefore been the more securely lashed to his pack-saddle. When unladen at night, he will sometimes frisk about with most grotesque antics; and surely, there is no more absurd sight in the world than a "larky" camel.

To ride a camel is at first no easy matter; when you have climbed on to his hump, and laid hold of his pack-saddle, the "*ont-wallah*" gives the word, and the animal rises on his hind knees, with a "send "forward that will pitch the rider over his bows if he does not hold fast; before he has properly recovered his seat, the camel rises on his fore-feet, with a worse struggle than before, that threatens to send the rider flying over his stern; and a third "pitch" brings the camel on to all fours.

But now commences a most trying discipline, for the beast begins to trot, and each step appears to dislocate every bone in your body, and it is only by practice that you learn to rise in the rope stirrups with each unexpected motion, so that at last the riding is even pleasant. The camel has large pad feet, whose natural cushion prevents this jarring from damaging the animal himself, and keeps his feet from sinking in soft sand: camels are at all times guided by a string attached to a wooden toggle passed through the nose, which in a caravan is fastened to his precursor's tail. At night, the camels of each regiment kneel down in a circle, their young ones and pack-saddles by their sides, their drivers in the centre, and thus they sleep on their stomachs, many of them are very vicious, and if approached too closely by strangers, give a nasty tearing bite.

The elephant is a far nobler and more intelligent creature; viewed as a piece of animal architecture, he is perhaps the most wonderful on earth. The largest of living creatures, his enormous proportions require corresponding support, which is found in his straight and massive legs; his arched back enables him to bear heavy burdens; and his strong head, set close on to his shoulders, enables him to concentrate his strength into a push. But the absence of a neck precludes him from putting his head to the ground, unless he kneels down, and therefore Providence has given him his marvellous trunk; with this he will pluck herbage from the ground, or tear down tender branches of trees for food; when directed he will pull down a house with it, root up a small .tree, or chastise a bad brother; with this he drinks water; holding a branch in it he will fan away flies; or attacked by a tiger, with one blow he will break its back.

At the end of a day's march, one elephant goes to the nearest jungle, and assists the *mahout* in cutting down branches for the food of the others; when these lie in a heap on the ground, he lifts up one foot, and so disposes his trunk as to make a stair for his keeper, who gets on his back with a long cord; now the beast passes up the branches one by one to him, and assists in stacking them on his own back, where they are secured by the mahout. Elephants delight in water, and will stand for hours squirting it over their own, or each other's backs, and washing their thick dark skin, and its few coarse black hairs. They have no

175

front teeth in the lower jaw, but the under lip protrudes, so as to form a sort of spout, into which they pour water from their trunks when drinking; the end of the proboscis is exceedingly sensitive, and affords to this huge beast the power of great delicacy of manipulation.

On a more intimate acquaintance, he is found to be by no means as awkward or ugly an animal as might be expected; his large flabby ears are very correct, and can not only distinguish the various inflections of the human voice, but also distant sounds which are to us inaudible: his black eyes, though very small, sparkle with unmistakeable intelligence. Many elephants have no tusks, from some they have been cut off for sale, and the stumps are tipped with brass to prevent their splitting: in combat with each other, they generally lock their tusks and push head to head.

The motion of riding an elephant is not unpleasant; their pace is a shambling trot, with which they get over a good deal of ground, but soon become footsore if worked too hard. Perhaps, if there is one way in which an elephant shows its intelligence more than another, it is in its dislike to gunpowder. Formerly they were much used in native warfare; but now, at the scratch of a bullet or sound of a gun, the sensible animal, having no Victoria Cross to gain, or spurs to win, starts off in the opposite direction as hard as he can run, regardless of the tent on his back, or the 68-pr. in tow. As no tame elephants will breed, each has to be caught and tamed separately. The mutual dread that exists between the elephant and horse is most unaccountable, familiar with each other as a campaign must make them; they never pass without both exhibiting signs of fear, which the former sometimes gives vent to in a shrill trumpeting sound.

December 29th.—Eram Cusserai. Yesterday, at noon, we arrived at this place and do not march again today, nor, I believe tomorrow, on account of a bridge ahead of us having been broken down. I cannot succeed in getting a comfortable saddle, and English saddles are very scarce; my pony is spirited and restless, and my saddle so uncomfortable that I have several times been nearly thrown; he never walks quietly over a little ditch, but clears it with a sudden bound that nearly unhorses me; he is very clever in scrambling over the low mud walls of this country; he has learnt the not very agreeable trick of giving the stirrup a sharp, vicious ringing kick just as one puts one foot into it when mounting, so I have to be extremely careful, or I should get my ankle broken.

The aspect of the country through which we have been marching has not changed; in some places are little brooks, clumps of nice trees, fields of wheat, tobacco, or cauliflowers; the country is nearly level with but few undulations; the trees are well grown, affording delicious shade, and generally begin to branch out at about ten feet from the ground; birds are abundant and noisy, especially green parrots; some of the houses of the natives are tastefully adorned with wood carving, and we pass others with very prettily ornamented porches, the whole of which on inspection prove to be worked in dried mud.

TOMB AT ERAM CUSSERAI

After the day's march, as soon as we arrive at our halting-place, we pile arms and sit down on the grass to wait for the elephants with the tents; they generally come in about twenty minutes, and when we have got our tents pitched, we go to sleep on the ground inside until the carts arrive with the baggage, which is sometimes as long as two or three hours; then we have some breakfast cooked, perform our respective toilettes, unpack a few things and spend the rest of the day in walking or riding, reading or writing. We go to bed at about 8 p.m., and the next morning rise at about five, pack up our things, have a cup of coffee, and are off again before it is light This afternoon I rode out with Captain Peel, Captain Oliver Jones, Lieut. Lind, Messrs. Garvey

Watson, and Lascelles. Captain Jones is a young half-pay captain in the navy; he was formerly commander of the *Hannibal* in the Black Sea, and is now up here for his own pleasure.

MUD PORCH AT ERAM CUSSERAI.

We went to see the ruins of an old town, about two miles N.N.E., called Kunnoj; this town is said to be older than Babylon, and its ruins larger than London; it was once the chief city of India, but of the old town nothing now remains but mounds of earth and bricks, which show that it must have been a place of great magnitude and importance. These mounds have in many places been tunnelled by the Hindoos, and treasure has been found in sufficient quantity to encourage people still to go on mining in peaceful times. There are many tombs and temples at Kunnoj of a comparatively modern date, although still upwards of eight hundred years old; this we ascertained by the architecture which was Hindoo, and in some places where it had been repaired, the alterations were Mussulman: the Mahommedans came into India about the year *a.d.* 1000,

December 30th.—This afternoon I went to Kunnoj to try to make a sketch of a gateway and the tombs of two holy men: they were built of old red sandstone, which is chiefly found at Agra. Today Brigadier Adrian Hope's brigade, consisting of the 42nd and 93rd Highlanders and 53rd arrived from Bithoor.

December 31st.—6.15 a.m. Struck tents. 7.30. Proceeded on the march, p.m. 2. Halted and encamped after a march of fourteen miles. To find the exact spot where we are now encamped, follow the trunk

178

road up past Kunnoj until a by-road turns off to the right, crossing a branch of the Ganges; we are in the angle between the two roads; the enemy have broken down the bridge across the river about five miles off; the by-road leads to Futtegurh, distant about twenty-four miles. This place is called Goosaigunge. "*Gurh*," as in Futtegurh, means "fort;" "*Futteh* "means "victory;" "*gunge*," as in Goosaigunge, means "market" or "bazaar;" "*pore*," as in Berhampore, means "city." The ignorance that existed in England a few years ago about Indian terms, and indeed everything relating to this country is amusingly illustrated in the following story: it is said that an English M.P. read an account of a battle in the Punjaub, in which it was stated that after the engagement *doolies* carried off the wounded from the field. The indignant gentleman said:

> Picture to yourselves the feelings of the sick and wounded, when just as the trumpets were sounding for victory, the ferocious *doolies* rushed down from the hills and carried them off.

It is to be hoped that our representatives are better informed by this time. An Indian army on the fine of march is a sight affording much interest and amusement; such a menagerie of men and beasts, footmen and cavalry, soldiers and sailors, camels and elephants, white men and black men, horses and oxen, Marines and Artillery, Sikhs and Highlanders.

When we first leave the encampment all is shrouded in darkness, and everyone naturally feels a little grumpy, but when the first streaks of dawn appear, and we have been an hour on the road, the welcome note is heard in the distance of the bugles sounding the "halt;" with great rapidity it passes from regiment to regiment and dies away in the rear; cavalry dismount, infantry pile arms in the middle of the road, and for a few minutes the whole army disperses on each side of it; the favourite refreshment of officers is bread, cold tongue, and "brandy-pawnee," which find their way out of innocent-looking holsters; and now we all take off overcoats or monkey-jackets which were needed when we started in the cold and damp night; the blue jackets fasten theirs over their shoulders, and the officers strap theirs to their saddles; the brief halt is too quickly at an end, and we enjoy a ten minutes' rest, when the "advance" sounds again down the fine from bugler to bugler; all at once fall in, arms are un-piled, and enlivened by our band, we again step out; now feet begin to ache and boots to chafe, but the cheery music of the bands, bugles, or drums and fifes of the regiment

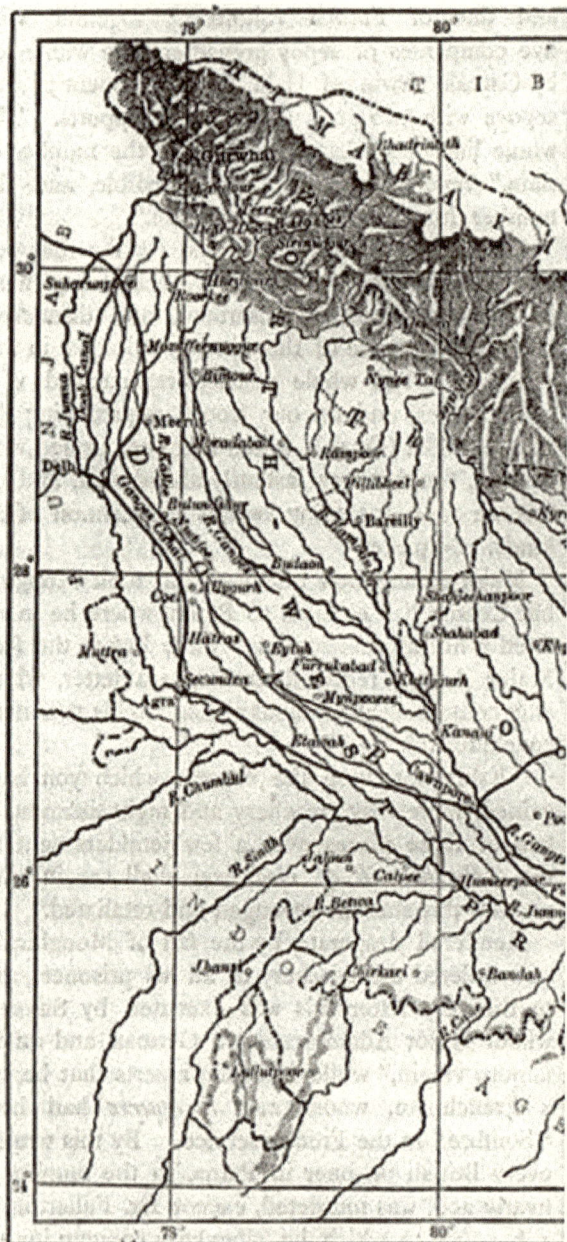

80°

M A

A K

Badrinath

Ghurwha

Srinug

30°

Hurdwar

Saharunpore   Roorkee

Mozufferngger

Bijnour   Nynee Tal

R. Jumna Canal

Meerut   Moradabad   Ramjoor

Delhi   R. Kalee   Pillibheet

Ganges Canal   Bareilly

Bulundshur

28°   Bulaon

Coel   Allygurh   Shahjehanpoor

Shahabad

Muttra   Hattras   Etah   Furrukabad   Fattyurh

Secundra   Mynpooree   Kanag

Agra   Etawah   Cawnpore

R. Chumbul   R. Ganges

R. Sinh   Jhansi   Calpee   Hummeerpoor

26°   R. Betwa   R. Jumna

Jhansi   Chirkari   Bandah

Jullulpoor

24°   78°   80°

NORTH-WEST PROVINCES

AND

OUDE

English Miles

0   50   100   150

N   S

UCKNOW

Oude

Busti   Goruckpoor

R.Rapte

Tandah

Sultanpoor

Azimgurh

Ray Bareilly

Jounpoor   R.Ganges

Portabgurh
Manikpoor

ALLAHABAD

Benares

Mirzapoor

Agori Khas   R.Sone

Singpoor

Buraech

Jonra

Bastee

marching next to us, generally the Rifles, infuses energy into the most footsore.

We make three halts in a march of thirteen or fourteen miles, of which the last is the longest, to allow the quartermaster-general and his staff to ride on and mark out the camp. A day or two ago, an officer of a distinguished Highland regiment was observed passing the Naval Brigade on a camel; now to ride a camel at all requires some experience, but to ride one in a kilt can hardly be accounted among the pleasures of life: the individual in question, so far from appearing to enjoy himself, appeared much distressed, and in imminent danger of slipping over the camel's tail; at last his feelings became too much for him, and letting go his hold, he fell sprawling on the grass amid shouts of laughter.

As the sun rises, the heat rapidly increases, and the camels and elephants are seen making short cuts across the fields, and keeping always clear of the road; when our bands have blown as much wind as they can spare into their instruments, our men strike up a song, and old windlass tunes, forecastle ditties, and many a well-known old ballad resound through the jungles or on the fertile plains of Bengal, and serve to animate our sailors and astonish the natives. The dust now becomes almost stifling, and rises in a thick cloud for eight or ten feet above the road; occasionally a staff-officer gallops by, kicking up a terrible dust; or again, a slight declivity and slope in the road shows the long and varied line of march; generally, however, it is very level, with a broad grassy glade on either side, bounded by handsome spreading trees.

Our guns and ammunition follow in rear of the brigade, under the charge of a lieutenant, with a strong guard; the small-arm ammunition is carried on camels in charge of a midshipman with a small guard. Perhaps one of the least romantic and most important offices is that of baggage-master, and every officer of the Naval Brigade will long remember the friendly care bestowed on our baggage by the Hon. Hugh Hare, an officer of the Indian army, attached to us in that capacity: owing to his exertions, it rarely happened that our baggage was not among the first to reach the new camping ground, the luxury of which will be appreciated by many an old campaigner.

January 1st, 1858.—10.30 a.m. Lieuts. Wratislaw and Lind, and Mr. Garvey, mate, with two 24-prs. and one 8-in. howitzer, and double gun's crews, under command of Lieut. Vaughan, have gone to form part of a small column under Brigadier the Hon. Adrian Hope, to cover the sappers and miners while repairing a bridge over the Kallee-Nuddee, four or five miles distant. Just before Lieut. Vaughan went away, Lieut. Young and Mr. Daniel returned with the party that accompanied General Wyndham; they had blown up a large fort called Detea, shot away five or six *sepoys* from guns, and hung up seventeen or eighteen of the chief men of the neighbouring villages.

I have this morning bought a goat for three *rupees*; she will yield plenty of milk, as I shall feed her in the fields of young corn which abound; at our last camping-ground, one regiment was encamped in a potato field. I am learning to milk a goat, but cannot quite manage it yet; I consider, myself, however, second only to Soyer in making omelettes. We get plenty of grapes, which come in caravans from Câbul, packed with cotton in little round wooden boxes; and very delicious they are too, on a dry, hot, dusty march,

January 2nd.—At 7.30 a.m., just as the suspension bridge was repaired, the *sepoys* opened fire upon our men, under Lieut. Vaughan, from a small gun in the opposite village, and our guns returned it,—the crews who were washing their garments by the riverside leaving their soap-suds and clothes, never to see them again. At eight we received orders to strike tents in half an hour; and the Naval Brigade, with their guns, the Artillery, Highlanders, Engineers, Probyn's Horse, and other regiments, were ordered to proceed immediately to the bridge.

11 a.m. Halted at the bridge. Here we found the village on the other side of the river occupied by the mutineers, with two guns. Our three guns, under Lieut. Vaughan, had crossed over the bridge, which had been repaired by the Naval Brigade during the night, and were firing from a yellow bungalow near the northern end of it, keeping up a heavy fire on the village, distant about three hundred yards; our guns now took up a position further to the left, and held in check a body of the enemy's cavalry visible beyond the village, behind the crest of some rising ground; the 53rd were lying behind the yellow bungalow, keeping up a withering fire from their skirmishers, for whom the ground afforded excellent cover from mounds and ridges of earth, and tufts of tall, coarse grass; and shortly afterwards the lancers, and a body of Sikh cavalry, crossed the bridge and took up a position on our left; Brigadier Greathed's division then crossed over, and also formed on the left of our guns.

Lieut. Vaughan now pointed and fired one of our guns at the small gun of the enemy, which was concealed behind the corner of a house, and annoying us much: his first shot struck the roof of the house; his second struck the angle of the wall about halfway down; and a third dismounted the gun and destroyed the carriage. Captain Peel, who was standing by, said, "Thank you, Mr. Vaughan; perhaps you will now be so good as to blow up the tumbril." Lieut. Vaughan fired a fourth shot, which passed near it; and a fifth, which blew it up, and killed several of the enemy.

"Thank you," said Captain Peel, in his blandest and most courteous tones; "I will now go and report to Sir Colin." I was only under fire for a few minutes, when I took some ammunition over the bridge to our guns, and Captain Peel then pointed out to me the remains of the gun and tumbril. The company to which I belonged was held in reserve; but when we afterwards marched through the village, we saw the bodies of *sepoys* lying near the remains of the tumbril, and fearfully burnt. After a good deal of firing, the village was stormed and captured by the 53rd, the enemy making no stand; the cavalry pursued them for some miles, capturing all their guns, eight in number, and cutting them up dreadfully.

It is said that a bugler of the 53rd sounded the "advance" without orders, which excited Sir Colin's displeasure. The whole army now crossed the bridge, and proceeded about two miles to the camping-ground, distant from Futtegurh twelve miles. Casualties in the Naval Brigade, one officer and two men wounded. Captain Maxwell, of the Bengal Artillery, was brought in wounded by a musket ball through the thigh, early in the action; he was attached to the Naval Brigade as interpreter, and we shall feel the loss both of his professional services and of his agreeable society. Captain Peel met with an adventure after the capture of the village, which might have been serious; when passing through a small street, accompanied by Captain Oliver Jones, three men of the 53rd, and one or two blue jackets, five *sepoys* jumped up out of a ditch on either side of the road, and rushed on them; they fought with desperation, but were all killed,—Captain Jones shooting the last man with his revolver; one man of the 53rd was dangerously wounded, but no one else on our side was hurt.

Mr. Watson, an officer of the engineers, had also a narrow escape this morning: last night he was in the village, and agreed with the head man for a hundred and fifty *coolies* to come to assist in repairing the bridge; this morning a message came to him that they were ready, and should be delivered to any officer who came to fetch them. Watson, having some suspicions, did not go; and this saved his life, as the *sepoys* were at that time in possession of the village. We reached our camping-ground at about 9.30 p.m., and parked our battery in a ploughed field, but no baggage or provisions had arrived, except the spirits, a cask of which is carried on some old limbers, and, under the charge of two quartermasters, is always foremost in the field or on the march; we were each glad to drink our day's double allowance, and even Captain Peel, who rarely drinks spirits, tossed off with gusto the abominable arrack that is served out in lieu of rum. Nearly famished, we ate every crumb in our haversacks; and I deemed myself lucky when I discovered two or three *bile-wallahs* making *chupatties*, one of which I bought for a *rupee*, and halved with a tent-mate.

At about midnight the elephants arrived with the tents, which were immediately pitched in the total darkness; but we had not a thing else, not even a candle, till about four, when the *hackeries* arrived with the baggage. Every tent was then illuminated, and roaring fires blazed in rear of the camp; and at about five, as the first streaks of dawn hove in sight, we sat down to a *late* dinner.

January 3rd. —This afternoon we marched to Futtegurh, where we arrived at 4 p.m., and encamped on the parade-ground; the enemy abandoned the town and fort with the exception of one native officer and thirty men, with two guns, who surrendered on our arrival. The road from Kallee-Nuddee to Futtegurh, and the fields on each side of it, were strewn with dead bodies, some of old men, some of young, and some of even boys, covered with ghastly wounds; and one could trace the tracks through the fields of the flying *sepoys* pursued by the relentless Sikhs, and see the trampled ground where the short, final struggle had taken place, and some of the wells we passed were choked with corpses. Near Futtegurh the road runs through groves and thickets, and among fields and. orchards, separated by walls or thick banks of mud, which might have been obstinately defended.

Chapter 6

Return to Cawnpore.

January 4th.—Futtegurh. This morning an order came out that no officer is to leave the camp without permission from the general of his division. The tents now supplied to us are square, and supported by a single pole, made of coarse canvas, and lined with blue cotton; the roofs are double, the upper one spreading out on two opposite sides into large eaves or wings. One of these is turned towards the south to keep off the sun, while the other forms the house of the native servants: on the two remaining sides are the doors, which, supported on little poles, form porches, while before the openings hang green blinds of finely-split bamboo. I have just returned from seeing a prisoner taken here, Madir Kahn; he remained in the fort till the last moment and fired a shot at us, and the commander-in-chief declared that if he was not given up he would burn the town down.

He was at the head of the cavalry, and commanded the day before yesterday at the Kallee-Nuddee. I do not, know what will be done with him, but I suppose he will either be blown away from a gun or hanged. When I saw him there was a crowd round him, some pulling his hair, and others throwing dirt in his face as he lay tied to some boards. He was a very handsome, strong-looking man, with black beard and moustaches, and richly dressed. I can hardly think it right or brave to torment a bound prisoner, however heinous his crimes may be. He lay there quite dignified and indifferent to the taunts, &c. of the crowd round him: it is said that he was a chief mover in the atrocities of Cawnpore.

January 5th.—I went today to see the fort of Futtegurh, which is not to be despised. The ramparts consist of two very high and solid walls of mud with a deep ditch between; but the houses outside approach very near, and would afford excellent cover for riflemen, while there is no protection on the ramparts for the men working the guns. The fort is not very large and appeared to be nearly a square, with round mud towers at the angles, but no redans or scientific fortifications. I afterwards rode across the bridge of boats over the Ganges, and about a mile beyond the videttes into the country. It is very sandy and barren, and little tributaries cross the road, or rather track, running into the Ganges, with here and there a quicksand.

When we leave Futtegurh, there are four roads open to us; the first, and I think the most probable, is that back to Cawnpore and thence to Lucknow; secondly, that leading across the country straight to Lucknow, which we are not likely to attempt with our heavy guns, as I suspect it is not a very good one; thirdly, the road to Bareilly, which I think we shall not take, as the rebels do not seem to intend to make a stand anywhere, and if we go on a wild-goose chase after them in the north, we shall leave our forces at Cawnpore and the Alumbagh unsupported.

If the rebels had intended to make a stand anywhere, they would have done so at Furruckabad, which I hear is a very strong place. We hear that there are only about two thousand *sepoys* gone to Bareilly, with a great mob of *budmashes* and rabble. Our fourth road would be that to Mynporee and Agra, where it is said that some rebels are congregated. I saw Ceely of the 42nd today, and he presented me with three pairs of socks, a most acceptable present, although I hear that socks are to be bought at 16*s*. a pair. Madir Kahn is to be seen hanging by the neck from a tree in the principal bazaar of Furruckabad; he said, just before he was executed, that he died with a clear conscience!

January 6th.—11 30 am. Interred the remains of Thomas Gregory, R. M. in the station churchyard. Lieuts. Young and Wilson and Mr. Daniel, midshipman, an 8-in. howitzer and 24-pr., with a double number of oxen, proceeded with a force, under Brigadier Adrian Hope, to Mhow, on the Bareilly road, to procure rum, of which there is a large store here, for the use of the army. Our chaplain, Mr. Bowman, is a capital shot with a gun or rifle, and sometimes brings home peacocks from the neighbouring jungle, which when roasted make no contemptible addition to a camp repast.

January 8th.—p.m. Marched out for exercise; halted in an open plain, and exercised first, second, and third companies at light infantry drill. A walk through the camp in the morning is very amusing; eve-

187

rybody breakfasts at about nine, and hence at half-past eight all the world is dressing, &c.; in front of every tent door are one or two gallant officers enjoying their morning's bath, which ceremony is performed in this wise: the devotee, attired in the lightest conceivable dress, squats on his marrow-bones on a small board at his tent door, and his *bheestie* then proceeds to torture him by first letting the chilly water trickle slowly over him from the neck of his pig-skin; in vain does the victim shriek out" *geldie, geldie koroo!*" (quicker, quicker!) the *bheestie* knows his duty, and will at first only perform it in detail; gradually, however, the stream increases, and at length the very last drops are emptied in a deluge over the now shivering wretch; his bearer then presents him with towels, slippers, and brushes, and he retires from the chill morning air into his tent invigorated and refreshed as he needs be, who has the duties of a campaign to perform under an Indian sun.

And passing to and fro among the tents are the charming young "*dood-wallahs*," every now and then repeating their musical cry "*buck-rie-dood*," (goat's milk); these young ladies, with brass or silver bangles on their ankles, and bracelets on their wrists, contrasting with their polished black skins, and dressed in white robes with bright-coloured shawls round their heads, supply the camp with milk, and their jetty, sparkling eyes, and tail, graceful figures, surmounted by the shining brass chatty, form no unattractive addition to camp scenery.

And now while their masters are breakfasting, the *syce* grooms and caparisons the horse of the field officer, and the bearer of the captain or subaltern gives his sword an extra rub up for the coming parade; the little cooking fires in rear of the officers quarters send up grateful odours of curries and omelettes, and little pots hiss and bubble, slyly lifting their lids, daring you to guess their contents, and shut up again with a defiant little puff of steam; and while burning green twigs crackle, subs and captains prattle, plates and dishes rattle, the bugles for parade summon all to duty; and now for a time the camp is quiet; only the native servants are left cleansing the breakfast things, the *maters* (sweepers) sweeping out the tents, the *bheesties* catering the floors, and the voices of commanding officers of different regiments break the comparative stillness; now orderly officers proceed to the headquarters, distinguished by the union jack floating in front of the commander-in-chief's tent, and the camp seems deserted until regiment after regiment is dismissed, and those who are not on duty spend the heat of the day under the shadow of their tents.

January 10th.—8 a.m. Mustered by companies and performed Divine service. H.M. 9th Lancers, Carabineers, Royal and Bengal Artillery attended; our chaplain, the Rev. E. L. Bowman, officiating. I have been two or three times to Furruckabad, distant three miles, and to the splendid palace which belonged to its *nawab*. This is built upon a high rock, and commands a beautiful view in a northerly direction; it was intended to blow it all up, but when the mines were completed, happily the authorities changed their minds, and it is to be left standing; it is a strong fortress, and must at the same time have been a most picturesque residence, but the actual palace has been burnt.

I bought from some soldiers a pair of gold-embroidered drawers, a silk table-cover, and a turban: I also took a velvet saddle from the *nawab's* coach-house, where were two or three English barouches and other carriages. I found in one room a book which I brought away, and which proved to be the "little *Koran*" corresponding in some degree to our prayer-book. I also inspected the *nawab's* garden, where amongst other things, were two tigers in cages. The city of Furruckabad is very picturesque, and fortified in the old fashion with gates and drawbridges; it is entered through several fortified gateways from which a street or boulevard runs right through the centre of the town, with trees and walks on either side, occasionally opening out into squares. It is the handsomest Indian town I have seen, its streets are broader and its houses less squalid than those we have hitherto passed through.

January 11th.—10 a.m. General parade, p.m. Exercised first and second companies at gun drill.

January 12th.—a.m. Lieutenant Young and party returned from Mhow, having hung one hundred and twenty-seven rebels on one tree at that place. These dreadful though absolutely necessary severities are most painful to recollect and to commemorate. 4 p.m. Marched out for exercise, and exercised first, second, and third companies at light infantry drill.

January 13th.—A party consisting of Lieutenants Hay and Wratislaw, and myself, with fifty-five men left the camp with a brigade under the command of Brigadier Walpole.

January 14th.—Yesterday morning we marched away across the Ganges on the road to Shahjehanpore to the Ramgunga River, a tributary of the Ganges, on whose banks we encamped yesterday afternoon. The first part of our march was over very swampy country near the Ganges, and it was only by putting all hands on to each gun separately that we were able to proceed. We have sent our 24-pr. and 8-in. howitzer down to the banks of the Ramgunga. This river rises in the Himalayas and falls into the Ganges opposite Kunnoj; the stream here is narrow but deep, there is no ford near, and four days ago the enemy burned the bridge of boats, so that we are puzzled to know how to get over with our guns; there is talk of bringing boats overland from the Ganges, a distance of eight miles.

The enemy seem to be in some force on the opposite side, with, I should think, three guns and about a hundred and fifty cavalry; they fired at us last night for about an hour, and although some of their shot pitched over our guns, no damage was done. Our brigade consists of two thousand five hundred men under command of Brigadier Walpole; Sappers, Horse Artillery, Rifle Brigade, 23rd, and detachment of Naval Brigade. Noon. About an hour ago I went down to the river with fourteen men to try to raise a sunken boat, but when the enemy saw us, they opened fire, and one shot plumped into the water about three yards from where we were all standing, which,-not meeting with the approval of the engineer officer in command, he sent me and my men back again. During the night, the sappers have thrown up a pretty little breastwork in front of our guns, with the ornamental railing of a neighbouring garden forming the rear. A shot has killed three of our gun-bullocks, which we have accordingly eaten; rather an improvement on the inferior beef served out as rations.

January 17th.—The day before yesterday Lieut. Vaughan brought up Lind and Garvey with two 24-prs. and their crews, so our present force here consists of six officers, one hundred and sixteen men, three guns and a howitzer. We have constructed a raft of wood and casks, under the direction of Captain Peel, who has ridden over here two or three times, and it now lies on the bank of the river all ready for launching: there is a good ford two or three miles farther down, where a boy of twelve years old could cross without being wetted above the waist: the raft is rather long and tortuous; there are besides eight boats, three of considerable size, protected by three 9-pr. guns and a very strong picquet. It is said that we are waiting here until Sir Colin receives further orders from Calcutta. We have received two elephants to draw one of our guns instead of bullocks. Yesterday we had a few drops of rain, the first intimation of the showery week that is generally met with at this time of year: the cold weather will now soon be over.

January 20th.—The day before yesterday, a Sikh belonging to Hodson's Irregular Horse was severely wounded in the leg, since amputated, by a round shot, when on parade; in consequence of this, we shifted camp further back yesterday afternoon. We are now just waiting for orders from the commander-in-chief, and are able to cross at any moment. We frequently receive visits from our messmates in camp at Futtegurh, but *we* are not supposed to go outside our own picquets.

January 22nd.—Yesterday afternoon I rode down to the ford, and saw the eight boats which we have there; the river winds a good deal, so that to go to the ford by water would be a journey of perhaps five or six miles, while on this side it is only three. The country seems well cultivated, and in several places we saw topes of fine trees, but it was rather marshy. Two bodies of irregular Sikh cavalry are attached to the main army; one is distinguished by wearing red turbans, is commanded by Captain Hodson of the Indian Army, and is known as Hodson's Horse; the other wears blue turbans, is commanded by Lieut. Probyn of the Indian Army, and is known as Probyn's Horse; their dress consists of the whitey-brown "*kharki*;" each man is armed with a *tulwa* and brace of pistols, and one or two troops with lances.

To command a regiment of these semi-barbarous troopers requires no small ability, tact, and personal courage, as well as knowledge of the native character, and both Probyn and Hodson are beloved by their wild horsemen. They are generally splendidly mounted, and each horse is the private property of his rider.

January 25th.—Yesterday fell the first of the rain that generally comes at this time of year: today is cloudy, and this morning the rain fell heavily. Yesterday afternoon I rode over to the camp at Futtegurh, slept there, and returned this morning. Everything was much the same as usual, only the camp had been shifted since we left. I had a nice ride there, but my poor horse had to stand in the rain all night, and it poured all the way back this morning. I took a rug with me for the horse, and at night had a couple of doormats put over him; the poor fellow has had a bad cold, and his wetting has made it no better. We are much in want of books to read, we can carry only a very few, as our baggage is limited to one camel's load.

It is said that the enemy have got another heavy brass gun, which. I suspect must be an 18- or 24-pr. We have roofed over a couple of mud houses near our battery for guard rooms, one for the officers and one for the blue jackets, and the former has been fitted with a table against the wall, a bed-place, and a round mud fireplace, with a hole in the roof to do duty as chimney. Yesterday a shot grazed along the roof of the guard-rooms, but did no damage beyond enlarging the chimney, and covering me with dust. The accompanying rough plan will give you some idea of our position. The enemy generally fire at our reliefs as they are marched down, but have never hit them.

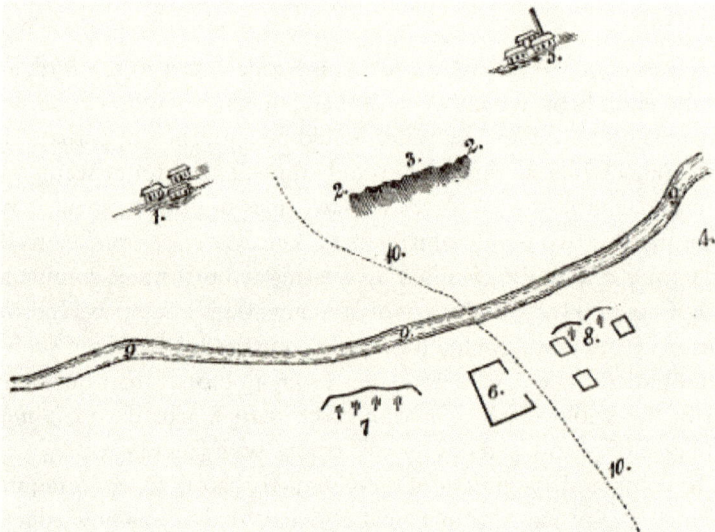

THE RAMGUNGA.

1. A village whence the enemy fire.	6. Guard-rooms.
2. 2. Are rifle-pits.	7. Naval Brigade Battery.
3. A field of sugar-cane.	8. Horse Artillery Battery.
4. Our rifle-pits.	9. The Ramgunga river.
5. A village where the enemy have guns, one of which is a 9-pr.	10. The road to Shajehanpore.

Yesterday a large quantity of planks and beams came from Futte-gurh, and I believe that it is in contemplation to build a bridge lower down the river, where the boats are. For the future our baggage is to be carried on camels instead of in *hackeries* (waggons). The following is my household, a staff of six servants; first, one of our bandsmen, who is of course able to do but little for me, having to look after himself; second, my *kitmagar*, cook, and *valet-de-chambre* by name Sularoo, who receives a salary of ten *rupees* a month; third, my *syce* who looks after the ponies, brings my meals down to me in battery, cleans my shoes, and receives a salary of seven *rupees* a month, by name Ramjean; fourthly is my *bheestie*, who pours a skin full of water over me every morning, provides water for cooking, drinking, and for the horses, goat, and dog, at a salary of five *rupees* a month, by name Rosun: fifthly and sixthly are my two grass-cutters, who look after the ponies under the super-intendence of the *syce*: the one of most exalted rank, who attends on the black horse is known as Mongou, and the junior one who looks after the little white baggage pony is called Beychou; they each receive a salary of five *rupees* a month. A *rupee* is of nearly the same value as a florin, and is a most convenient coin for calculations, being one tenth of a pound.

January 28th.—Yesterday evening I was to have dined with Captain Fremantle of the Rifles, in his tent, but a couple of hours before din-ner time he was ordered on picquet on the Futtegurh road: I begged that the invitation might be allowed to hold good to dine with him on picquet, which he kindly agreed to: accordingly at about seven in the evening, I started on my pony through the rear of the camp. Few things are more puzzling than the geography of a camp, especially by night: fires and lights are abundant, but circles of camels, rows of elephants, and streets of tents are very much alike; by dint of repeat-edly asking my way, I at last came in sight of the little grove where the picquet lay; I was challenged by the sentry and led to the fire by which my friend was sitting; here a few branches had been cut down, and disposed so as to form a roof to keep off the dew, and the floor of this improvised hut was swept and strewn with hay: on this was placed a knapsack covered with a white napkin; we each brought our own knife and fork, our own servants were in attendance, and by the light of the picquet fires and a small dark lantern, the arms of the sentries glancing among the trees, the remainder of the guard sitting round their watch fire with song and jest, I enjoyed as good a dinner as ever I had in my life.

February 2nd.—Yesterday at 3 a.m. we struck tents, and at 4 marched for our old camping ground at Futtegurh, where we now are; and so I suppose that the *sepoys* will boast that they have driven us off. At the same time that we left Ramgunga, the main body of the army marched from this place, and were to proceed to Cawnpore.

February 3rd.—Futtegurh. My little horse has at last recovered from the very serious cough that has laid him up for the last fortnight: I sometimes rig up a hurdle on the parade ground for him to jump over, which he does admirably. The *sepoys* have crossed the Ramgunga

River on whose bank we were encamped, and are now not far from the N E. bank of the Ganges: perhaps our late retrograde movement has increased their confidence, as well as the fact that the floating bridge has been taken to pieces for the purpose of moving it lower down the river.

The habits that Europeans acquire in this country are certainly most luxurious: for instance, even when campaigning, unless we are actually under weigh, the first thing that awakens me in the morning is my *kitmagar* with a cup of delicious coffee: I drink this, half awake, and go to sleep again on the other side, and presently have visions of a warm water lather on my face, and the light touch of a keen razor, wielded by a skilful and unerring hand; a soft handkerchief dipped in warm water seems to be gently passed over my chin, and when I wake about an hour afterwards, lo! I am shaved.

February 4th. —This morning we left Futtegurh and marched twelve miles. I saw this afternoon an enraged elephant, commonly called a "*bobbery-wallah*." He walked straight through the two sides of an uninhabited house, and then with his tusks and trunk began unroofing and pulling down the next one, throwing the pieces of mud and wood in all directions; the owner of the house sat on a neighbouring wall wringing his hands, and uttering the most piteous lamentations: the *mahout* sat quietly on the animal's neck kicking its head to make it go away; after some time this discipline took effect, the animal became more quiet, and returned by the way that it came.

February 5th.—This morning we passed the suspension bridge over the Kallee-Nuddee, where we licked the *sepoys* on the 2nd of January. Between this place and Futtegurh, the sides of the roads were ornamented with the skeletons of *sepoys*, whose grinning skulls were as clean as a knife-handle, having been skilfully picked by the jackals. From being constantly led on the march, and having always to make his home where I make mine, my horse has learnt to follow me like a dog; and this tameness shows itself in most other horses; they do not wish to run away, because they have nowhere to run to.

We hear of reports circulated of the barbarities practised by the *sepoys* upon our countrymen and women, which we believe to be greatly exaggerated; this is a war in which the worst passions are likely to be excited, and without doubt dreadful scenes have been enacted; but I have heard of great cruelties being perpetrated by our own people during some of the sieges in Spain and elsewhere, yet we claim to be the most enlightened nation in the world, and the *sepoys* are comparatively savages. It seems to be a general opinion that in this case a war of extermination *must* be carried on, at any rate for the present, but I feel the greatest compassion for our enemy.

It is idle to speak of the benefits we have heaped upon them; they regard every Christian as lower than a dog, and therefore every benefit is an additional insult; if a European makes use of a native drinking-pot, no Hindoo will drink out of it again, but will throw it away, unless it be of brass, and then he will kindle a fire in it to purify it. The Hindoo is not by nature such an abject being, but circumstances have made him simulate it up to the present time, and I regard them with pity and almost admiration, though this is a sentiment that I cannot expect to be shared by those whose dearest friends have been their victims.

February 8th.—Castor-oil bushes abound on this road; the nut is by no means of a disagreeable taste, but rather the reverse, and is, I believe, as efficacious a medicine as the oil; I wish the doctors would give us the nut instead of its most nauseous extract. We halted this afternoon about thirty-one miles from Cawnpore, and hope to arrive there the day after tomorrow. We hear that the *sepoys* we left at Ramgunga have all gone to Lucknow.

February 9th.—Today we passed the ground where we were encamped on Christmas Day. Nothing can be more desolate than the appearance of a deserted camping-ground; it is astonishing to see the harm that ten thousand men and their followers can do in one night; in an old camping-ground one can trace the lines of the several camps, the places where the horses were picqueted, and where the elephants slept; the ground is strewn with worn-out shakos and accoutrements, broken pots and kettles, old boots and rags, the ashes of camp-fires, and other *debris;* altogether, I think it is one of the most doleful sights in the world, calling up, as it often does, a few happy hours spent there when it was teeming with life, the camp-fires burning brilliantly, and the merry laugh and jest passing from tent to tent; perhaps an hour or two afterwards the spot is peopled with loathsome, howling jackals, who have been prowling about waiting to pick up any or all offal that may be left behind. Shortly after our camp was pitched, a hare started up and ran through it, and eventually escaped, though chased by various men and dogs; about half an hour afterwards, a small deer started up, and, after being nearly caught, also succeeded in making its escape.

February 10th.—I rode into Cawnpore this evening in advance of Brigadier Walpole's brigade, to announce their vicinity. I dined with Captain Peel, who showed me a wonderful hen; every evening she comes into his tent, and cackles until he places his portmanteau across one corner, when she retires behind it for the night, and the next morning lays an egg.

February 11th.—This morning the whole of Brigadier Walpole's brigade—*i. e.* the 2nd and 3rd battalions of the Rifle Brigade, H.M. 23rd, and detachment of the Naval Brigade with four guns, under command of Lieut. Vaughan—rejoined the main army, which tomorrow morning starts for Lucknow, towards which place Mr. Church, with two guns, under the command of Lieut. Wilson, have gone with an advanced brigade this evening; we are now encamped on the south side of Cawnpore.

CHAPTER 7

Capture of the Dilkushah

February 12th.—4.30 a.m. Struck tents and proceeded across the bridge of boats over the Ganges towards Lucknow. These bridges of boats over the Indian rivers are very remarkable, and it is only by this plan that they can be bridged, except at a very great expense; they have to be reconstructed every year. As soon as the floods, brought on by the rains, begin to fall, a number of large boats, of some fifteen or twenty tons, are securely moored across the river, with the exception of two in the middle, which can be removed to allow trading craft to pass; planks are laid across from one end to the other, and covered with straw and earth; large platforms are then laid down on the soft mud from the bridge to the firm ground. When the river begins to swell in autumn, the platforms are floated away and secured for the succeeding year, and all the barges are moored together. After marching twelve miles, we encamped at Unao. H.M. 53rd accompanied us, also our siege-train, consisting of six 24-prs., six 8-inch 56-prs., two 8-inch howitzers, and eight rocket tubes.

February 13th.—Unao. The right wing of H.M. 93rd Highlanders arrived in camp. Yesterday morning, on our arrival here, all the men of the 53rd left their tents, came out to meet us, and gave us a cheer; when the 93rd arrived this morning, our men with one consent ran out to meet them, and as they approached gave them three cheers; when they passed our guns, where Captain Peel was standing with his officers, they carried arms, and our band played "*Auld Lang Syne.*"

February 15th.—Unao. Today the Naval Brigade races took place, and Captain Peel was umpire; I rode my pony in a steeple-chase, but when going over the course for the fifth and last time, with both stirrup-leathers broken, in taking the last hurdle, neck and neck with the leading horse, my pony fell, and we rolled over and over in the dust together: I was stunned but not hurt, but my pony sprained his shoulder rather severely. Much amusement was created by two of our blue jackets racing on water-buffaloes, urged on by half a dozen men before and behind.

February 17th.—Unao. Every evening we have battery drill, and run our very heavy battery about near the camp; sometimes we form square to receive cavalry, with guns on three faces and the limbers in the rear, and at other times we change the front of the battery with great rapidity, as in light infantry drill. The commander-in-chief witnessed our parade this evening, and expressed his approbation of the way in which our men worked the guns. With drag-ropes, and eighteen or twenty men to each gun, we run them about very well, and really Captain Peel has a splendid command.

On the march our guns are each drawn by twenty-two bullocks, or two elephants; if a gun sticks in the mud, it becomes a most serious matter, as it is no easy task to persuade eleven pairs of bullocks to pull together; but, by taking them out, manning the wheels and drag-ropes with blue jackets, and having an elephant to push behind with his forehead, we never fail to extricate a gun from the worst swamps.

February 21st—Unao. The third battalion of the Rifle Brigade arrived from Cawnpore. Performed divine service; present the Naval Brigade, Royal Artillery, and 42nd Highlanders.

February 22nd. —Unao. We are still waiting for orders to proceed to Lucknow; the usual routine of the day is a ride before parade; at 9 a.m. parade with drill, then breakfast, and sedentary employments throughout the day; at four in the afternoon, parade followed by battery drill, and this succeeded by dinner finishes up the day. Lieut. Vaughan has been promoted to the rank of commander.

February 25th.—4.30. a.m. Struck tents and proceeded on the march, twelve miles, to Buntera: at Bunny Bridge, Lieut. Wilson, with his detachment, joined us, and proceeded with the 79th Highlanders and ourselves to the camping ground. The march of an army at four o'clock in the morning is a very picturesque sight. At about three you are awakened by your servant bringing in a cup of hot coffee and a *chupattie*, a sort of cake, and then you perceive that everything in the tent has been packed up, except the clothes about to be put on: the carpets he rolled up in a corner; the tables and their folding legs are tied together, ready to be placed on the elephant that carries the tent; all the tent pegs have been knocked out except four which just keep the pole from falling; and as we wish each other good morning and sip our coffee, the boatswain's mates pipe "down tents;" we hurry on our things, but before we are dressed our *charpoys* (light bedsteads) are carried out, and the bedding rolled up, and as the last of us steps out of the door, the *calassies* (tent-men) drive out the remaining pegs, and down falls the tent: now all appears to be chaos: large fires are burning, consuming the refuse of the encampment; their fitful lurid glare distorts all shadows, and only seems to make darkness visible; the cries of the natives, the moanings and gurglings of camels, the trumpetings of elephants, the buglings of neighbouring regiments and the shrill pipe of our boatswain's mate add to the confusion: and occasionally a frightened bobbery elephant rushes past in the darkness, regardless of the sharp iron point which the *mahout* is driving into the back of his neck; presently a few lances glimmer in the firelight; we hear the jingling of accoutrements, and the commander-in-chief rides swiftly by, attended by his staff and a small cavalry escort.

At last the boatswain's mates pipe all together—a pause—and we hear "Hands fall in:" immediately everything must be left, baggage, tents, or breakfasts, and we all find our respective companies in the darkness. Captain Vaughan's clear voice rings out: "*Naval Brigade, attention!*" "*Fours right*" "*By your left, quick march!*" and away we go, our band playing the Rifle Brigade March "*I'm ninety-five.*" News has arrived that Brigadier Grant, with a force, went out from Buntera and attacked the rebels at a place about twelve miles off, called Meangunge, taking four guns, and killing four hundred and fifty *sepoys*. The Queen's Bays have today joined the army; as they passed our tents, one horse reared, and rising perpendicularly on his hind legs, overbalanced himself and fell back on his rider; to my astonishment both got up and shook themselves, the trooper remounted and took up his place again in the troop. The breech-loading carbine, with which this regiment is armed, is very heavy even if held with both hands but yet is intended to be fired with one hand only.

February 26th.—Buntera. The great question in England now seems to be "How are we to govern India?" Ought it not rather to be "What sort of people are now thrown upon our hands to be governed?" There seems to be some idea that, since we have shown our military superiority, we can govern India as we like; but this is far from being the case; the rebellion, except, in Oude, has been confined entirely to the one class, the *sepoys*; over them only have we shown our superiority, and not over the mass of the Hindoos. I do not believe that the mutiny has been caused, by the Civil Government, though that may also have been defective, but by military misrule, and the contempt for the natives so universal among the English in the country. If any indiscreet measures are introduced by the new form of government, whatever that may be, I should not be surprised if they were followed by a revolt more serious than the present mutiny.

Some few Hindoos have commanded my respect and sympathy, for all I feel much pity. They contain the elements of a fine and noble people, and it remains to be seen whether religion and civilisation will precipitate the dross, or whether harsh measures are indispensable. The accounts we hear of the fertility of India, its aptness for railroads, the abundance of water for agricultural purposes, and its various climates suitable for the production of every tree, vegetable, or flower in the world, are in no degree exaggerated. The governing of such an invaluable country as India might become, is a subject which cannot receive too much consideration, and so inexhaustible that a life-time would not be thrown away upon it. I think that much harm is done in this country by Englishmen who have made a good deal of money out here, and encourage a feeling of contempt for the natives.

It is indeed a great puzzle how India is to be governed; at present, the English in the country are *all* gentlemen; there is no class that is considered as the aristocracy, except a few officials at Calcutta; there is no lower class, except a very few English servants; the country is therefore ruled by the magistrates and a few of the richer natives, while all the labouring work is done by the Hindoos: from all which I gather that the simplest way to rule India would be to colonise it; to *make* a lower class who would farm and cultivate the land themselves, which in many parts might be done, except perhaps during the three hottest months. I can see too that the English in the country despise the Hindoos, especially since the mutiny, quite as much as the Hindoos despise them: one great difficulty with which the government has to grapple is the attachment to caste.

February 28th.—Today the sacrament was administered by the Rev. Mr. Ross, in the mess-tent of the 42nd Highlanders, and amongst others present was Brigadier Adrian Hope. This holy rite, performed in a foreign land, amid the bustle and hurry of a camp, on the bare earth, with a few yards of canvas for a covering, was most impressive, and conveyed a lesson of the omnipresence of the Almighty, which will long be remembered by the few who knelt together on that day. This morning, Sir Colin Campbell left Cawnpore, and passed us on his way to Alumbagh, returning here in the evening, a ride of upwards of sixty miles. The activity of our veteran chief, tires out many younger members of his staff.

March 2nd. —Yesterday I went to see the Alumbagh, and paid a visit to my friend Major Guise of the 90th. The Alumbagh was formerly the residence of the queen-mother. For a palace the house is rather small; it is at present surmounted by a telegraph and surrounded by a walled garden: the latter has been almost completely destroyed, and is cut up in all directions by zigzags leading to batteries at its angles, There is also a battery in front of the main gate. The Alumbagh is about three miles from Lucknow, and from the top of the house the beautiful domes and minarets of the city are plainly visible. No firing, except from small arms, was going on during my visit. The palace must formerly have been beautifully ornamented, as the walls are still prettily painted.

Afterwards we rode to Jellalabad, which is about one mile distant from the Alumbagh; it is a curious old fort, with very strong thick mud walls, which we are now putting into a tolerable state of defence, to be used as a large depository for all sorts of commissariat stores. On my return to camp, the news arrived of Captain Peel's appointment as A.D.C. to Her Majesty, and receiving the decoration of K.C.B. Yesterday morning, there was an alarm that the *sepoys* were attacking us, and the whole army got under arms; but it turned out to be all a mistake. Captain Peel went away this morning at four o'clock, with two guns and two howitzers, under command of Lieut. Young, and I believe that he is gone with Sir Colin and other troops to occupy the Dilkushah, which will probably give them a little fighting.

March 3rd.—Last night, at half-past ten, just as we had all comfortably turned into bed and were enjoying our first doze, orders arrived to strike tents and proceed on the march; so there was no help for it but to turn out again. We marched the whole night in company with the 93rd and 42nd Highlanders, and did not reach our camping-ground, in rear of the Dilkushah, until 10-30 a.m. Our march was only seven miles, but it lasted twelve hours, on account of the narrowness and bad state of the roads, losing our way in the dark, and the difficulty we experienced in getting our guns through the tortuous approaches of the ancient fortress of Jellalabad. The Dilkushah was taken yesterday afternoon, with but little loss; we had two men mortally wounded. I went there today; it is a fine-looking old house, commanding a splendid view from the upper balconies.

On the right is the blue winding River Goomtee, an inconsiderable stream at this time of year, with fertile plains stretching beyond it. On the right front is that splendid building the Martinière College, having two guns at one corner doing a good deal of mischief to our battery of four guns. In front of the Martinière is a loop-holed wall, used by the *sepoys* as a rifle-pit, and opposed by a similar one for our riflemen. In front of the Dilkushah is another gun, partially concealed by trees; in the distance are seen the domes and minarets of Lucknow, looking not unlike a view of Stamboul from the land side: on the left stands our camp. I remained in our battery for about an hour, the firing not being very heavy, or the enemy's guns particularly well aimed.

CHAPTER 8

Siege of Lucknow

March 4th.—Today our guns all came into park, being replaced by four artillery guns, which took up the position. We have buried one of our petty officers, named Terry, who. had been doing duty as sergeant-major; he was severely wounded by a round shot in the upper part of the leg; the same shot wounded another man, who still survives, carrying away a portion of his skull and brain. Captain Oliver Jones, who is serving as a volunteer with H. M. 53rd, has distinguished himself, being the second to mount a breach at the capture of a neighbouring fort; he received a wound on the knuckles, but cut down the fellow who gave it to him. A bee has made herself a nest in a hole in our bamboo tent-pole, and there she lives as snug as possible; in the day time she comes out and flies about, at night creeps into her nest, and on the march travels in her tent-pole; I am not sure that we have not got a pair; we frequently see one passing in or out, the hole being of about this size and shape.

I hear that we have with us pontoons, and when at Jellalabad the other day I saw a portable raft on empty casks floating on a pond with a gun on it.

March 5th.—Here is a rough plan to give some idea of our battery, *a*, is the River Goomtee; *b*, is the Martinière; *c*, the Dilkushah; *d,* is the battery I visited the day before yesterday, which was then held by our guns, but is now in charge of the siege-train, *e,* is the position of Lucknow; *f* of our camp; *g*, represents two bridges across the Goomtee,

RELIEF
LAKHN
ENEMY
IN GROVES AND
HIGH CROPS
INFANTRY
INFANTRY
PARK WALL
KÁNÉGOIA
VILLAGES
VILLAGES
VILLAGE
Lines of Retreat
Lines of Retreat
GOOMTI
RIVER

Cawnpore Road

Clole Bridge, Bridge

CITY OF LAKHNAO

GROVES
OCCUPIED BY
ENEMY

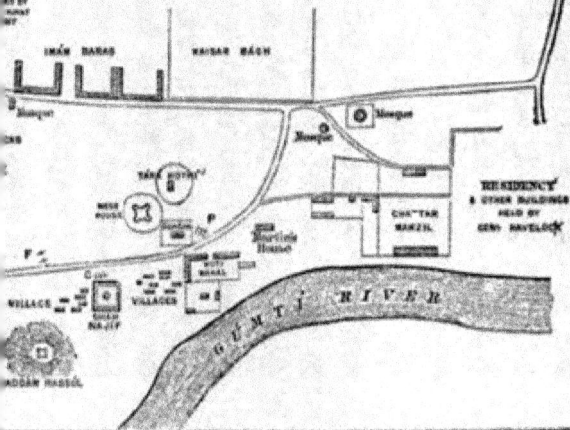

REFERENCES.

A.	Heavy Horse Artillery	E.	Naval Brigade breaching Mess House
B.	Breaching Battery	F.	Mortar Battery shelling „ Do.
C.	Naval Brigade breaching the 61th Regt.	P.	Naval Brigade breaching Palace Bldgs
D.	Mortars shelling the 61th Regt.		

NOTE.

In Artillery positions the ‼‼‼ does not denote the correct number of Guns,
only as general terms, that it is an Artillery Battery.

IMÁM BARAS

KAISAR BÁGH

Mosque

Mosque

Mosque

TÁRÁ KOTHI

MESS
HOUSE

RESIDENCY
& OTHER BUILDINGS
HELD BY
GENL HAVELOCK

CHUTTAR
MANZIL

Martins
House

VILLAGE

VILLAGE

GUMTÍ RIVER

only one of which is as yet finished.

The artillery guns are marked ✝ ✝

Those of the Naval Brigade ⚲ ⚲ ,

And the enemy's guns, as near as I could guess, ⚲ ⚲ .

PLAN OF THE *SHANNON'S* NAVAL BRIGADE BATTERY.

We left camp this morning at half-past nine, with two guns and four guns crews under the command of Lieut. Wilson, with Lieut. Wratislaw and Mr. Richards, who passed for a midshipman about a fortnight ago: we had not brought our guns into position ten minutes, before the *sepoys* opened fire on us from their two guns at the corner of the Martinière, and the second or third shot struck the ground within six feet of where I stood and enveloped me in a cloud of dust; my comrades thought I was killed, and were surprised to see me standing in the same place when the dust cleared away. I should not wonder if an attack were made on the bridge tonight; it is constructed of wood lashed on empty casks, and appears to be well and strongly put together: the enemy are keeping up an occasional fire of round shot on it, but are doing no damage, as it is protected by the banks of the Goomtee. At 8 p.m. the enemy opened fire with shells made of brass, which we did not return, and they were then quiet for the remainder of the night.

March 6th.—Here is another rough outline of our position: *a,* is the Dilkushah; *b,* the Martinière; *c,* is Lucknow; and *d,* the Goomtee; *e,* shows the position of the two bridges, and *f,* of the guns which annoyed us yesterday; this morning at 2 a.m. thirty guns of Horse Artillery, H.M. 23rd Fusiliers, and 79th Highlanders, the 1st Bengal Fusiliers, and Cavalry, under command of Sir James Outram, began crossing the river, and, proceeding by the track I have marked *g*, took in rear the guns marked *f*, and are now marching towards where the old cantonments stood. While the troops were crossing, I observed a young man in spectacles on a small pony, riding unobtrusively about, giving a quiet order here and stopping a dispute there, always listened to with, respect; I inquired who he was, and learned that it was General Mansfield, the Chief of the Staff.

OUTLINE OF THE SHANNON'S
NAVAL BRIGADE POSITION

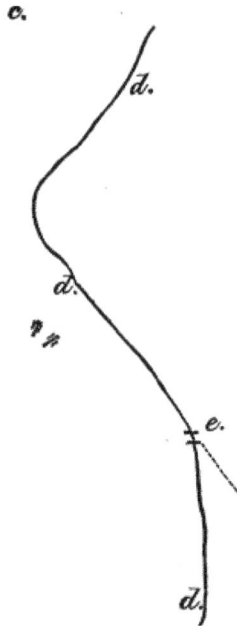

At daylight the enemy opened fire upon the troops crossing, which we returned, and then changed the position of our guns further to the left. At 10 a.m. we observed the Horse Artillery and Cavalry engaging the enemy among the *topes* of trees on the other side of the river from which they were effectually driven and their guns captured. Sir James Outram has siege guns with him, so Lucknow will be threatened from three points—the Alumbagh, the Dilkushah, and the cantonments where Sir James is in force. We slept very comfortably in battery last night, except when a little rain fell. .

March 7th.—This day has been comparatively quiet, an occasional

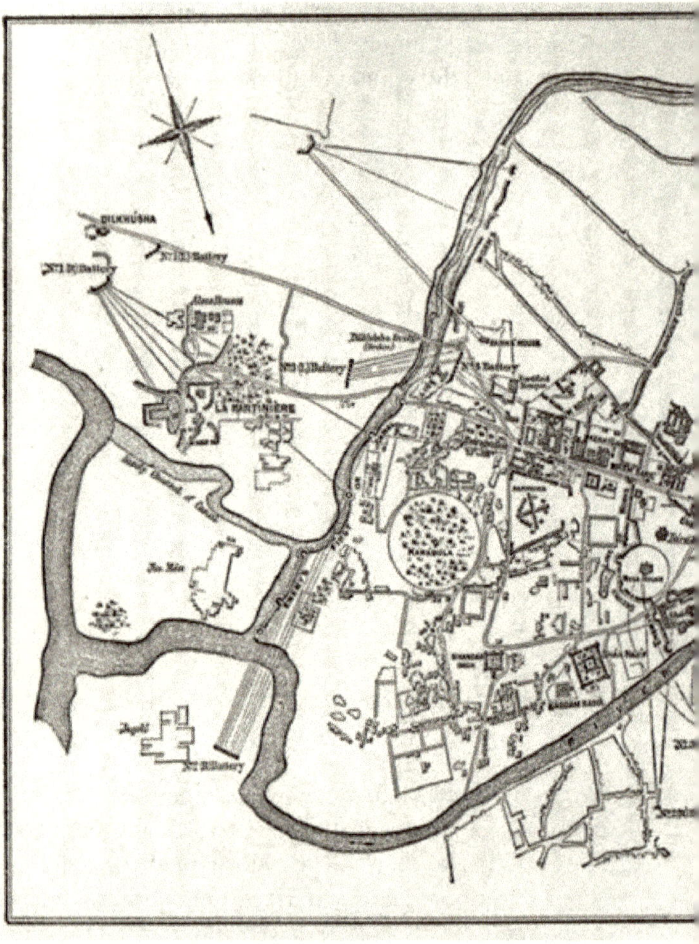
DILKHUSHA
LA MARTINIERE

PLAN
to illustrate the operations of the
BRITISH ARMY
BEFORE
LAKHNAO
IN MARCH 1858.

fire only being kept up on the Martinière.

March 8th.—This afternoon we withdrew our guns from the river, so now all our battery is together in park.

March 9th.—At 3 a.m. our six 8-in. guns and two 24-prs. went down in front of the Dilkushah, with four rocket *hackeries*, the whole under command of Captain Vaughan, accompanied by Lieuts. Young, Salmon, and Wratislaw, Mr, Daniel, and Lords Walter Kerr and Arthur Clinton, midshipmen; Captain Peel is also down there with his two A.D.C.'s Watson and Lascelles. In giving the strength of the Naval Brigade, I have heretofore forgotten to mention two brass field-pieces, a 6-pr. and a 24-pr. howitzer, also eight rocket tubes mounted on *hackeries*. When General Grant was away with his brigade, and took the fort of Meangunge, about seven hundred mutineers were executed, and to save ammunition five were placed one behind the other; it was then found that a Minié bullet passed through the bodies of the first four and killed the fifth.

Yesterday I rode over the Gurkhas' camp, but did not find them such short men as I had been led to expect. With their celebrated knives, they are said to cut off a bullock's head with one blow. Even now, as I am writing, Watson, Captain Peel's A.D.C. arrives with the news that he has been wounded; he went out with his usual nonchalance to find a suitable place for some guns to be posted to breach the outer wall of the Martinière, when he was shot in the thigh by a musket ball; he was taken to the Dilkushah, and the bullet extracted by the surgeon of the 93rd Highlanders. The wound is dangerous, it having been necessary to cut the ball out from the opposite side of the leg to that at which it entered: this news causes us all the deepest concern, as we have such great admiration and regard for him.

At 2 p.m. several regiments marched to the Dilkushah to be ready to storm the Martinière: at 3, the 42nd and 93rd Highlanders with some artillery and Sikhs left the Dilkushah and got under cover of a wall two or three hundred yards from the Martinière; a heavy fire of musketry was kept up by the enemy as the troops marched down, but no casualties occurred: after a short time the Highlanders rushed into the open and crossed the field to the Martinière, hardly a shot being fired: as soon as the enemy saw us preparing to storm they withdrew their guns, evacuated their trenches, and fled to the rear of the Martinière, leaving that building in our possession without the loss of a man. As soon as we had occupied it, a heavy fire was opened upon us from the first line of defences in its rear, but this, being enfiladed by Sir James Outram from the opposite side of the river was stormed and captured by the Highlanders on the same evening.

March 10th.—This morning one of our men was slightly wounded in the lower part of the leg; this is our first casualty, with the exception of Captain Peel's wound of yesterday, and the two men mortally wounded at the capture of the Dilkushah. We know very little of what goes on in the front, as we are obliged to remain in camp in case we are wanted, and we cannot believe all the reports that reach us. Tomorrow I am ordered down to relieve the battery with Richards, midshipman, and the whole of the first company under command of Lieut. Wilson: our guns have now pushed on to Banks's bungalow. I went this afternoon to see that palatial building the Martinière; it is indeed splendid in design and perfect in execution, and the view from the top is very extensive and magnificent. Captain Peel is going on as well as can be expected.

Several regiments have moved today into the park in front of the palace of the Dilkushah, which, as well as the Martinière, will be used as a hospital. I went to the corner of the latter where the enemy had those two guns that did them such good service: a bank rising on one side afforded good natural protection, and accounts for our having been unable to dismount their guns with our shot. In front of the college is an artificial lake from the centre of which rises a single column on an arched foundation, water in this climate being an essential in a "*parterre.*"

March 11th.—Opened fire on the *begum's* palace, and advanced an 8-inch howitzer on the right. 1 p.m. Advanced two guns on the right front to within about a hundred and fifty yards of the Begum Kothee. 4.30. The Begum Kothee stormed and captured by H.M. 90th and the 93rd Highlanders, and regiment of Feroozepore, supported by H.M. 38th and the 42nd Highlanders.

March 12th.—Yesterday, about the middle of the day, I came down with the first company to relieve battery. We found our men at (1), where we had three guns; we had also guns at Banks's Bungalow (2); at the same time Captain Vaughan commanded another battery at about (4); while we were busily employed breaching the wall of the Begum's palace at (6) from (1), and Captain Vaughan was breaching another wall at (5) from (4), we heard the sad news that poor Garvey had just been killed by a shell from one of our own mortars at (15).

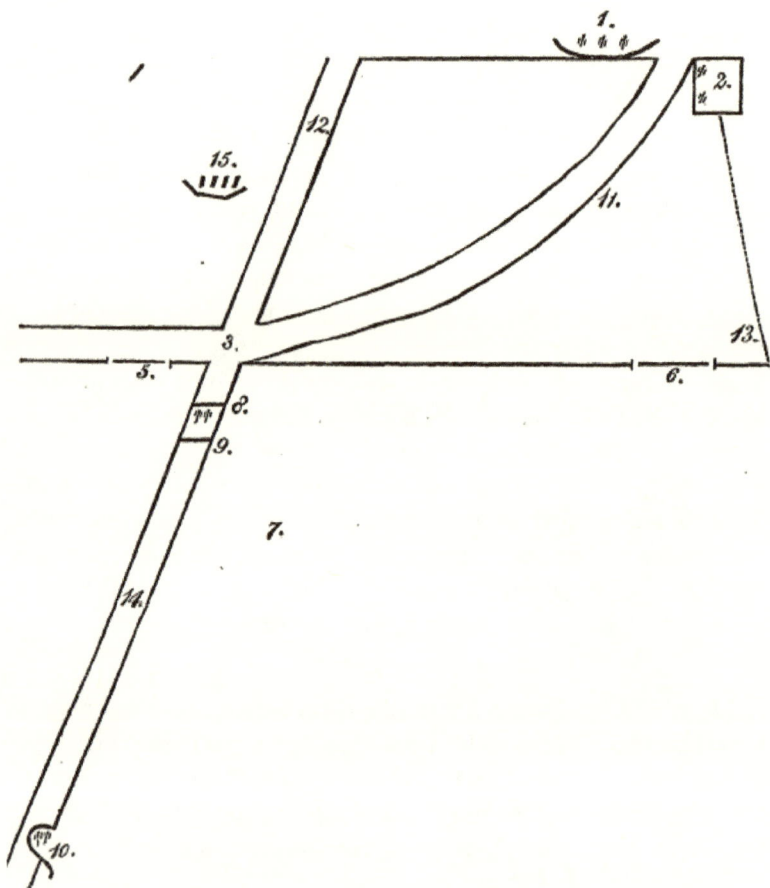

PLAN OF ATTACK ON THE BEGUM'S PALACE.

He was riding very fast to deliver a message, and had occasion to pass before a row of *cohorns*; he did not see that the quick-matches were alight until too late to stop, and the charges igniting, one shell struck him on the head, causing of course instantaneous death; the horse on which he was riding escaped unhurt. Thus for the second time we have lost one of our most promising young officers, and I have lost an intimate friend and affectionate messmate. Poor Garvey! he had a warm heart. At about 5 p.m. the breach was considered practicable; General Sir Robert Napier decided on the precise moment when the firing should cease; officers commanding batteries, and those told off to lead the storming parties compared their watches.

At this moment an officer, in a half-Oriental half-European uniform, mounted on a magnificent Arab, galloped up, followed by half-a-dozen native officers gorgeously dressed and also mounted on Arabs; it was Captain Hodson of Hodson's Horse, and this was the last time we were to behold the gallant fellow. It was a sight worth seeing that Englishman commanding and holding in check such a wild body of Sikhs, and yet beloved by them and admired by all who knew him; and even his dress was striking, the red turban on his head, and the cashmere scarf round his waist showing his connection with his wild horsemen. He dismounted, and leaving his horse in our battery, exchanged a few pleasant words with us, and walked cheerily down to where the storming party were anxiously awaiting the agreed-on moment.

A few seconds before their time, the storming party of the gallant 93rd rushed from their cover, led several yards ahead by their noble commander Captain Clarke, who ran up to the breach waving his sword and shouting out "Come on, 93rd!" His men gave one loud and continuous cheer, some hoisting their bonnets on the points of their bayonets, and in a few moments the space between our battery and the breach was swarming with kilted Highlanders. Suddenly, however, came a check, as they found that a deep trench had been cut in front of the wall: this however had been foreseen by Sir Robert Napier who had ordered a house to be knocked into where he supposed it would be (13); to this point the troops now swarmed, and crossing the ditch disappeared behind the wall.

From this time little more could be seen from our battery; occasionally a few *sepoys* would be observed clambering over a wall or along the roof of a house, and one would make good his escape, and another would fall back shot through; and occasionally a soldier ap-

213

pearing on the wall, perhaps in pursuit of a fugitive, would be greeted with a sailor's cheer; the air resounded with the cries of the wounded and dying, the cheers of our soldiers, and the echoes of a dropping fire, it was at this time that Captain Hodson was mortally wounded. Gradually, as all became still, we knew that the enemy's second line of defence was captured, and the Begum Kothee was in our hands; at the same time that the 93rd stormed at (6), another party stormed opposite Captain Vaughan's battery at (5), and were equally victorious.

A gun from our battery, and a gun from the battery at (4), then advanced down the road to (3), Captain Vaughan coming by the road marked (12), and we by that marked (11); thence we began firing over the *sepoys'* earthwork at (8), back through their own embrasures, at a confused multitude of them retreating down the road, (14) to (10), where they had a semi-circular battery: once safe in this they opened a smart fire on us, which would have done much harm, as they knew our distance so accurately, had we not been protected by their own earthwork: we could not see over it to point our guns, but Captain Oliver Jones, at no small personal risk, planted himself on the top and directed our fire.

We took the *sepoy* guns at (8), and during last night moved our two guns round to a breastwork we had thrown up at (9), where they now are, and the rest of them into park in a neighbouring garden. The *sepoys* in derision have hoisted the union jack over their circular battery. Last night I went into the breach that we had made, and found the courts and gardens covered with the bodies of slain *sepoys*: I went there again this morning, and saw a deep ditch full of them. At the back of the palace was a small chapel, full of *Korans* and chandeliers, such as are to be seen in every mosque. The palace had been fitted up beautifully, the walls ornamented with splendid mirrors and the ceilings with chandeliers; everything of this kind was of course smashed, but those men who first got in found numbers of cashmere shawls, valuable silks, &c, and even a few gold *mohurs*. Last night we slept at our guns, which we did not find unpleasant, the weather being quite warm, but the flies and mosquitoes rather uncourteous.

March 13th.—This afternoon I went down to our guns, and found that they had advanced, as in the plan: *a* is the advanced wall of the *begum's* palace which was taken on the 11th; *b* is an entrance we made in it for our guns to advance to the court *c*, having a mosque in the centre; they then passed through the wall by a hole *d* into the yard *m*,

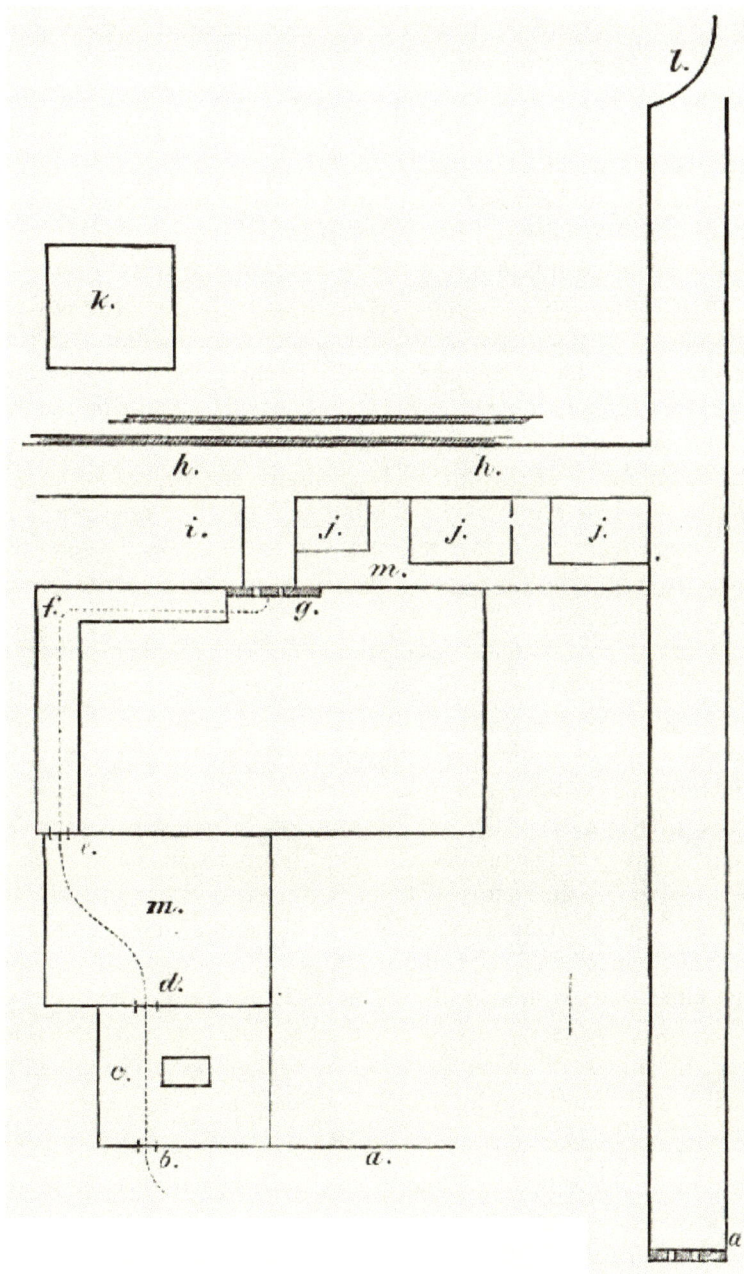

MORE EXTENDED PLAN OF ATTACK ON THE BEGUM'S PALACE

and thence by a breach at *e*, through a long shed *f*, to a gate *g*, where a breastwork was thrown up for them; our troops then took possession of the houses *j* and the garden *n*, and commenced a withering fire upon the *sepoys* who were in the house *i*, and all along the opposite side of the street *h*, which is about twenty yards wide; *k* is the small Imaum-barah, the immediate object of attack, to reach which it is first necessary to breach two walls.

The Imaum-barah is a large square building, containing but one room, which is used as a sort of mosque, and is profusely decorated with gilding and enormous coloured glass chandeliers: *l* is a *sepoy* semi-circular battery, and *o* is the battery we took possession of yesterday. I was not on duty, so I went with Kerr into the house *j*, nearest to *k*, to reconnoitre; suddenly we heard a yell and a cheer, and the *sepoy* bugles from two different quarters sound successively the alarm, the assembly, the advance, and the double; Kerr and I rushed back to our guns at *g*, the skirmishers evacuated their advanced post, and also fell back upon the guns, where we found all the troops drawn up under arms, the officers with swords drawn and pistols in hand; we waited for a few minutes in breathless anxiety, but the *sepoys* only set on fire the house *i*, and then retired.

I waited until our guns again opened fire, and was then compelled to return into camp; immediately after my departure, some sand-bags, forming the front of our battery, caught fire. A coloured man, of the name of Hall, a Canadian, gallantly jumped out and extinguished some, and threw far away others that were burning; in the performance of this exploit, under a heavy fire of bullets from loopholes not forty yards distant, he was severely wounded, and Her Majesty has since been pleased to award to him the Victoria Cross; he was always, a man remarkable for his steady, good conduct, and his athletic frame; at a foot-race in camp, he had distanced by far all competitors, and I have never seen his superior either as. a swimmer or diver. This evening we buried poor Garvey under some cypress trees in the garden of the Dilkushah; all the brigade in camp attended the funeral, and many military officers to whom he had endeared himself by his frank and affectionate character.

March 14th.—This morning, having advanced our guns to within fifty yards of the Imaum-barah, it was captured with very little loss. At about noon I rode down towards our guns with Captain Vaughan, Kerr, and Lascelles, when we saw two or three officers on horseback, apparently unable to find their way across the canal; Kerr suddenly called out, "Why that is Sir James Outram," and so indeed it proved to be; he had crossed the lower bridge over the Goomtee, ridden past the Residency and through the Kaiser Bagh into our lines; we directed him to the headquarters, and rode on. The rebels had only prepared for the attack on the town from the direction of the Dilkushah, and had thrown up three strong lines of defence in that direction; but Sir James Outram, crossing the river, not only attacked the town on the side on which it was almost totally undefended, but enfiladed the defensive works, one after the other.

On arriving at our guns we dismounted, and proceeded on foot, leaving our horses to the care of our *syces*; we passed through the court of the Imaum-barah, which was strewn with the dead and dying, through breaches in walls and fortifications, through the remains of Oriental gardens, and through all the horrible indications of the recent skirmishing, until, on nearing the Kaiser Bagh, we met Sir Colin Campbell; he desired Captain Vaughan to bring up a gun's crew of blue jackets to man an abandoned gun, which was to be turned against the retreating enemy; Kerr was sent back for the gun's crew, and we proceeded on to the gun itself, which was at a gate of an outer court of the Kaiser Bagh. We found that a body of *sepoys* were defending themselves in an adjoining court, and it was necessary to blow away the gate of it that the troops might storm, and it was for this object that Sir Colin ordered the guns to be turned against them; in the meanwhile, however, they kept up a continual fire on us from the walls over and round the gate when we approached the gun.

Captain Vaughan then fired a few rounds at the gate, I sponging and loading, three of the *Shannon's* bandsmen bringing up the powder and shot, and some men of the 38th, under command of Lieut. Elles, running the gun up after every round; our position at this time was very hazardous, as on our right was a house containing very large quantities of gunpowder, in some rooms lying in loose heaps on the floor three or four feet high, and in others contained in huge earthen *chatties*; moreover, the adjoining house to this was in flames, probably purposely kindled by the *sepoys*; a sentry was, however, posted to give warning in time, if the flames approached the loose powder.

Captain Vaughan now went back to meet the gun's crew that had been sent for, and to show them the way, leaving orders with me to keep up the fire; the *sepoy* charges were so heavy that the shot went clean through the solid gate every time we fired, merely leaving a small loophole, through which the enemy fired at us; by reducing the charges with every shot, the firing at last began to tell; when the party of blue jackets came up, under command of Lieut. Hay, the gate was blown open, and the court captured by the company of the 38th, I then proceeded further to explore the palace: I forced open the large door of a building, which I discovered to be the King of Oude's coach-house; this was full of carriages, some of which were very curious; one was a long car, a sort of roofless omnibus, with gaudy decorations, very like the car drawn by an elephant, a cameleopard, and a pair of ostriches, which heads the procession of a travelling menagerie making its triumphal entry into a quiet country town.

But there was one carriage, evidently the work of European hands, of a style of magnificence that I have never beheld before or since: all parts of the carriage, the wheels, the springs, and the frame, that are usually painted and varnished, were covered with thick plates of solid silver, and the appearance of the whole was perfectly dazzling, as the brilliant sunlight of an Indian spring poured upon it; the inside and the cushions were covered with the richest white silk, and in the box stuck a silver whip, with a lash of silver wire, of which I possessed myself. About an hour afterwards, I again passed this coach-house; the white silk had all been cut or torn off and carried away, nearly all the silver had disappeared, with the exception of one or two places where men were busily engaged hammering it off.

I now climbed on to the roof of a neighbouring house to try and gain some idea of the geography of the palace: at my feet was a garden, on the opposite side of which stood another house; four or five men were running among the bushes, exchanging shots with men in the opposite house; at first it was difficult to tell which were English and which *sepoys*, but the men in the garden soon came directly under me; they did not perceive me looking down on them, but I saw that *they* were *sepoys*, and could easily have shot one had I had my revolver, but I carried only my sword; at last two of them were shot, and the remainder escaped through a side door.

After this I went over some portions of the Kaiser Bagh, but really an attempt to describe it would be vain: my wildest dreams of Oriental splendour were more than realised: I saw luxury, wealth, priceless silks, cashmeres, pictures, gilding, glass, and china, to an extent I hardly believed to have existed, and room after room was fitted up in a style of lavish magnificence devoid of taste: the principal court of the palace was of very great extent, containing gardens, aviaries, and conservatories; in the centre was an artificial lake spanned by a bridge of white marble, and fined all round with the same; at one end stood a pavilion of the most beautiful coloured marbles, and at the other a white marble mosque, much discoloured, however, by fire.

I entered a detached building in flames, which had been used as an armoury, and in spite of the great heat, succeeded in bringing out a helmet of Damascus steel inlaid with gold, and having Persian characters worked on various parts of it; hence also I brought away a *tulwar*, some bows and arrows, a powder-horn of inlaid mother-of-*pearl*, and two standards: I also found a long straight sword of very curious workmanship, and meeting my servant I gave it him to carry up to camp for me; a quarter of an hour later he was walking with another man, when three *sepoys* attacked him; they had no arms but this sword, and with it they killed one *sepoy* and put the the others to flight; my sword, however, was broken, and my servant severely wounded in the hand.

Shortly afterwards I met a *doolie-wallah* carrying a red standard with the King of Oude's arms embroidered on it in gold: now I thought that this being a trophy of war, was hardly a proper possession for a non-combatant, and I suggested this to him; as he made no opposition he apparently viewed the matter in the same light, so, with as little discourtesy as possible, I seized it. In another part of the garden, I saw a crown lying on the ground; it was made of cardboard and red satin, stiffened with rusty iron wire, and sewn all over with dull white beads; it appeared to have been used either for private theatricals or for a child's toy: I tore off half a dozen of the beads which I put into my pocket as mementos of the day.

I saw a room full of little cabinets, every cabinet was fall of little drawers, and every drawer was full of little bottles containing scents and spices, some were liquid and some solid; some agreeable and some very nasty, some like pills and others like their concomitants, but as there were none that I liked, I left them for the next comer. I met a man with a little bag full of gold coins, which he had just found and bought one for half a sovereign; at last, thoroughly wearied out, I returned to camp, and gave away the beads I had plucked off the tawdry crown; but imagine my astonishment, when I was told that they were most beautiful pearls. I afterwards received one of them back, and estimated, at a rough guess, that the whole crown must have been worth two thousand pounds.

Facsimile of gold coin.

Chapter 9

Siege of Lucknow Continued

March 15th.— Two guns were advanced up to the mess-house, which was stormed and taken by the 42nd Highlanders. We hear that many lives have been lost by powder blowing up, which was left about loose in large quantities by the *sepoys*, probably on purpose. One of our engineers, Henri, purchased a sword and belt from a Sikh for 1*l.*; the knowing Sikh had touched the hilt with a file to see if it was silver gilt, but finding it the same colour throughout, sold it: Henri was much astonished to find that the hilt and mountings of the scabbard and belt were all of solid gold; some jewels which had been inlaid in the hilt were extracted before he bought it.

March 16th.—3. p.m. Four guns were advanced and got into position in the Residency, and the Great Imaum-barah was captured. 7. Opened fire on the city with shells and rockets. This afternoon I went to the Kaiser Bagh with Lieut. Young, and we climbed to the top of a large building containing a throne room and hall of audience. Here was a gallery which had been used as a look-out place; but before we had been there many minutes, we found ourselves the centre of general attention; a number of *sepoys* who were still hanging about the palace opened fire upon us: of course at that great elevation, and from their rude matchlocks, the shot were very erratic, but still on the whole we deemed it prudent to descend: in some storehouses at the base of the building we found large crates of crockery emblazoned with the King of Oude's arms, which had never been opened, and were evidently of French manufacture: we sent into camp as much as we needed for our own use; a day or two later I passed the same spot, and saw that the whole of this beautiful china had been wantonly smashed. From one of the rooms, I cut a couple of pictures out of their frames, but almost all of them had been destroyed or defaced by swords and bayonets. In one of the courts I picked up a plated bit mounted with the royal arms of Oude.

March 17th.—Yesterday evening six of our guns were advanced to the Residency, where they now are, occasionally firing a shot over the town: all seems quiet, and there is a report that the inhabitants are going to ransom their city, and turn the *sepoys* out. I have purchased several arms that have been looted in the city; amongst others an old flint lock fowling-piece the stock and barrel of which are most beautifully inlaid with silver and gold, the sights and flash-pan being of pure gold. I have been into the Dilkushah to see Captain Peel and to give him a *tulwar* which he asked me to procure for him; the halls of that palace were crowded with sick soldiers, most of whom were burnt all over from head to foot by the dreadful explosions that have taken place in the city; they were covered with cotton wadding, and by the side of each sat a native with a paper fan to keep off the flies: the sighs and groans of these poor fellows, reduced to mere pieces of burnt flesh, were those of men who literally felt life to be a burden, men without hope of recovery to whom death could be but a relief: the scene was most harrowing.

Yesterday morning I went down from our battery in the Residency to the Goomtee with Lieut. Wilson, to have a bathe, but the river was so choked with *sepoy* corpses that we could not make up our minds to jump in. Some of our men caught a goat, milked her and drank all the milk; I then asked for some, but they had none left; however they took her down to the Goomtee, where she drank her fill; they then passed a bowline round her horns, ran her up and down the battery half a dozen times, milked her again, and brought me the milk, which I drank; it was rather watery, but passable under the circumstances. In battery in the Residency we have suffered from a plague of flies; I never before appreciated how terrible a thing a plague of flies could be; they have been bred by the innumerable dead bodies of men and animals; the moment one sits down they settle on every exposed part of the body; they drown themselves in tea and gravy, immolate themselves on the end of cigars, accompany to one's mouth all one's food, and render sleep next to impossible: indeed the only way to obtain any rest is to get under a mosquito curtain; at about sunset the mosquitoes relieve guard, and the flies have their watch below.

I was sent down to the Great Imaum-barah this afternoon to bring up a prisoner from the guard-room. Instead of going through the main street, I tried a shortcut through the native town; I had not ridden five hundred yards from the Residency before I found myself an object of great attraction to numbers of *budmashes* who were skulking about the deserted town, and amused themselves by firing at me from every available window or door. This was not pleasant; so with my revolver in my hand I put my horse into a gallop and dashed along considerably at random, as in those narrow and tortuous streets it was not easy to keep one's dead reckoning; no one attempted to stop me, and I was considerably relieved when I saw the tall minarets of the Great Imaum-barah towering over my head, and heard the sentry's challenge.

From these minarets a beautiful view of the city can be obtained, and its appearance is very picturesque from every house being built round a court containing trees, gardens, and sometimes fountains and greenhouses; thus, when viewed from any height, it looks like succession of gardens. The body of the building of the Great Imaum-barah, which is now used as a barrack, is of white stone, and remarkable for the extreme beauty of its architecture and the delicate tracery of its adornments; it contains a high pulpit covered with exquisitely embossed plates of silver, which is fortunately under the charge of a sentry.

March 21st—We have now in the Residency, four guns and eighty men, who are relieved every forty-eight hours: the town is all apparently quiet, but we know there are still many rebels about. Since we left Calcutta, a drill-sergeant of the 78th Highlanders has been attached to us; yesterday he was sent to rejoin his regiment, with a camel to carry his traps &c.: passing through a portion of the native town, at some distance from our guards, about a dozen *sepoys* suddenly rushed out, killed the camel and its driver, and took his things: providentially he was following a little distance astern, and just escaped with his life.

March 22nd.—The last body of rebels evacuated the town. I have visited the Shah Nujeef, and seen the spot where poor Daniel fell and was buried. The Sikhs are very knowing fellows: a Sikh sergeant will watch a party of Europeans enter a house for the purpose of plundering, and immediately plant sentries all round, and as each man comes out, he is told that there are strict orders against looting, and that he must disgorge his plunder; this of course he does with a very bad grace, and walks away looking sadly crestfallen: as soon as the whole party have thus gone off, the sergeant calls in his sentries, divides the loot, keeping the lion's share for himself, and they all go on their way rejoicing.

March 25. —Captain Peel's wound is still going on favourably. To-day I visited the observatory, which was formerly one of the best in India: it is now little better than an empty house, a few rooms of which have been furnished for the use of General Sir Edward Lugard. When returning to camp, I passed two ladies in a carriage drawn by a pair of oxen; these were Mrs. Orr and Miss Jackson. Mrs. Orr saw her husband, Captain Orr, and Miss Jackson her brother, Sir Mountstuart Jackson, murdered by the *sepoys* at the outbreak of the mutiny. These two ladies were then carried into Lucknow, where they have been kept until a few days ago when they were discovered and released by some English soldiers.

The cruelties to which they have been subjected, are enough to extinguish any feeling of pity that one may retain for the rebels: at one time they were confined in a mud hut containing two rooms, in one of which they were placed while their guards occupied the other; they overheard the wretches talking and agreeing that it was quite right they should be killed, but neither was willing to do the deed: at last one of them got up and went away saying that he would leave the other to do it, and while they sat momentarily expecting their death, the other man arose and also departed, and thus at this time their lives were spared.

When they were first made prisoners Mrs. Orr had a little daughter with her, in connection with whom occurred a remarkable manifestation of Divine Providence. Mrs. Orr first gave out that her child was sick and afterwards that it was dead, and it was then conveyed in a bundle of dirty linen to her brother-in-law in the Alumbagh by a faithful native; when she stated that it was sick, some medicine was given her for it, wrapped up in a piece of torn paper: on examining this, it proved to be a piece of the leaf of a large Bible, and on one side was written:

I, even I, am he that comforteth you; who art thou that thou shouldest be afraid of a man that shall die, and of the son of man which shall be made as grass: and forgettest the Lord thy maker, that hath stretched forth the heavens, and laid the foundations of the earth; and hast feared continually every day because of the fury of the oppressor, as if he were ready to destroy? and where is the fury of the oppressor?

On the other side was written:

Thus saith thy Lord, the Lord, and thy God that pleadeth the cause of his people, Behold, I have taken out of thine hand the cup of trembling, even the dregs of the cup of my fury; thou shalt no more drink it again: but I will put it into the hand of them that afflict thee; which have said to thy soul, Bow down, that we may go aver; and thou hast laid thy body as the ground, and as the street to them that went over.

Surely it is not presumption to regard this as a direct message of consolation from our Heavenly Father to one of His afflicted children.

March 26th.—I rode down to the Residency today. A palace stands on the banks of the Goomtee called the Chutta Munzil, consisting of the usual conglomeration of courts, gardens, and rooms fall of chandeliers; and through this a straight road has been cut to the Bailey Guard Gate of the Residency. I rode first through a court, then a hall, a throne-room, a garden, an artificial pond partially filled up, through more rooms, and at last out through a court and gateway, and it was by this road that our guns were brought up, and all subsequent supplies of ammunition, &c. When I returned, I rode along the banks of the Goomtee; the river was full of dead bodies that had caught among the weeds, and swamped near the Chutta Munzil was a miniature frigate, the ruined houses and palaces gave the city altogether a melancholy air of desolation.

March 27th.—There is a wonderful rhinoceros in the camp, the property of the 53rd; he was found in Lucknow and is very tame; every day he is driven to a well to drink, guided by little taps from a twig which one would have thought could hardly have been felt through his thick hide: if, however, any one ventures to do more than touch him very lightly with it, he at once gets angry. He is very old, poor fellow, and suffers from some sort of ophthalmia, which has rendered him all but blind.

March 28th.—Last night our four guns were withdrawn into park from the Residency. This morning Captain Peel has been out for a little exercise in a *doolie*, and is considerably better. One of our men, who was wounded in the thigh by a musket-ball, died last night of disease of the heart. Poor fellow! he was just recovering from his wound.

March 29th.—Amongst other *souvenirs* of Lucknow, I have got from the palace a very handsome glass chandelier, with four branches; for each branch are two shades, one red and the other clear. We always use two branches; and when we have company to dinner four, which make our tent look very handsome. We hear that Captain Peel is going on as well as can be expected, but his severe wound will take some time to heal. Today we have sent our two 8-in. howitzers and six 8-in. guns into park in the small Imaum-barah; the latter are the guns we brought from the *Shannon*, and we have now handed them over to the artillery; and here they will remain, may I say it with pardonable pride, a memorial of what sailors *can* do on land. The word "*Shannon*" is cut deeply into each carriage, and must last as long as the wood does.

March 30th.—A few days ago I was sent in to the Kaiser Bagh with ten men to bring out one of the King of Oude's carriages for Captain Peel's conveyance to Cawnpore. I selected the best I could find; and, having brought it into camp, our carpenters padded it, lined it with blue cotton, made a rest for his feet, and painted "H. M. S. *Shannon*" over the royal arms of Lucknow: when, however, he saw it today, he declined making use of it, saying that he would prefer to travel in a *doolie* like one of his blue jackets.

CHAPTER 10

Return of the Naval Brigade

April 1st.—This morning at 2 a.m. we struck tents, and passing in the dark through the sleeping camp commenced our march to Cawnpore. Yesterday, in the Kaiser-Bagh, I got a two-wheeled vehicle called a buggy out of the King of Oude's stables, emblazoned with his arms. I have harnessed one of my ponies to it, and it does capitally for carrying crockery and light baggage.

April 2nd.—At 2 a.m. struck tents and proceeded on the march, encamping again at 6.30 on the Lucknow side of Bunny Bridge, which spans the only river between Lucknow and the Ganges. We have this morning had our first taste of the hot winds, and most remarkably like the continued blast of a furnace do they feel.

April 4th.—Encamped at Unao.

April 5th.—This morning Captain Vaughan went away with two companies and two guns to see after some rebels in a neighbouring village. In the meantime we are encamped under the trees of a snug little garden, whose walls afford some protection from the dust and hot winds. At night we have to send out picquets, which is rather dull work.

April 6th.—This morning we marched into Cawnpore. A general order of this evening directs that arrangements be made for sending the Naval Brigade down to Calcutta by bullock-train, which will probably be a journey of about three weeks. Our two guns which left Unao yesterday morning found that the rebels had fled, so they had merely a man-of-war's cruise "there and back again;" the *sepoys* were, however, chased by some Sikh cavalry, who cut them up a good deal. We are to leave here all the remainder of our battery. I have seen the monument erected over the well into which the bodies of the murdered women and children were thrown. This plain and beautiful memorial consists of a stone cross bearing the inscription:

> In memory of the women and children of the 32nd Regiment, who were slaughtered near this spot 16th July, *a.d.* 1857. This memorial was raised by thirty men of the same regiment who were passing through Cawnpore, Nov. 21st, 1857.

Round the circle by which the cross is connected is written:

> I believe in the resurrection of the body.

April 7th.—Tomorrow at 3 a.m. we leave Cawnpore for Calcutta; we depart in three detachments: the first company and the Marines go tomorrow, under command of Lieut. Young; the officers are Captain Gray and Lieut. Stirling, R.M., Lieuts. Wilson and Wratislaw; Way and Richards, midshipmen, and myself. I am sorry to say that one of our midshipmen, Lord Arthur Clinton, is lying dangerously ill at the house of the Rev. T. Moore, the excellent chaplain of this station; another midshipman, Way, is, and has been for a long time very unwell. Among the arms I have brought from Lucknow is a *tulwar* of Damascus steel inlaid with a verse of the *Koran* in gold; a native gentleman here assures me that it must have cost at least 2000 *rupees (200l.)*; I have also a cashmere dressing-gown, which must have been once worth a hundred pounds, although it is now old, worn out, and moth-eaten.

April 8th.—This afternoon we have halted for dinner about twelve miles from Cawnpore, which, we left at 3 a.m.; we have drawn up the officers bullock waggons a little on one side of the road, among some trees; we have spread out our dinner-table on the altar of a picturesque little road-side temple, while a stream running close by furnishes us with water for cooking or bathing, and is most grateful to the eye and ear; we tarry here until the great heat of the day is passed.

April 10th.—Allahabad. We arrived here yesterday evening at about nine, and took up our quarters at the permanent camp; our tents are wonderfully different to what we have been accustomed to up country, far more luxurious: the one in which I am is divided by-a curtain into a dressing and sleeping room, and is double all round; the air between the inner and outer tent, being most efficacious in keeping us cool.

Yesterday we had a specimen of how things are managed in India; we reached Futtehpore at about 10 a.m., and immediately an officer was sent to the railway station to report our arrival, with the number of men and amount of baggage requiring conveyance; in the meantime a letter came, ordering us to be there by three, to go down to Allahabad in the same train with Sir Colin Campbell; accordingly at about half-past two we arrived at the terminus, and found a small train near the platform capable of containing one hundred and twelve men; there was also a long train of trucks containing guns and ammunition waggons which a very stupid *baboo* was landing with a few *coolies*, and a great deal of noise, at the rate of one in twenty minutes: our commanding officer went from one railway official to another, but nobody seemed to know anything about us, or care whether we reached Allahabad or not; he went to the military and commissariat authorities, but they seemed afflicted with the same inertia as everyone else, and said that if there was not room for us all in this train, they supposed we must leave an officer behind to bring the rest of the men on in some other; so when Lieut. Young saw we could get no satisfaction out of any of them he set all our blue jackets to work, and in less than half an hour they had cleared every gun and ammunition waggon from the long train, and stowed all our own baggage in the trucks, and thus we all got down to Allahabad together.

Sir Colin Campbell came down in the same train with us, and made a very complimentary speech to our men, who cheered him heartily. Today the second detachment of the Naval Brigade arrived under command of Capt. Vaughan. Lord Canning, the Governor-General, is here.

April 11th.—5-30 p.m. The third detachment arrived under command of Lieut. Hay. 6. The first detachment started by bullock-train for *Benares*.

April 13th.—8 a.m. Halted for breakfast under a *tope* of trees. 1 p.m. Proceeded. 7.30. Arrived at *Benares*, and took up our quarters at the Mint.

April 14th—6 a.m. The second detachment, under Captain Vaughan, arrived by bullock-train. I have seen a field devoted to what in England would be considered a very extraordinary purpose, namely, the manufacture of ice. The whole field was full of square holes about six inches deep, and between every two was an earthen jar; in the winter, commencing in November, these holes are filled with straw, covered with about fifty shallow earthen-ware saucers; the jars are then filled with water, from which the saucers are filled with a large ladle; the water in the saucers will not freeze unless the straw is kept perfectly dry; early in the morning, the ice is taken out, pounded into lumps, and then put into the ice-houses; if a small piece of pottery accidentally gets in with it, it will eat its way to the bottom of the pit. It freezes at *Benares* about ten nights in the year, during which time, sufficient ice is made to last the inhabitants all the hot season.

April 16th.—The building in which we are quartered was formerly the Mint, and still retains its name though now converted into barracks. We are waiting here for conveyance, all the bullock-waggons being detained somewhere between this and Raneegunge. The day before yesterday, we had a specimen of a real dust-storm; in the evening we first saw a thick brown cloud advancing from the north. Immediately every window was closed and door shut, and presently the air was so darkened that it was impossible to see the road; clouds of dust were whirled round and round, and the ground was soon covered with leaves torn from the trees. At length the storm seemed to abate a little, when suddenly a rushing sound was heard, and the ground became perfectly white with hailstones, many of them as large as a good-sized marble; after a time it all subsided, leaving the air clear, calm, and deliciously cool.

April-17th.—9 a.m. The detachment under Lieut. Hay arrived.

April 18th.—4 p.m. Proceeded by bullock-train across the bridge of boats over the Ganges towards Calcutta.

April 20th.—8 a.m. Arrived at Sasseram, a large but squalid village containing one or two interesting ruins of mosques. 4 p.m. Half the detachment, under command of Lieut. Young, proceeded by bullock-train.

April 22nd.—This morning at 6 a.m. we arrived at Shergotty: a telegraph has arrived directing us all to rendezvous at Raneegunge, as the council at Calcutta desire to give us a public reception. It is very gratifying that the services of the Naval Brigade, especially at the relief of Lucknow, are to be publicly recognised. Marching by bullock-train is not bad fun when one gets used to it, although bullock-waggons are not provided with springs. Carriage is provided for only two-thirds of the men, but for all the officers; one waggon drawn by two bullocks is allowed for every fifteen men; into this their bags and traps are put and ten men get in; the remaining five march as a van and rear-guard and are relieved every four hours; the bullocks are changed about every ten miles.

There is one waggon for every two officers, and all are supplied with roofs and curtains at the sides. The perils and dangers of bullock-tram travelling are as follows: between two stages a bullock may take it into his head to lie down, and thus he will, insist on remaining, regardless of pricks, blows, or blandishments until such time as he sees fit to get up; the consequence is that the unfortunate inhabitants of the waggon are deprived of their rest, and do not reach the next station until it is time to leave it again. Or a bullock may be frightened or pretend to be frightened at anything or nothing, and will rush violently off the road, in spite of all the "*bile-wallah*" can do to stop him, down an embankment, into a river or swamp, sometimes overturning the waggon; such an animal becomes known as a "*bobbery-bile*," one of our men lost his life in consequence of an accident of this kind; on these occasions the whole train has to be stopped, the guards assemble and drag the waggon or what is left of it on to the road again.

Or a wheel or pole may break, and then the contents of that waggon have to be transferred to some other, until some place is reached where one may be procured. Or a *bile-wallah* may fall asleep, and this may lead to any of the afore-mentioned calamities. A bullock-train generally starts at about 4 p.m. and averages two miles an hour. Half an hour before sunset, a couple of servants descend from the waggons, and run on ahead with a bundle of wood and a large kettle; they select a snug spot by the road side near a stream, light the fire, fill the kettle, and put it on; when the last waggon of the train reaches them, the "halt" is sounded, and grog served out to the men; the moment the water boils, perhaps in ten minutes or a quarter of an hour, the "advance" is sounded, the waggons move on, and the officers remain behind to drink their tea; then the servants gather up the traps, and run after and catch up the train.

The van and rear guards are now told off for the night, and the men and officers walk by their waggons smoking and yarning, or at once turn in. The first attempt to sleep in a bullock-waggon is rarely successful, for once or twice during the night the bullocks are changed, and it requires practice to sleep through the shouts of the "*bile-wallahs*," the glaring of the torches, the bellowing of oxen, or occasional anathema of a blue jacket whose temper is put to a more than usually severe test. But all welcome the first rays of dawn, the singing of birds, and the delicious feeling of the fresh morning air, to which many a man passes his whole fife a stranger; there is no more exhilarating hour of the four-and-twenty than this, when all nature around seems bounding with life and enjoyment of the mere act of living, and at no time is the heart more filled with gratitude to the great Creator for the bountiful provision He has made, not only for man's necessities, but for his enjoyment, in clothing this earth with such all-pervading beauty.

Now beds are rolled up and stowed, and we stop behind at any brook we pass to enjoy a hasty wash, catch the train up again, and so proceed joyfully on our way, until we reach a station about noon; here sheds, erected on purpose, receive the men, and the *dâk*-bungalow the officers, and after due attention to the *toilette* we assemble for the one meal of the day, and four hours welcome rest. This is bullock-train travelling in Bengal.

April 23rd.—Chumparun. We arrived here this morning; the last part of our journey has been through very hilly country, and we had great difficulty in getting the heavy bullock-waggons up the hills, some parts of which, covered with thick jungle, were very picturesque; they form part of the Rajmahal range. The day before yesterday we saw a few hills, but were not in a hilly country; it appeared more like a plain with hills stuck on afterwards.

April 27th.—Burkutta. We are now about sixty miles from Shergotty, on the road to Calcutta, from which last place we are distant two hundred and thirty-three .miles. Yesterday we had a sudden whirlwind of rain, dust, and hail, which blew away my writing portfolio, and scattered its contents far and wide. We arrived here on Saturday, and on Sunday proceeded forty miles further to a place called Nimiah Ghaut, where we received an express, ordering us to return to this place. We hear that Koor Sing has crossed the Ganges with a force of four thousand five hundred men; five hundred men of the Indian Navy were sent against him, but were entirely cut to pieces and their guns captured. We have, therefore, been ordered to remain here until the whole of the 6th shall have passed up, and then we are to return to Shergotty. We are now in three detachments: this one is under the command of Lieut. Young; Captain Vaughan commands another at Gyah; and the third is at Shergotty, under the command of Lieut. Wilson. The aspect of the country has entirely changed since we left Shergotty, having become picturesque and hilly.

April 28th.—Today we have had another storm and whirlwind, but not such a bad one as the last. The first detachment of the 6th Regiment arrived by bullock-train from Calcutta this morning, and will proceed in the evening; we have no proper barracks here, but our men have to put up in open sheds, while we live in the public room of the *dak*-bungalow; at about 10 a.m. every day, a detachment arrives by bullock-train on its way up country, with perhaps four or five officers; to these we, of course, show all the hospitality in our power, and they remain with us until about 4 p.m., when they take their departure, and we are alone until the following forenoon. We live in a delicious air among the hills, and, though far from cool, have not the oppressive heat that we have elsewhere experienced; if the sun was a little less hot and burning, we might enjoy expeditions and picnics among the hills.

I heard a reason assigned for the mutiny the other day, which was new to me; the King of Oude was in the habit of keeping all men in his employ—soldiers, officers, or civilians—two or three years in arrears of pay; but when Oude was annexed, the king declared that he had no money wherewith to pay these arrears, and the Company refused to do so, on the ground that they had not contracted the debt, and so it remained unpaid. Now all these creditors had brothers, cousins, or near relations in the *sepoy* regiments, and some of the *sepoys* themselves were amongst the creditors; this gave rise to a feeling of discontent, which, if it did not cause the mutiny, at least exercised no small influence over the excited minds of the mutineers; the rebels thought they had a better chance of revenge against the Company than against the ex-king of Oude snugly ensconced at Calcutta.

April 29th.—Today another detachment of the 6th has passed up, and we hope to get away on Sunday evening. Although we shall only go as far as Shergotty, we shall be sixty miles nearer to the actual seat of war. It is curious to see how independent the Naval Brigade is, compared with infantry regiments; the Naval Brigade can be sent anywhere with a small body of cavalry, but an infantry regiment must be accompanied by detachments of artillery, cavalry, and sappers and miners. Now, with all humility, I would venture to suggest that the following staff of ten men might with advantage be attached to every regiment of foot, as every man-of-war carries a certain complement of artificers; and as, when any heavy work is to be done on board of a particular ship, all the artificers of other ships in company are sent to her, so, when three regiments are brigaded together, they might have a superior staff of thirty skilled artificers for employment in building bridges, pontoons, temporary barracks, &c.:

1. There might be a sergeant, understanding something of the trades of each of the nine men under his orders, and receiving good pay.

2. There should be a wheelwright, who in a few hours might build up some sort of waggon for conveying *materiel,* and, besides having the general supervision of all vehicles attached to the regiment, would be always able to assist other carpenters.

3. A shipwright, who could construct punts for a bridge of boats, have some sort of idea of sailorising, and be able to assist other carpenters.

4. A cabinet-maker, understanding fine work, who might be of great use in keeping barrack furniture in repair, and store-chests in the field, but able to assist in heavier work if required.

5. A caulker and cooper, who would assist in making pontoon bridges.

6. A house-carpenter, who would help the cabinet-maker, and might add much to the comfort of men in barracks by making rough articles of furniture.

7. A mason, who could use a spade and assist in throwing up an earthwork.

8, 9. An armourer and blacksmith, men whose trades are perhaps more different than is generally supposed, and without whose assistance carpenters would make but slow progress; the former of these would, of course, have the care of all spare arms, &c.

10. A painter, whose trade is quite as useful as ornamental, as no permanent woodwork ought to be exposed to the weather without a coat of paint. Major Guise, of the 90th, bought a very good double-tent, but the piece of wood which kept the two roofs apart was accidentally broken; so the tent became very hot, indeed, quite unbearable, and no one was able to repair it until Captain Vaughan sent one of our carpenters, who fitted another piece of wood, and put it all to rights in an hour. A sovereign was considered a fit recompense for this hour's work.

April 30th.—Today we have been much distressed to learn the death of our noble captain. He fell a victim to small-pox on the 27th, when just recovering from his wound; he refused to go from Lucknow to Cawnpore in the carriage that was prepared for him, saying that he would sooner travel in a *doolie* like one of his blue jackets, and it is supposed that his *doolie* must have been previously used for a small-pox patient. The information was brought by Lieut.-Col. Wells,

V. C, of the 23rd, as he passed us on his way down to Calcutta.

I cannot say what a sad loss we all feel this to be, and how deeply his death is felt and regretted by every officer and man; the mainspring that worked the machinery is gone. We never felt ourselves to be the *Shannon's* Naval Brigade or even the *Admiralty* Naval Brigade, but always *Peel's* Naval Brigade. He it was who first originated the idea of sailors going one thousand four hundred miles away from the sea, and afterwards carried it out in such an able and judicious manner, I do not doubt that his worth will be appreciated and his death deeply lamented by the people of England.

Burkutta is the most retired, out-of-the-way place it is possible to imagine. It is true that troops arrive day after day; but, as they have been perhaps a week on the road, they look to us for news. Occasionally someone, travelling down rapidly by horse-*dâk*, flashes upon us like a meteor, perhaps leaving behind him some shadowy scattered piece of news, delivered with an air of the most vital importance, such as *"Koor Sing has crossed the river; goodbye"* and instantly the carriage dashes on again. What river? when? who heard him say so? Nobody knows. It may be that he has crossed back again to the east side of the Ganges; or our informant may have only just become aware of his having crossed at all; or it may be that he has crossed the Soane, coming south, or going north; or it may be that the eyes of all India are fixed (metaphorically) on the banks of some river of which we have as yet heard nothing: so we shut out the big world altogether, as being, under the circumstances, beyond our comprehension; and we concentrate our hopes and fears on the few sheds containing the little garrison of Burkutta.

This place is really so small, that the post-office authorities will not even recognise its existence; the one European resident has his letters directed to a friend at Shergotty, who kindly sends them back in a waggon. By the following method we keep our rooms tolerably cool:—The wind blows steadily all day with scorching heat from one point of the compass: the windward door is stopped up by a thick mat called a "*tatty*," made from the root of the "*cuscus*" grass, strengthened with bamboo. Outside sits a native with a large tub of water by his side, and from this he continually sprinkles the mat, keeping it always wet. The hot wind blowing through it is effectually cooled by the evaporation; and, by using a *punkah* at the same time, a room may be made almost cold.

From this date my continuous journals of the proceedings of the

Shannon's Naval Brigade cease. On the 4th of May the detachment with which I was serving left Burkutta, arriving at Shergotty on the 6th. On that same evening I again left for Calcutta with a large party of sick and invalids, and returned to the *Shannon* on the 12th of May.

June 13th.—Lieut. Young, writing from Shergotty, says:

They are at last building barracks for us here, but they cannot be finished for a month. The heat has been excessive, 102° at night in the coolest bungalow in the place. One of our poor fellows, Flynn, a foretopman, actually died of the heat; he went to bed all right and sober, and by all accounts had not been in the sun, but was found a few hours afterwards in a dying state, with the symptoms of sunstroke.

June 30th.—This evening Captain Marten, who has been appointed acting captain of the *Shannon*, went up country to take command of the Naval Brigade, taking with him Mr. Digby, naval cadet, as his A.D.C.

July 27th.—This morning I left the *Shannon* with Mr. L. P. Willan, naval cadet and thirty-five men, as a reinforcement to our Brigade at Gyah, and in the afternoon reached Raneegunge by rail.

July 28th.—This afternoon left Raneegunge by bullock-train.

July 29th.—5 a.m. Arrived at Toldangah. We are most thankful for fine weather, but the River Burâka, which I passed as an insignificant stream on my way, was this morning so swollen by the rains, that we had to cross it in ferry-boats. The stages have been shortened, so that now seven days are allowed for performing a distance, for which only five were previously granted; this makes our travelling more agreeable.

August 1st.—At 5 a.m. we arrived at Burkutta, and a note was put into my hand from Lieut. Young, ordering me to return to the ship, as the whole brigade is on its way down country, so this afternoon I start again for Calcutta.

August 2nd.—Arrived at Doomree. A dog belonging to Captain Dansey, commissariat officer here, who showed us such cordial hospitality when we were at Burkutta in April, was killed last night by a leopard, it was therefore left in a field for bait, and when the animal came to devour it, he was shot by a native: he must have been a very fine fellow indeed, with enormous fangs and claws.

August 5th.—Arrived on board the *Shannon*, in the middle of a shower of rain.

August 12th—At 3 p.m. I crossed the Hooghly with all the *Shannon's* men, who served in the interior, to the railway station, to meet the brigade coming down country: at five they arrived, we all formed together on the railway platform, and then embarked on board the steamer; a detachment under command of Lieut. Young was still in the interior, but altogether we numbered about two hundred and twenty: as we steamed across the Hooghly, all the ships in that mighty stream dressed with flags, some bearing the word "Welcome;" on reaching the opposite pier we were enthusiastically cheered, the wharves were decorated with flowers, flags, and evergreens, surmounted by the inscription "Welcome, hearts of oak," all the houses on the Strand, as far as the *Shannon*, a distance of about a mile were similarly decorated, the road was lined by almost the entire population of Calcutta, European and native: all the thoroughfares leading to the Strand were blocked up and a double row of native policemen, dressed in white with red turbans and *cummerbunds*, kept the road.

We landed on the pier, and passing between two rows of ladies, formed on the road; the order "fours right," was then given, and we marched off, our band leading, escorted in front and rear by the Calcutta Volunteer Cavalry: Fort William saluted with twenty-one guns, and the people all cheered as we passed, the ladies showering down flowers and bouquets on us: at length we emerged on the Maidân, the public promenade, where the road on each side was lined with carriages, the horses unharnessed, and troops who presented arms as we passed; amongst others were the 77th, the Calcutta Volunteer Guards, the Calcutta Volunteer Artillery, the Calcutta Volunteer Rifles, the Indian Naval Brigade, the ship's company of H.M.S. *Pylades*, Captain M. de Courcy and small remnant of the crew of H.M.S. *Pearl*, who were still serving in the interior under Captain Sotheby.

A bridge of boats had been constructed from the shore to the *Shannon's* gangway, and each company marched on board and fell in on the quarter-deck as if they had been on shore for a day's drill instead of a year's service. The order was given to "ground arms" and then the pipe rang through the decks, "hands cheer ship;" in a moment our lower and topmast rigging were swarming with men and three such mighty English cheers rolled over that old Maidân, as the Indian soil had never echoed to before, and probably never will again. And where all this time was our old companion in arms who had planned our enthusiastic reception, Sir James Outram, well named the Bayard of India?

As we stepped over the gangway of the *Shannon,* perhaps we hardly noticed a figure dressed in the plainest of plain clothes, whose eagle eye scanned every bronzed face as it appeared, welcoming one with a nod, and another with a cordial shake of the hand; yet this was Sir James Outram, and in this simple way did he welcome us all.

August 24th.—This evening Sir James and Lady Outram gave a grand ball to the officers of the *Shannon,* at which almost the whole of Calcutta society was present.

August 25th.—Lieut. Young returned on board with the remaining detachment of the *Shannon's* Naval Brigade.

September 1st—This evening a banquet was given in the Town Hall, to the seamen of the *Shannon's* Naval Brigade; it was attended by a large number of people, and several very fair speeches were made by our chief petty officers referring to the transfer of the government of India to the Crown, which took place today.

September 15th.—H.M.S. *Shannon* sailed from Calcutta.

CHAPTER 11

The Return of H.M. S. Shannon to England

Early in the morning of the 15th of January 1858, H.M.S. *Shannon* sailed from Calcutta, under the command of Captain Marten. She touched at Trincomalee, and reached the Cape of Good Hope on the 6th of November: on the 13th she left the Cape, and touching at St. Helena and Ascension, anchored at Spithead on the 29th of December. The behaviour of her ship's company on the passage home was what might have been expected as the result of the fellow-feeling and mutual esteem engendered by the vicissitudes of an arduous campaign: and indeed it was no easy matter for her varied crew, many of whom had been merchant seamen, to fall in at once to the routine of a man-of-war; the ship was inspected in Portsmouth harbour by Sir George Seymour, the port admiral, the Naval Brigade passed before him in review order, and he addressed them in a short but hearty speech. The officers of H.M.S. *Excellent* entertained the officers of the Naval Brigade at dinner, on the 15th of January 1859, at 3-30 p. m. the last man of the *Shannon's* crew was paid off.

The officers of H.M.S. *Shannon* received the following promotions:—Lieut.Vaughan was promoted to the rank of commander, and after serving for one year, to that of captain; Lieuts.Young,Wilson, Hay, Salmon, and Wratislaw were promoted to the rank of commander; Dr. Flanagan, assistant-surgeon, was promoted to the rank of surgeon; Mr.Verney, mate, was promoted to the rank of lieutenant; Mr. Comerford, assistant-paymaster, was promoted to the rank of paymaster; and each of the engineers and warrant-officers received a step. To the midshipmen and naval cadets were promised their promotions to the rank of lieutenants on their passing the requisite examinations, which has in each instance been performed.

The Victoria Cross was presented to Lieuts. Young and Salmon and three blue jackets "for valour" at the relief of Lucknow, mentioned in despatches by Sir William Peel. Commander Vaughan received the order of C.B., an honour never before accorded to any naval officer below the rank of captain.

The Indian medal, with the Lucknow clasp, was presented to each officer and man who formed part of the Naval Brigade. The following officers, who were present at the relief of Lucknow, on the 17th of November, received also the "Relief of Lucknow" clasp:—Lieuts. Vaughan, Young, and Salmon; Capt. Gray, E.M.; Rev. E. L. Bowman; Dr. Flanagan; Mr. Comerford, assistant paymaster; Messrs. M. A. Daniel, E. St. J. Daniel; Lord Walter Kerr, Lord Arthur Clinton, and Mr. Church, midshipmen: Messrs. Bone and Henri, engineers, and Mr. Bryce, carpenter. Never was medal more highly prized, or clasp more nobly won.

Appendix

Camp, Futtehpore,
3rd November, 1857.

Sir,

I have the honour to lay before His Excellency the Commander-in-Chief the details of the Battle of Khujwa with the circumstances that preceded it.

Detachments amounting to 700 men under the command of Lieut.-Col. Powell, of H.M. 53rd Regiment, in charge of siege-train guns and a large convoy were proceeding from Allahabad to Cawnpore, and had arrived on-the 31st of October, after a march of twelve miles, at the camping-ground of Thurrea. The same afternoon intelligence was received from Futtehpore that the *sepoy* mutineers of the Dinapore Regiment with three guns had passed the Jumna with the intention of either attacking Futtehpore or crossing over into Oude. The camp was immediately struck, and we arrived at the camping-ground of Futtehpore at midnight.

Colonel Powell then made arrangements for marching at daylight upon the enemy, who were reported to be about twenty-four miles distant at Khujwa beyond the village of Binkee. The column of attack consisted of 162 men of H.M. 53rd Regiment under *Major Clarke;* 68 of the Royal Engineers under *Captain Clarke;* 70 of a depot detachment under Lieutenant Fanning of H.M. 64th Regiment, and 103 of the Naval Brigade under Captain Peel. It marched at daylight and was joined from the garrison of Futtehpore by a company of the 93rd Highlanders, 100 in number, under Captain Cornwall, and two 9-pr. guns under Lieutenant Anderson, Bengal Artillery. After marching for sixteen miles, the column halted for refreshment and then resumed the march at a rapid pace passing the village of Binkee at about 1.30 p.m., when the intelligence was confirmed that the enemy was at hand.

The troops pressed on without interruption, the Highlanders advancing in skirmishing order supported by the Royal Engineers and followed by the 53rd in column, and then by the Naval Brigade; the depot detachment was with the baggage. We advanced along the road which led straight for the village of Khujwa and saw that the enemy's right occupied a long line of high embankments on our left of the road, which embankment, screened by a grove, continued towards the village, and that their left was higher upon the other side with their guns posted in the centre on the road, two of them in advance and one on a bridge near the village.

A round shot coming down the road opened the battle at about 2.20 p.m. and the column was ordered to edge to the right and advance on the guns through the corn-fields. The skirmishers of the 93rd and the Royal Engineers pushing on both sides of the road. The enemy's artillery was well served and did great execution, and the flank fire of musketry was very severe. The gallant Colonel Powell himself on the left of the road, pressed on the attack, and had just secured two guns of the enemy when he fell dead with a bullet through his forehead.

In the meantime the Naval Brigade had advanced on the right of the 53rd, and carried the enemy's position in their front. It was then that the death of Colonel Powell was reported to me, and I was requested to assume the command. The great force of the enemy, the long line of their defences, and the exhaustion of both officers and men after such long marches rendered our position truly critical. The front of the battle had become changed to the line of the road, and the enemy with all their force behind their embankments threatened to intercept our rear.

I left Lieutenant Hay, R.N., supported by two 9-pr. guns to hold the position which his party had gallantly carried, and which secured our flank, and collecting as many fresh troops as were available, assisted principally by Lieutenant Lennox, Royal Engineers (Captain Clarke being unfortunately severely wounded), and by Ensign Small of the 53rd we marched across the road, and passing round the upper end of the embankment divided the enemy's force and drove them successively from all their positions. The enemy then retired in confusion, leaving us masters of their camp and with two of their guns and a tumbril in our possession.

The late hour of the evening (it was half-past four when the enemy fired their last shot), and the excessive fatigue of the troops prevented any pursuit; we therefore spoiled their camp, and leaving it with cheers, formed on the road by the bridge near the village, and sent out parties to collect our dead and wounded.

With the body of the colonel on the limber of the gun he had so gallantly captured, we then returned and encamped near the village of Binkee. Our loss in the action was very severe, amounting to ninety-five killed and wounded. Enclosed are the returns of the column of attack,

The behaviour of the troops and of the Naval Brigade was admirable, and all vied with each other and showed equal courage in the field. The marching of the 53rd, and the accurate firing of the Highlanders, deserved especial commendation.

I received the greatest assistance from Captain Cox, H.M. 75th Regiment, whom I wish to bring to the favourable notice of H.E. the Commander-in-Chief; and the arrangements of the field-hospital, under Dr. Grant H.M. 53rd; and those of the quarter-master's department under Captain Marshall, were everything I could wish. The total number of the' enemy was reported to be about 4000 men, 2000 of whom were *sepoys*, who fought in their uniform. Their loss was estimated at above 300 killed.

  I have the honour to be. Sir,
    Your very obedient servant,
  (Signed)   William Peel, Capt., R.N., Commanding.

I have the pleasure to inform His Excellency that the remaining gun of the enemy with three tumbrils was brought in this evening by the police, having been abandoned by the rebels in their flight about eight miles beyond Khujwa; and that the *sepoys* have dispersed in all directions pursued by the villagers.

EXTRACT FROM THE *LONDON GAZETTE*, MAY 25, 1858.

No. 17.—*Nominal Roll of Officers of Her Majesty's ship Shannon's Brigade serving under Captain Peel, K.C.B., who are deemed worthy of promotion, or of honourable mention, for their services during the campaign, and* m *the capture of Lucknow, March* 1858.

Lieutenant Thomas J. Young, gunnery officer of Her Majesty's ship *Shannon.*—This officer has been distinguished in every engagement by his cool courage and admirable skill as a gunnery officer: has been specially employed on all critical occasions, and has been named for the Victoria Cross.—Recommended for promotion,

Lieutenant Nowell Salmon.—An excellent officer; distinguished himself in the *Shannon's* Brigade at the relief of Lucknow, was severely wounded, and named for the Victoria Cross.—Recommended for promotion.

Mr. Edmund H. Verney, senior acting mate, zealous and well-conducted.—Recommended for promotion.

Officers not eligible for promotion, but worthy of honourable mention:
—

Lord Walter T. Kerr, midshipman.—Has had an independent command.—Is very highly recommended.

Lord A. P. Clinton, and Mr. E. J. Church, midshipmen.—Have behaved admirably, and are very promising officers.

William Peel, Captain, R.N.,
Commanding *Shannon's* Naval Brigade.
Lucknow, March 31, 1858.

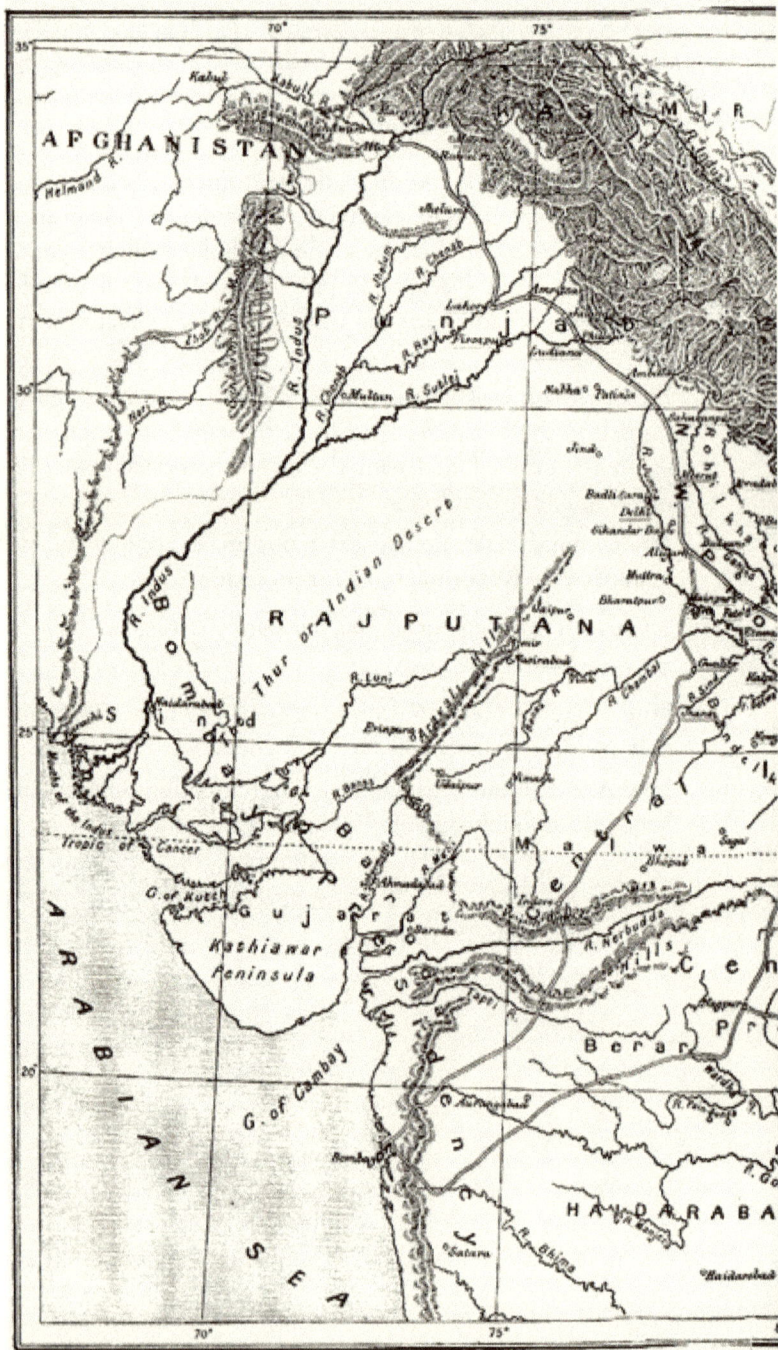

AFGHANISTAN

KASHMIR

Kabul

Kabul R.

Helmand R.

P u n j a b

R. Jhelum

R. Chenab

R. Ravi

Lahore

Amritsar

Firozpur

Ludiana

Multan

R. Sutlej

Ambala

Malba

Patiala

Sind

Badli Saray

Delhi

Sikandar Bala

Aligarh

Muttra

Bharatpur

Hari R.

R. Indus

R. Indus

Thur or Indian Desert

R A J P U T A N A

Jaipur

Ajmir

Nasirabad

R. Luni

Erinpura

Udaipur

R. Banas

Neach

R. Chambal

B o m b a d

Haidarabad

S i n d

Mouths of the Indus

Tropic of Cancer

G. of Kutch

G u j a r a t

Kathiawar
Peninsula

Ahmadabad

Baroda

M a l w a

Bhopal

R. Narbuda

hills

C e n

B e r a r

ARABIAN

SEA

G. of Cambay

Bombay

Satara

R. Bhima

HAIDARABA

Haidarabad

35°

30°

25°

20°

70°

75°

70°

75°

NORTHERN INDIA

THE MUTINY 1857-9.

English Miles

REFERENCE

The principal centres of the Mutiny are underlined thus, Benares
Railways are shown thus, ———
    The line from Calcutta to Ranigunj was open in 1857,
    that from Allahabad to Cawnpore in 1858.
The Grand Trunk Road is shown thus, ═══
Other Main Roads are

LEONAUR

ALSO FROM LEONAUR
AVAILABLE IN SOFTCOVER OR HARDCOVER WITH DUST JACKET

ESCAPE FROM THE FRENCH *by Edward Boys*—A Young Royal Navy Midshipman's Adventures During the Napoleonic War.

THE VOYAGE OF H.M.S. PANDORA *by Edward Edwards R. N. & George Hamilton, edited by Basil Thomson*—In Pursuit of the Mutineers of the Bounty in the South Seas—1790-1791.

MEDUSA *by J. B. Henry Savigny and Alexander Correard and Charlotte-Adélaïde Dard* —Narrative of a Voyage to Senegal in 1816 & The Sufferings of the Picard Family After the Shipwreck of the Medusa.

THE SEA WAR OF 1812 VOLUME 1 *by A. T. Mahan*—A History of the Maritime Conflict.

THE SEA WAR OF 1812 VOLUME 2 *by A. T. Mahan*—A History of the Maritime Conflict.

WETHERELL OF H. M. S. HUSSAR *by John Wetherell*—The Recollections of an Ordinary Seaman of the Royal Navy During the Napoleonic Wars.

THE NAVAL BRIGADE IN NATAL *by C. R. N. Burne*—With the Guns of H. M. S. Terrible & H. M. S. Tartar during the Boer War 1899-1900.

THE VOYAGE OF H. M. S. BOUNTY *by William Bligh*—The True Story of an 18th Century Voyage of Exploration and Mutiny.

SHIPWRECK! *by William Gilly*—The Royal Navy's Disasters at Sea 1793-1849.

KING'S CUTTERS AND SMUGGLERS: 1700-1855 *by E. Keble Chatterton*—A unique period of maritime history-from the beginning of the eighteenth to the middle of the nineteenth century when British seamen risked all to smuggle valuable goods from wool to tea and spirits from and to the Continent.

CONFEDERATE BLOCKADE RUNNER *by John Wilkinson*—The Personal Recollections of an Officer of the Confederate Navy.

NAVAL BATTLES OF THE NAPOLEONIC WARS *by W. H. Fitchett*—Cape St.Vincent, the Nile, Cadiz, Copenhagen, Trafalgar & Others.

PRISONERS OF THE RED DESERT *by R. S. Gwatkin-Williams*—The Adventures of the Crew of the Tara During the First World War.

U-BOAT WAR 1914-1918 *by James B. Connolly/Karl von Schenk*—Two Contrasting Accounts from Both Sides of the Conflict at Sea During the Great War.